D0343040

BERNARD GREBANIER

Playwriting

BARNES & NOBLE BOOKS

A DIVISION OF HARPER & ROW, PUBLISHERS

New York, Hagerstown, San Francisco, London

Acknowledgment is gratefully made as follows for permission to reprint copyrighted material:

The *New York Herald Tribune*, for the quotation from Walter Kerr's review of *The Connection*, in the issue of June 5, 1960.

Random House, Inc., and S. N. Behrman, for passages from *Biography*, copyright 1933 and renewed 1960 by S. N. Behrman, reprinted from *Four Plays by S. N. Behrman*, by permission of Random House, Inc., and for a passage from *Second Man*, copyright 1925 and renewed 1952 by S. N. Behrman, reprinted from *Four Plays by S. N. Behrman*, by permission of Random House, Inc.

Coward-McCann, Inc., and Edward Albee, for a selection from *The Zoo Story* by Edward Albee © 1959, 1960 by Edward Albee. Used by permission of Coward-McCann, Inc., Publishers. *The Zoo Story* is the sole property of the author and is fully protected by copyright. It may not be acted either by professionals or by amateurs without written consent. Public readings, radio and television broadcasts likewise are forbidden. All inquiries concerning these rights should be addressed to the William Morris Agency, New York.

FOREWORD

༄༅༅༅༅༅༅༅༅༅༅༅༅༅༅

My own wish was to call this book *How to Write for the Theater* since that is precisely what it is about. But my publishers have an understandable objection to the recent deluge of "How To" titles, and I have yielded to their preference with the proviso that I open this foreword as I have now opened it. My purposes are now stated.

I do not pretend it is impossible to write a fine play without having first objectively mastered the science of playwriting. I have too much respect for the creative imagination to believe that. I do not forget that it was not Aeschylus and Sophocles who read Aristotle, but he who read them. But he did read them with great profit, great profit to everyone who has come after him. And it is enough measurement of the universality of the truths about tragedy which he discovered through his analysis of Aeschylus and Sophocles that though Shakespeare assuredly never read the *Poetics*, his great tragedies satisfy Aristotle's basic concepts quite as much as do those of Sophocles.

Nor is it, perhaps, beside the point to add that the author of *Titus Andronicus* and the co-authors of *Timon of Athens* might have done better had they consciously been aware of the principles enunciated in the *Poetics*.

Chekov, who was so much the master of the art which conceals art that he is often erroneously supposed to have composed casually, fully acknowledged the existence of aesthetic principles and their importance to the creator. One might collect, he suggested, "all the best works of art that have been produced throughout the ages," and by analysis "discover the *common* element in them" which "conditions their value. That *common* element will be the law. There is a great deal that works which are called immortal have in common; if this common element

v

were excluded from each of them, a work would lose its charm
and its value. So that this universal something is necessary, and
is the *Conditio sine qua non* of every work that claims to be
immortal." (Letter to A. S. Souvorin, November, 1888.) The
method Chekov proposes is precisely the method Aristotle employed in arriving at the *sine qua non* of tragedy.

While by no means setting myself up as a modern Aristotle,
I think it no disgrace to have arrived at the principles of playwriting hereinafter discussed by doing as he did in arriving at
the principles of tragedy—that is, analyzing what the best plays
have in common. To this expedient I was forced. During some
fifteen years of teaching playwriting I have never been able to
recommend to my students a textbook on the subject. Those
available are so full of vague platitudes (such as "Keep your
characters convincing," "Make your dialogue interesting," and
so on—without a hint on how these worthy objectives are to be
achieved) as to be of no use to anyone. After much experimentation, some trial and error, I have, I believe, been able to evolve
the fundamental principles of writing for the theater, as well as
not a little in the way of specific information on the craft. While
not willing to hazard such a declaration on novel or short-story
writing, I have found playwriting to be eminently teachable.
Indeed, I make this averment with a certain chagrin. Playwriting
is so much of a craft that I have discovered, alas, that I could
teach people possessing a modicum of literary talent to write
a quite acceptable play—a consummation, to a lover of literature, hardly to be wished. (Nevertheless, there have been
twentieth-century Broadway dramatists aplenty who, knowing
their craft, have achieved considerable success despite their almost intolerable prose!) On the other hand, many a brilliant
writer among our professional contemporaries has composed a
play far below his abilities only because in the particular case
the creative imagination failed; had the dramatist had sound
objective knowledge of the principles of playwriting, he might
have been able to understand what was amiss in the work. I
must confess that it is vexing to find an authentically poetic
work permitted to emerge feebly constructed when it could
easily have been a great play had the author known something
about dramaturgy; or to discover an extremely gifted author

utterly ruining an otherwise brilliantly written play with an inadequate last scene.

In any case, it must be agreed that a dramatist is in a happier situation when he can identify, by principle, the shortcomings of his work. It would be important to know these principles even if he deliberately decided to violate them. Certainly, the mere expedient of trying directionless rewriting again and again is both wasteful of time and discouraging to enterprise. It is like being adrift on a raft in mid-ocean and trusting that somehow one will be wafted to shore.

But there is another factor involved here. This book makes no apologies for concentrating entirely on technique—on form, if we may be so bold as to use that disgraceful word. There exist other books on the *ideas* to be found in plays—such books being intended for the reader, not the writer, of plays—and some of them, such as Mr. Eric Bentley's brilliant *The Playwright as Thinker*, one of an incomparably valuable series by the same critic, may be recommended without reserve. But this book has nothing to say about our dramatist-to-be's philosophical, ethical, or political notions; we assume that he is entitled to nurture his own. We assume that this dramatist has something to say—let it be grave, let it be light. What we do undertake to teach him is the dramatic form.

However—and this will be no news to the practicing creator in any of the arts—form is not to be thought of as a cold receptacle into which intellectual concepts are poured. Form itself not only conditions the idea but also, when mastered, invites hosts of new ideas. Any poet will tell you that meter and rhyme, matters of form, so far from being constricting, are actually enlargers of the poet's intellectual horizon. When a poet is searching for a rhyme for, let us say, the verb "content," as he rapidly thinks of the possibilities (for example, circumvent, resent, pent, lineament, blent, frequént), he is at the same time rapidly rearranging his thoughts to see how the rhyme may be introduced; and in this process he constantly expands the horizons of his ideas. This is why few, if any, real poets can resist toying with rhyme. Form itself, they know from experience, is creative of idea. So, too, as the reader will later observe, considerations of dramatic form will inevitably condition—and therefore, more often than not, enlarge—the "contents" of the play. For this reason alone a study of form justifies itself.

Mr. Louis Kronenberger in a trenchant analysis (*New York Sunday Times Magazine*, February 5, 1961) of the deplorable state of affairs which has obtained for some years on Broadway, has complained that "Broadway excels at things with holes in the center." Nothing, unfortunately, could be truer. The hole in the center has been due, above all, to a general collapse of respect for dramatic form. When the shape of a play goes to pieces (to change the image) so do the ideas and characters. For some time now many dramatists seem to have expected the audience to supply the lapses in the play itself. This is carrying the Do-It-Yourself vogue too far.

It is my purpose to be practical. I therefore assume throughout that I am addressing the beginner. I intend no insult when I include in that group those who are practiced in forms other than the drama and those who, conscious of some talent for the theater, have not found themselves when attempting the dramatic form. In the Appendix I propose a series of exercises, which I suggest be *all* undertaken and in the order in which they appear. Long experimentation has proved the value of these. At the moment in the text when I feel such an exercise would be apropos, I indicate by a small numeral the corresponding exercise in the Appendix. I may be forgiven for having gone so far in some of these as to suggest the topic itself upon which the reader is to write. The emphasis, I repeat, is solely on technique; these are but exercises; and the serious apprentice, possibly even the genius, will not seriously object to being thus challenged. He can reserve his own, better ideas for complete plays later.

To follow the course of the argument it is necessary, naturally, that the reader become familiar with the plays I use as illustration. I have deliberately recurred again and again to certain plays in the interests of time and concentration. Concurrently with reading this volume it is necessary, therefore, that the reader study with attention the following plays so that he may understand the points which they are intended to illustrate:

Shakespeare's *Romeo and Juliet*, *Hamlet*, and *Othello*
Racine's *Phaedra*
Ibsen's *Hedda Gabler*, *The Wild Duck*, and *Ghosts*

Rostand's *Cyrano de Bergerac*
Wilde's *The Importance of Being Earnest*
Chekov's *The Cherry Orchard*
Strindberg's *The Father*
Synge's *The Playboy of the Western World*
Behrman's *Biography*
Howard's *The Silver Cord*
O'Neill's *In the Zone*
Albee's *The Zoo Story*

Most of the plays written by Ibsen and his successors can be conveniently found in the many fine anthologies which Mr. John Gassner has edited; the most recent translation of *Phaedra* is my own verse-translation (1958). In addition there are, as the Index will indicate, copious references and quotations from a vast number of other plays, nearly all of them modern.

It should be remarked that Chapter Eleven, on Tragedy and Comedy, contains a number of passages which I have but slightly rewritten from analogous portions which I had composed not very long ago for *Introduction to Imaginative Literature*. There are also a few paragraphs which appear in this book substantially the same as they do in my recent *The Heart of Hamlet*. These instances of self-plagiarism add but to a very few pages in this work. It seemed idle to attempt rephrasing what I had already said in a manner fairly satisfactory to me.

I am deeply indebted to my good friend and colleague, Dr. Seymour Reiter, for a number of valuable suggestions, as well as to my esteemed editor, Mr. Philip Winsor of the Thomas Y. Crowell Company, for a number of others. I wish also to thank Mr. John Lynch for his good judgment and taste in a number of matters; I have never had his peer as copyeditor.

BERNARD GREBANIER

To

JOHN WESTERN,

*who, if he vows a friendship, will
perform it to the last article.*

CONTENTS

CHAPTER ONE

The Theater vs. Life

. . . the purpose of playing, whose end, both at the first and now, was and is, to hold, as 'twere, the mirror up to nature.   *Hamlet*, III, ii

If this were played upon a stage now, I could condemn it as an improbable fiction.   *Twelfth Night*, III, iv

Fiction carries a greater amount of truth in solution than the volume which purports to be all true.   THACKERAY, *Steele*

> *All the world's a stage,*
> *And all the men and women merely players.*

What a pity that this is not in fact the case! If all the world were a stage, how much more exciting all the eventualities of life would be (for no excitement, no theater!)—how much more exciting and also how much more endurable. There would be no dull stretches of months, weeks, or days; and we should all know how to hold "eternity in an hour." Moreover, a concentration of the most irresistible mirth would have the grace to cease at about 11 P.M., so that we might breathe a while, or the most overwhelming catastrophe would halt at the same hour; * if we were cast but as the spectators in such a world, we should rise from our chairs refreshed, depressed, or chastened, according to the play, to encounter other matters; if as the actors, we should rise up from our tragic posture where lately we had lain slain by the wrath of god or man, wipe the false dye from the false wound— remove the putty from the nose, the clown's white from the face,

* The audience must not be delayed beyond this, for there is always the last train for the suburbs to consider. The dramatist must be either a classic or a celebrity to dare ignore this restriction.

the simulated wrinkle or the flush of youth from the cheek—
divest ourselves of robes of state or rags—remove the powdered
wig or the luxuriant raven locks or the monk's tonsure to take on
again our own scant or redundant hair—if we may assume that
we are granted an intermission between this play and the next.

If all the men and women were merely players, there would
never be an overtaxed host, for again that eleven o'clock summons
would be a Cinderella's midnight warning that the coach is waiting. . . . But there! The idea that all the men and women could
be players is sheer nonsense, for then there would be no audience.
No audience, no theater!

And, which is more to our affair, if it is untrue that all the
world's a stage, it is even less true that all the stage is the world.
This is a fundamental fact to which we must frequently advert.

Let us, to begin with, merely consider that domination of
time under which we all live. In the world, you are constantly
put to the necessity of consulting the minute hand of your watch.
Miss your train by a minute and you may lose your sweetheart
or your job or both. Miss your boat by two minutes and you may
have to wait two months for the next reservation. Such tyrannies
are unknown in the theater.

Consider the first scene in *Hamlet*. When it opens it is midnight. The guard before the castle is changed. Horatio and
Marcellus come in; the men discuss an apparition which has twice
appeared; Horatio is skeptical about the existence of ghosts. Suddenly the Ghost appears in the likeness of the late king. Horatio
addresses it but it declines to answer, and vanishes. Horatio explains the current haste in preparing for war, and tells how the
late king slew the King of Norway in open combat, and how the
latter's son is busy collecting an army to win back the lands lost
by his father. The Ghost interrupts the talk by appearing again,
seems about to speak, but disappears at the crowing of the cock.
It is dawn.

Thus in 175 lines, which on the stage consume some fifteen
minutes by the clock, Shakespeare asks his audience to live
through intense experiences lasting from midnight to dawn. And,
if you are not hampered by the possession of the soul of a clock,
you do feel at the end of the scene that you have lived through
a stirring night.

Fifteen minutes of the theater can indeed represent the transactions of six hours of actual living. This kind of paradox is true of all the arts. For the "scientific" spirit is as much at home in the realm of aesthetic experience as a hippopotamus in a parlor; its intrusion in matters aesthetic only annihilates what is basic to the arts. In the sciences, truth can be achieved only by the closest adherence to fact; in the arts, truth can be achieved only by a certain deliberate distortion of fact.

It is, for example, a common objection to certain schools of painting that in their canvases the world is not presented as our eyes give it to us. The uninitiate, having had a grammar-school discipline in drawing milk bottles and cracker boxes in interesting attitudes, criticizes adversely a Cézanne cup on the grounds that one could not drink out of it, a Matisse chair that no one could sit on it—worse yet, praises a hideous chromo of a bunch of roses on the grounds that one "can almost smell them." Dismissing the amazing assumption that Cézanne and Matisse knew less than our critic about the laws of perspective (as demonstrated by captivating milk bottles and cracker boxes "correctly drawn"), we find it yet astounding that he never considers the painter's purpose in painting a canvas—that it was not Cézanne's ambition to create a cup for drinking purposes, not Matisse's to make a chair to sit in, not the possibility of a picture to offer flowers to the nose. If our critic is interested in such uses of a cup, a chair, or a bouquet, it would be far more practical of him—and considerably more thrifty!—to purchase the most expensive obtainable on the market rather than to invest in one of those pictures.

A painter may or may not acknowledge the laws of perspective, just as a dramatist may or may not be limited by the tickings of a clock. He accepts such limitations if they further the kind of reality he is striving to achieve. If the laws of perspective or the tickings of a clock stand between him and the truth he is trying to portray, he banishes them as though they had never existed, and rightfully does so. For *the artist operates under conditions which are essentially at war with the world of fact*—every art is by its nature coexistent with certain inescapable conventions; that is, coexistent with certain arbitrary procedures. A painter pretends to represent a three-dimensional world on canvas, board, or wall, which in fact allows him a surface of only two dimensions; a sculptor undertakes to represent in eternal rest and immobility the human form in attitudes which the mortal nervous system would find it difficult to maintain for half an hour; a composer writes operas or music-dramas about the basic emotions of life on the pretense that when people are agitated or delighted they sing—and this convention is no less true of the Wagnerian tenor crying *O heil der Mutter!* than of the Italian tenor caroling *Il mio tesoro* (whose enchanting vocalization the Wagnerian school affects to despise as "unrealistic"); a dramatist, restricted among other matters by the 8:30–11 P.M. limitation, undertakes to present within the few hours of a theatrical performance a complete life cycle. We should certainly not thank Shakespeare if, out of respect for the world of fact, in the opening scene of *Hamlet* he were to detain us in the theater from midnight to dawn.

Fifteen minutes by the clock may by condensation create the reality of a whole night on the stage; or, if the creator so chooses, by expansion fifteen minutes in the theater may correspond to the reality of only a fleeting minute. Such is the witchery of art, and such the meaning of reality in the arts. *The illusion of reality is their only reality.*

(It is, for instance, beside the point to settle whether or not ghosts exist in order to understand *Hamlet;* it is also beside the point to ask whether or not Shakespeare believed in them. He might very well not have believed in them, but it is an issue not worth arguing. What is of moment is that he believed in them for the purposes of that play, where the reality of the Ghost is an essential part of the drama's truth. We may, like Horatio, approach the first scene of *Hamlet* disbelieving in ghosts; but, like Horatio, when the apparition appears before us, we believe in it too.)

This is not to imply that the arts are in any way divorced from the world in which we live. Everything the arts have to say has bearing upon that world. In short order any play would become intolerable if *all* the characters walked on the walls instead of upon the floor, greeted one another affectionately with a kick instead of a kiss or a handshake, talked unremitting gibberish in the course of the dialogue, or laughed and cried without motive. For a work of art to have meaning, it must have its roots in the values of the world in which we live—the values of the world as they are or as they should be. But it is the conventions under which all arts operate that must decide the way in which those values are presented.

Perhaps no art is closer to the world in which we live than that of drama, for the theater must create the illusion of men and women actually living and breathing before the audience's eyes. But because of the conditions under which plays are presented, the conventions of drama are manifoldly more severe than those of any other kind of literature. That is why playwriting *can* be taught.

For example, people attending a theater expect, quite justly, to have their interest engaged throughout the performance. They will not tolerate even a quarter of an hour of boredom. If one is reading a novel and comes upon pages that suddenly seem dense, one can put the book aside for a while, or skip pages to discover whether the rest of the work tempts one to persevere. But there is only one recourse for an audience bored by a play being enacted before it, and that is to leave. Audiences have no compunction about doing just that. Above all forms of literature, therefore, drama requires the maintaining of unflagging audience interest. And herein is one of drama's chief differences from the facts of everyday living.

For the purpose of reinforcing this point, we have made a number of notes of conversations overheard in public. Here is an exact transcript of a conversation we recently overheard in a bus:

THE MAN IN FRONT OF US

Hey, Charlie!

> (He is calling out to a man who has just got on. CHARLIE is too busy paying his fare to hear that he is being addressed.)

Hey, Charlie!

> (CHARLIE looks around bewildered.)

Here, Charlie, over here!

> (CHARLIE sees THE MAN IN FRONT OF US.)

CHARLIE

Oh, hello. Hello, Gus.

GUS

Hello.

(CHARLIE wanders over to GUS.)

CHARLIE

How're you?

GUS

All right. How're you?

CHARLIE

All right. How're you?

GUS

(Moving over.)

C'mon, sit down.

(CHARLIE sits down beside him.)

How's the wife?

CHARLIE

All right. How's yours?

GUS

All right. How're the kids?

CHARLIE

All right. How're your kids?

GUS

All right.

(A pause.)

How come you're on this bus?

CHARLIE

What d'ya mean?

GUS

You don't usually take this bus, do you?

CHARLIE

No, not generally.

GUS

Then how come you're on it?

CHARLIE

I missed the one before.

GUS

Oh.

CHARLIE

I missed it by a coupla seconds.

GUS

I know how you feel when that happens.

(A pause.)

This is early for me.

CHARLIE

Yeah. I sometimes miss the other bus and catch this one. I ain't
seen you on a bus for weeks.

GUS

No, that's right, you haven't. I ain't been this early for weeks.

CHARLIE

Is that so?

GUS

Yeah. I go in later now. This is an exception for me today.

CHARLIE

Yeah, I guess it must be. I would have bumped into you otherwise.

GUS

That's right. I go in later now.

CHARLIE

I thought maybe you moved or somethin'.

GUS

No, I ain't moved.

CHARLIE

Still livin' in the same place?

GUS

Yeah. Still livin' in the same place. Why not?

CHARLIE

It ain't so easy to find a place these days.

GUS

No, it ain't. We're satisfied where we are.

CHARLIE

Yeah, you gotta nice enough place.

GUS

We're satisfied. It ain't much, but it's all right.

CHARLIE

Yeah, your place is O.K. But I thought maybe you moved, because I ain't been bumping into you.

GUS

Well, I don't take the early buses now because I come in later.

CHARLIE

No, I guess you don't.

(A pause.)

I'm a little late myself.

GUS

I'm early.

There was more of the same, but we spare our readers. We intended to bore you—but in a good cause—and there is no need of extending the punishment. However tempting such a conversation might be to a naturalistic novelist, to a dramatist it could only prove fatal. Though "true to life," the passage *shows* noth-

ing of interest or consequence and *says* nothing of interest or
consequence. At its end we know no more about the two men
involved beyond the fact that one is late and one is early. A few
such passages, with nothing to divert either the eye or ear, would
be enough to ruin any play. The audience in a theater would
begin to be restless and to lose interest in the entire work. A
continuation in the same style would be enough to encourage a
general exodus from the premises. If used as material in a play,
this passage would have to be thoroughly reworked; perhaps, in
a style something like this:

THE MAN IN FRONT OF US

Hey, Charlie!

> (He is calling out to a man who has just
> got on. CHARLIE is too busy paying his fare
> to hear that he is being addressed.)

Hey, Charlie!

> (CHARLIE looks around bewildered.)

Here, Charlie, over here!

> (CHARLIE sees THE MAN IN FRONT OF US.)

CHARLIE

Oh hello, Gus, it's you.

GUS

It's me all right. C'mon over here.

> (GUS makes room for CHARLIE, who saun-
> ters over very slowly.)

C'mon, sit down.

CHARLIE

I suppose I might as well.

> (He sits down beside him.)

GUS

How're you?

CHARLIE

Gus, let me say here and now—I'm all right, my wife's all right, my kids are all right, and I suppose your family's all right too.

GUS

They are.

(A pause.)

How come you're on this bus?

CHARLIE

My bum luck. I missed the earlier one by just a coupla seconds, damn it!

GUS

It don't make that much difference, does it?

CHARLIE

Oh yes it does, it sure does! I *like* the earlier bus, it's almost empty when I catch it.

GUS

This one ain't crowded.

CHARLIE

Too crowded for me! Say, I thought sure you musta moved or somethin'. I ain't bumped into you for weeks. But I guess you ain't moved, after all.

GUS

No, we ain't moved. It's just that I most always go in later now.

CHARLIE

Later? *That's* good.*

While not especially enthralling, this rewriting shows some
sparks of interest and purpose. The two men, at least, exhibit
symptoms of being differentiated. Charlie is plainly bored with
Gus, and his enthusiasm for catching the earlier bus seems not unconnected with a desire to escape meeting him. Superfluous lines
have been discarded and others have been combined. Such a
passage at best could be only incidental to a play, and therefore
ought to be compressed until it communicates a maximum of
meaning in the fewest possible lines—even though the first version is much "truer to life."

In the first version both men were bores and boringly presented. The problem posed by drama can be illustrated very
simply by this fact—that in drama a bore must be depicted *in a*

---

* The point of the rewriting might be reinforced for the reader
by equipping Charlie with some emotional cues, as thus:

(Wearily.) Oh hello, Gus, it's you. . . .
(With a sigh.) I suppose I might as well. . . .
(Turning around to face GUS; firmly:) Gus, let me say here and now—
I'm all right, my wife's all right, and my kids are all right, and I suppose
your family's all right too. . . .
(With exasperation.) My bum luck. I missed the earlier one by just a
coupla seconds, damn it! . . .
(Shaking his head, meaningfully.) Oh yes it does, it sure does! I *like*
the earlier bus, it's almost empty when I catch it. . . .
(Bitterly.) Too crowded for me!
                    (Hopefully.)
Say, I thought sure you musta moved or somethin'. I ain't bumped into
you for weeks. . . .
                    (Sadly.)
But I guess you ain't moved, after all. . . .
(With renewed spirits.) Later? *That's* good.

Such emotional cues are often helpful, but it is to be hoped that
they were not really necessary for catching the drift of the passage. Good
dialogue should require but few of them. It is our earnest advice to the
student-playwright never to put them in until after the dialogue has
been polished to the maximum. It is a very bad habit to depend upon
them to deliver the emotional force of the lines. A well-written play
reveals the drama in the lines themselves, not in the stage directions
and emotional cues. Notice the scarcity of the former and the total
absence of the latter in the plays of the world's greatest dramatists—
Shakespeare, Sophocles, Aeschylus, Molière, Racine, Ibsen, Chekhov.

manner which is interesting. One must present him for what he is without boring the audience. In our rewritten version Gus is made to appear a bore because Charlie clearly finds him to be one. It would of course be possible so to rewrite the passage that Gus would reveal himself as a bore without, however, oppressing the audience.[1] *

An actor performing such a role would, naturally, face the same problem as the dramatist. It would be his duty to portray a bore interestingly. For many twentieth-century actors this would prove an impossible feat: these days actors sin in being entirely too natural, entirely too much themselves. They saunter on and off the stage as though they were drifting in and out of our living rooms. I am grateful to anyone who avoids making a scene in my living room, but I have no thanks for anyone because he never makes one on the stage. That is what he is there for! A friend of ours once observed that you can always tell when the universally admired Miss H. has reached the high point of the drama, for at that moment her nostrils begin to quiver! I take no pleasure in watching actors as they shuffle or lounge about the stage in their own natural walk, stand limply, hold a hand in a pocket, scratch their heads or noses, or fuss with their hair, as the whim may seize them. I should take no pleasure if they behaved this way in my living room. But I am particularly indignant when they behave this way on the stage, and not merely because it is unattractive. *On the stage every gesture or move must have a meaning.* If a man scratches his nose, I at once try to find the meaning he is apparently conveying; if he lounges about, I wish to understand the meaning of that—though in a parlor these gestures mean no more than ill breeding. In their talk, too, actors are too tame. A number of them have made a career out of the questionable virtue of speaking throughout the evening in a monotone. The casualness of their tone implies that nothing being said is worth getting excited about. What they forget is that, in the theater, if nothing worth getting excited about is being said, there is also nothing worth listening to. To create the effect of even the casual, no actor himself can be casual. As in all art, *a certain heightening is necessary* to the best interpretation.

The arts do not attempt a carbon copy of life but an imitation of its values. *Imitation implies selectivity, and selectivity means heightening.* Thus, when Chopin wrote his exquisite *Cradle Song*

* Numbered footnotes refer to exercises in Appendix. See page 369.

for the piano, it was not his intention that a skillful pianist while performing it should put the audience en masse to sleep. A "real" lullaby—that is, one which is not a work of art—should put a baby to sleep; the dazzling chromatics of Chopin's composition would never do that. By the very terms of its existence no art can be truly naturalistic—least of all the art of the theater. Its only realism is, as we have said, the illusion of reality. Rob the theater of illusion and you rob it of drama.

Hamlet, urging a superlative performance upon the actors about to present their play before the King, reminds them that the whole purpose of playing (that is, playwriting and acting), "both at the first and now, was and is, to hold, as 'twere, the mirror up to nature." Holding "the mirror up to nature" has, since then, been cited as a justification for all kinds of literary crimes, including the writing of the baldly naturalistic novel. It seems to have escaped notice, however, that to "hold the mirror up to nature" is to indulge in a practice obverse to naturalism. When you hold the mirror up to it, you do not catch nature in a net, you catch rather its reflection.

Indeed, Shakespeare's figure of speech may be accurately applied to the method of all the arts. The arts are not concerned with catching Henry Jones and/or Mary Smith in a net so that we may know them as they "really are," or as they entirely are. That would be an enterprise both futile and useless. Futile, because Henry Jones and Mary Smith, being only themselves, will always retain an element of mystery decipherable neither to themselves nor to anyone else, retain some secret springs of motive and action the sources of which must be forever untraceable. And useless, because much of what we may know of Henry Jones and Mary Smith is uninteresting and valueless to know. But what is always possible, interesting, and valuable to know of them are their peculiar manifestations and variations of our common humanity. These we may catch by holding the mirror up to their actions. And what the mirror of art catches is, unlike life itself, complete, interesting, and decipherable.

The analogy of the mirror is, in truth, quite perfect. For, as we have said, because art is selective it is more vivid than life. So is the reflection in the mirror. The rose in the vase reflected in the mirror is a more vivid rose than the flower in the vase on the dresser before the mirror. The rose in the mirror is more vivid because it is selected out of the numerous details of the room, is heightened because it is cut off from the room by the frame of the mirror, while the rose on the dresser is part of a continuity in the room which the eye restlessly takes in without being able to isolate the flower from its contiguous environment. The rose in the mirror, more vivid than the "real" rose, gives a greater illusion of reality. Such is the paradox of art. The rose on the dresser is to the rose in the mirror as life is to art.

Let us now turn our attention to the kinds of heightening and selectivity which are imposed upon drama by the very nature of the medium. Plays worthy of the name are written to be presented in a theater. (We have nothing to say about plays which are not.) We have already remarked that because plays are written to be enacted by live people they undertake to come closer to a sense of actual living than does any other form of writing.

This fact results in a paradox. By cutting away a wall, the side of a ship, or the other side of the street, the theater invites the audience to witness and overhear scenes of such intimacy and privacy as no outsider is ever privileged to see or hear. Consequently, although plays are produced only because an audience is there to see and hear, drama usually pretends that no person other than the men and women on the stage are present. The audience, thus, at one and the same time, is supposed to be there and not there. If the audience were there, moments of such privacy and intimacy could not be taking place. If the audience were not there, there would be no reason for a play.

Because plays are written for a theater, they must be so written as to deliver their meaning, moment by moment, instantaneously. The novelist can, if he likes, manage his story with a certain amount of artistically conceived mystification: he can deliberately pretend to slight certain matters which later turn out to have been of cardinal importance. For his reader is always free to turn back to an earlier page and reread what he is unsure of. The novelist can also spring with the suddenness of a cat, by some unforeseen revelation catching the reader off guard and sending him reeling. At such times the reader is free to allow the book to rest in his lap while he re-evaluates what he has just read and what has gone before. In the theater there can be no such turning back. Anything missed at any moment is forever lost. The audience cannot, during a performance, cry out: "Stop,

please! Before the play proceeds would you mind doing the
middle of the first act over again? We seem to have overlooked
something." Nor can the dramatist afford to stun his audience
quite to the degree that the novelist can, since he would not want
them to be so much dazed by the unexpected that they are unable to follow the next fifteen minutes of the play. Here again,
the audience cannot demand: "A moment, if you please! We'd
like to consider the meaning of what's just been said!"

For these reasons (to which we must again revert) drama has
a tendency to be stripped of matters unessential to the plot. The
mind of the audience cannot be cluttered with irrelevancies, be
they ever so charming. Nor can a play indulge in those stretches
of philosophic abstraction which break out here and there on the
pages of some German novelists like a rash. In the best plays
everything counts. There is no place for tangential material or
merely graceful ornamentation.

Above everything else a dramatist must never forget that he
is writing for an audience under the special conditions which ob-
tain in a theater. Nothing can be presented in a way that the
audience cannot immediately absorb; nothing can be presented
too rapidly that is meant to impress; nothing can be extended that
is too unimportant to the meaning of the work; nothing can be
kept abstruse; nothing can be dull—and all because the audience
is there. It would be wise to remember, too, that everything that
is said on stage travels in a sort of triangle, of which the audience
is always the apex:

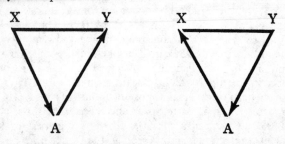

If character *X* is speaking to character *Y*, the remark can reach *Y*
only after it has passed through the audience, *A*. When *Y* re-
sponds, the remark will reach him, too, via the audience. To
forget this is to run the risk of excluding the audience. And when
this happens, drama departs.

CHAPTER TWO

~~~~~~~~~~~~~~~~~~~~~~~~~~~~~~~~~~~~~

Sources for Ideas for Plays

Je pense, donc je suis.*   DESCARTES, *Principes de la Philosophie*

Je suis, donc je pense.†   BANIERGRÉ, *Parler à Tort et à Travers*

Sempre il miglior non è il parer primiero.**   ALFIERI, *Don Garzia*

Quid rides?
Mutato nomine de te fabula narratur.††   HORACE, *Satires*, I

Boston therefore is often called the "hub of the world," since it has been the source and fountain of the ideas that have reared and made America.   F. B. ZINCKLE, *Last Winter in the United States*

Writers often have one of two problems confronting them: *What shall I write about?* or *Which shall I write about first?* Some people tend always to be facing the first question; many professional writers are perennially tortured by the second; but there are times when both sorts of writer are faced with one or the other difficulty. To have to decide *Which shall I write about first?* is not to be in a disastrous position—not much more serious, really, than having to decide among three equally agreeable invitations to a two o'clock Christmas dinner. One ought to ter-

---

* I think, therefore I am.
† I am, therefore I think.
** It isn't the first thoughts which are always the best.
†† Why do you laugh? Just change the name and it is of yourself that the story is told.

minate that difficulty by the simple expedient of deciding upon the choice which is most irresistible, and politely declining the others with thanks and with a sincere "Some other time, I hope." Nothing is more ruinous to a writing career than the practice of leaving behind a trail of half-begun, half-finished works. Naturally, when one has reason to be convinced that he has been following a false star, it is perfectly reasonable to abandon a piece of writing for good.* But that must be the exception. Generally speaking, it is very wise to insist upon seeing a work through to its end, even if one has to force himself to do so. It is this habit which above all others distinguishes the professional author from the would-be variety.

It is not, therefore, the writer whose problem is an embarrassment of riches whom we need advise, but he who is seeking ideas.

Obviously, when ideas suggest themselves it is usually from the thesaurus of one's own experience that they come. We hasten to add, however, that by "one's own experience" we do not mean exclusively the things which actually *happen* to one. It is perfectly sound to write only on matters that "one knows about." But pedants and schoolma'ams have foolishly limited what "one knows about" to mean only what the writer has personally experienced. According to that narrow rule, a man could never write about women, never having been a woman, or a woman about men; no one could write about death, never having died, etc. It is an unhappy fact that some American novelists of our time have seriously put themselves under the restraint of that rule, and seem unable to escape from the contracted circle of their personal experiences—almost as though they dared not deal with anything which has not come into actual contact with their own skins—which is the reason that they tend to write the same book over and over again.†

* As Jane Austen did, for instance, with *The Watsons*. In 1959 Mr. John Coates did an admirable job of finishing it for her.
† Mr. Moss Hart has testified in the strongest terms to the folly of taking as setting and characters "only the places and people you know best." He allowed this counsel to guide him in writing his first serious attempt at playwriting as a very young man and found, when he had finished, that he had created a piece of "hackneyed dreariness." He realized that in writing only about what was extremely familiar he had exiled his imagination. Such a play, built only on the familiar, lacks

"One's own experience" must be interpreted by a writer to include not only what has actually happened to him but also all that he has observed, all that he can remember of his dreams, all that he has heard tell about, all that he has read. All of this is part of him, and therefore part of his own experience (in the best meaning of that term). There are some dreams he has dreamed which are indelibly stamped upon his memory and are therefore much more part of him than thousands of happenings which, though they did actually occur during his waking hours, have left no impression upon his conscious thoughts. As for what he observes, hears, and reads—temperamentally, a writer is a creature with antennae all over him, ever reaching out to sense, to feel, to know whatever is going on about him. A chance phrase overheard or read in a book may open up whole perspectives, ever enlarging vistas of literary possibilities.

But there is no reason why any writer should not quite deliberately search out materials for his composition. It is a residue of romantic nineteenth-century nonsense to feel that the creator must wait until he is "inspired." He is just as likely to feel that exaltation which we call inspiration *after* he has found his materials and *during* the process of elaborating them as at the time he first discovered them. A vast number of the world's greatest paintings and musical compositions were created to the specific order of a patron. The inspiring circumstances, for example, under which Bach wrote his masterwork for the harpsichord, the *Goldberg Variations*, were these: a certain count was suffering from insomnia; he commissioned Bach to write a series of variations for his court harpsichordist; Bach sat down and wrote the *Goldberg Variations;* the harpsichordist played them; the count apparently slept—for he rewarded Bach with a cupful of louis-d'or. When Haydn came to London he signed a contract to compose a specified number of symphonies during his stay there. It was under similar conditions that the great painters of the Renaissance worked; indeed, they were not only supplied in advance with the subject but were also often required to work in the portraits of their patron and his family as part of the composition—which accounts for some of the hideous faces to

"breath of life and imagination, two necessary ingredients for what is usually called creative writing." (M. Hart, *Act One*, 1959, pp. 165–66.)

be seen in some of the world's greatest pictures. As for writers—
we have only to cite Shakespeare, who certainly seems to have
taken his materials from everywhere and anywhere, as though it
hardly mattered to him. From these facts we may very well conclude that, historically at least, a creator does not particularly
wait to be inspired; he is more likely to be in a constant state of
preparing to be inspired—willing to take on almost any subject
offered him—asking only the opportunity to create.

This being the case, a dramatist might very well look about
him in search of materials. Where are the sources for these
materials? A play may owe its inception to any one of three such
sources:

1. A theme to be illustrated.
2. A situation to be developed.
3. A group of characters to become involved in dramatic
   relationship.

THEME

The subject of a work is what the work is about. Here are
some possible subjects for a play: Love, Jealousy, Ambition,
Idleness, Social Rank, the Values of the Past, the Values of Big
Business. It will be seen that these subjects nowhere indicate the
presence of idea: indeed, all of them are susceptible of several
ideational interpretations. When a subject is so employed as to
exhibit an idea, it has a theme. *The theme of a work is its central
or governing idea.* A work, of course, may have several subsidiary themes in addition to the main theme.

Now, for each of the subjects we have mentioned there are
any number of possible themes. For instance, on the subject of
Love, there is this possible theme: Love can cause lovers to be
utterly reckless of the consequences of their acts. Or on Jealousy:
Jealousy is a sickness which can utterly destroy a human being.
Or on Idleness: A man or woman lacking direction in life and
with no work to do in the world may become a great menace to
others.

With any of these three themes as a point of departure for
thinking about a play, we have something which might turn out
to be quite important. Ibsen, apparently, began precisely this way
in the case of a play he wrote on the theme that "a man or woman

lacking direction in life and with no work to do in the world may become a great menace to others." The result was a very great play indeed, *Hedda Gabler*. But before that theme could become *Hedda Gabler*, Ibsen had to discover a situation and characters which would embody that theme.

Suppose we think for a moment about the theme that "Jealousy is a sickness which can utterly destroy a human being." We now need for the purposes of drama both situation and characters to embody the idea. After casting about for various possibilities, we decide on employing this situation: a man and a woman have married each other despite enormous barriers to their union; it is in the evolution of this situation that we are going to show the destructive power of Jealousy.

Having theme and situation, before we can begin we now are in need of our chief characters—at least the man and the woman. After considering various candidates for theme and situation, we at length choose these two characters: a noble, generous, pure-hearted man, a total stranger to the passion of jealousy; and an exquisite, refined, sensitive, but courageous woman. It is of her that he is to become jealous, and, exhibiting our theme, as a result to destroy himself.

By just such a process (though, as we shall have occasion to show later, this was certainly not Shakespeare's method) one might have arrived at the point where he was ready to plan the tragedy *Othello*.

Suppose we now think about the theme that "Love can cause lovers to be utterly reckless of the consequences of their acts." We first consider various possible situations in which this might evolve as a theme. At length we decide upon this one: two young people who are members of families which have for a long while been enemies, elope and get married; it is the evolution of this situation that will show the consequences of their recklessness.

With theme and situation chosen, we now need, at the very least, our young man and young woman. After rejecting various kinds of persons, we choose these two: a callow youth, in love with love, who has never known true love before he meets our heroine; she, we decide, is to be a mere girl, totally inexperienced, a dutiful daughter used to obeying the wishes of her parents to the letter.

By this kind of thinking we have arrived at a point where we should be ready to plan our play—if Shakespeare had not already written *Romeo and Juliet!* *

Again, let us try this theme: "One may be in total ignorance of his own potentialities if he has never had the opportunity to cultivate them." After some speculation, we hit upon this situation, in the evolution of which our theme will become embedded: a young woman has been living a rather bored, empty-headed life until an idealistic young man, sensing her capabilities, undertakes to educate her. For theme and situation, reflection recommends these two as our leading characters: the girl, taken out of the chorus by a rich gangster, is living the idle life of a kept woman; the young man is a free-lance reporter who is determined to write a series of articles exposing the gangster as a social menace. Through some such process Garson Kanin might very well have arrived at the point where he was ready to plan his delicious comedy *Born Yesterday*.

As we have said, for every subject there are innumerable possible themes. On the subject of Love alone, the available themes are almost endless. Let us list just a few:

Love can blind one to defects which he would loathe in any other human being. (Molière's *The Misanthrope*)

Proud people may mask their love by an open show of antagonism. (The Benedick-Beatrice story in *Much Ado About Nothing*)

People who truly love can forgive all and endure all for the sake of those they love. (The stories of Cordelia, Kent, and Edgar in *King Lear*)

Love can convert callow adolescence into passionate adulthood. (A theme in *Romeo and Juliet*)

Avenging a wrong to a loved one may cause one to commit an even more heinous crime than the wrong that he avenges. (Sophocles' *Electra*)

Deifying the love one has had from the dead may rob one of the rightful claims to a full life. (Tennessee Williams' *The Rose Tattoo*)

To give to others, no matter how generously, but without

* Employing a totally different situation and totally different characters, Shakespeare dealt with the same theme in *Antony and Cleopatra*.

love, may be only injurious to them. (Enid Bagnold's
The Chalk Garden)

Starting one's thinking with a theme is intelligent enough but
can be somewhat precarious too. It too easily may lead the writer
into contriving heavily moralistic or propagandistic demonstra-
tions of an idea, into merely manufacturing situation and character for purposes of *illustrating* the theme, in which case neither
situation nor characters will be dramatically convincing—so that
the play ends by being a kind of sermon, which a good play
should never be. Thus, if one wished to illustrate the theme
"Crime doesn't pay," he might contrive a situation in which a
penniless young man holds up a bank and is killed in the attempt
—with the resulting play sure to be either dull or even uninten-
tionally droll. Perhaps the best way to avoid this pitfall is to shun
themes that sound like slogans or Sunday-school mottoes. A good
theme should be an interpretation of life, not a lecture upon it.
The least an audience in the theater stipulates for is that a play
hold their attention and divert them—that is, entertain them—
as a sermon or lecture in the theater never can. The theme of a
play, in short, should never hit the audience between the eyes
by being too obvious; the theme should, rather, be deeply embedded in the action and the nature of the leading characters.
Certainly, it is in no obvious way that *Othello, Romeo and
Juliet, Antony and Cleopatra, King Lear, Much Ado About
Nothing, Electra, The Misanthrope, Hedda Gabler, Born Yesterday, The Rose Tattoo,* and *The Chalk Garden* embody their
respective themes. No man ever wrote with a more deliberate
intent of reforming than did Ibsen, but a study of his masterworks will reveal them to be, first and last, plays—not propagandistic lectures. If their ideas impress us by their power and
sincerity, it is only because our attention has been riveted upon
the characters in his plays and what those characters do.[2]

SITUATION

It will have been noted that in our consideration of the
several themes above, we always proceeded first to choose not
the characters but the situation. This was because the best point
of departure for thinking about a play is its action, and situation

is intimately connected with action. If one starts with either theme or characters, it is advisable to proceed at once to the consideration of possible situation. Situation is intimately connected with action, and action is intimately connected with plot; and plot, as we soon shall see, is the most basic of all elements in a good play. Situation, therefore, brings one closer to plot than can either theme or character.

We are making, it is to be observed, important distinctions between situation, action, and plot—and these distinctions will presently be made clear. With plot, indeed, we shall be dealing at some length, since the plot of a play is the very bone structure which holds it together. At the moment, let us say but this: plot can come into being only after situation has been at least tentatively considered.

Situation is a state of affairs. Obviously, at any given moment of a play there is, or should be, a situation. The action of a play contains a sequence of situations.* But in this chapter, when we speak of situation we mean to limit it to some state of affairs out of which the dramatist's thinking can evolve a plot, the chief characters, and a theme. (Such a situation, tentatively accepted as a beginning for one's thinking, may eventually not find a place among the situations in the finished play. It often happens that this tentative situation, as one considers plot and character, will be altered or even discarded. If so, it will nonetheless have served its purpose as the point from which one begins to plan the play.)

Let us consider some such situations (that is, states of affairs

* It is important to remember that a mere sequence of situations, though making for action, will not necessarily constitute a plot. (See the next chapter.) Thus: this sequence of situations certainly constitutes action:
1. Johnnie, after washing up, comes downstairs for breakfast.
2. He eats cereal and drinks a glass of milk for breakfast.
3. He goes to school.
4. At school he studies arithmetic and geography.
5. He comes home from school.
6. He chops up some logs for the fireplace.
7. He plays with his dog Rover.
8. He has his dinner.
9. He does his homework.
10. He plays checkers with his brother.
—but it emphatically does not constitute a plot.

out of which the dramatist's thinking might have evolved plot, characters, and theme):

A king, deeply concerned about the drought which is destroying his people, sends to the oracle to find out what can be done to save the country. (Sophocles' *Oedipus Tyrannus*)

A young man and his servant arrive in a strange country where his twin and the twin of his servant—both long believed dead—have been living most of their lives. (*The Comedy of Errors*)

An elderly monarch decides to divide his kingdom among his three daughters and to spend his declining years under their care. (*King Lear*)

A man of affairs, taken in by the hypocritical cant of a beggar whom he believes a saint, gives him the run of his house. (Molière's *Tartuffe*)

A virtuous woman has conceived an overwhelming passion for the son whom her husband fathered in an earlier marriage. (Racine's *Phèdre*)

When her husband was ill, a devoted wife forged the signature to a document in order to procure funds to restore him to health. (Ibsen's *A Doll's House*)

After living for years in self-imposed exile abroad, a woman comes back to her ancestral home when it is in danger of being sold to pay debts. (Chekhov's *The Cherry Orchard*)

An authority on dialects bets that he can convert a guttersnipe into a lady elegant enough to pass as a duchess by teaching her to speak and behave like one in a few months. (Shaw's *Pygmalion*)

A varied assortment of people have been invited to a house for a weekend because all of them wish to have a second chance in life. (J. M. Barrie's *Dear Brutus*)

A young woman who unknown to her father has been living as a prostitute in another city comes to live with him. (O'Neill's *Anna Christie*)

Having escaped the engulfing influence of his mother, a young man brings his new wife to meet her. (Sidney Howard's *The Silver Cord*)

A pretentious woman comes to live at the home of her sister
    and brother-in-law, a young laborer. (Tennessee Wil-
    liams' *A Streetcar Named Desire*)

A portrait painter of international reputation both for her
    art and her Bohemian life is asked by the editor of a
    popular magazine to write her autobiography. (S. N.
    Behrman's *Biography*)

If our dramatist has been able to start with a situation, he
will be wise to proceed next to his plot, and then to the characterizations. As for the theme, his tentative plans for one may help
him in deciding upon what to accept and what to reject in the
way of plot and characters.[3]

The techniques of planning a plot and deciding on the characters will be presented in chapters devoted to these cardinal matters. At the present the reader may reflect for himself upon the
characters and themes connected with the above-listed situations,
and note how each of those situations might have given rise to
the theme and characters employed by the dramatist.[4]

Let us consider this situation: "An authority on dialects bets
that he can convert a guttersnipe into a lady elegant enough to
pass as a duchess by teaching her to speak and behave like one
in a few months." The dramatist could have made, among others,
these choices of action and character:

1. The professor chooses a guttersnipe utterly unteachable
   and beyond redemption. Seeing her advantage, she pretends to be trying to learn, while she is busy laying plans
   with a gang of thieves with whom she is connected.
   When she disappears suddenly, so do all of the professor's
   most treasured possessions.

or

2. The guttersnipe is actually very brilliant of mind but cold
   and calculating. She learns very rapidly, and the professor
   falls madly in love with her. She encourages his love while
   it suits her, but only uses him to make a more advantageous match. He has succeeded only too well.

or

3. The guttersnipe learns very rapidly, becomes in every
   way a lady, but falls in love with her teacher. He, however, is never interested in her beyond the experiment.
   He is a born bachelor.

or

4. The professor's experiment, altruistically undertaken, is completely misunderstood by his fiancée and his friends. All sorts of complications are possible here, and various endings to the story too (reconciliation with the fiancée —with or without his pupil's voluntary withdrawal from his life; emergence of the pupil as the superior of the fiancée).

Shaw chose the third of these alternatives; his theme is that a guttersnipe *can* be converted into a duchess in a short time.

For the situation: "After living for years in self-imposed exile abroad, a woman comes back to her ancestral home when it is in danger of being sold to pay debts," a dramatist could have made, among others, these choices:

1. Faced with the challenge of losing everything, the woman rises to the occasion for the first time in her life. She accepts the offer of an enterprising real-estate operator to divide her land into building lots, and salvages everything.

or

2. Touched by the real-estate operator's lifelong worship of her, she swallows her pride and for the sake of her family marries him, determined to make the best of things in a changing world.

or

3. Unable to face the realities of a changing world, she procrastinates and temporizes, hoping for the miracle that does not arrive. In the end, she loses everything, and returns to her exile.

Chekhov chose the last of these possibilities.

For the situation: "A pretentious woman comes to live at the home of her sister and brother-in-law, a young laborer," a dramatist could have made, among others, these choices:

1. The visitor makes her sister aware of the uncouthness of her husband, and breaks up the marriage.

or

2. The husband falls in love with his sister-in-law, neglects his wife, and runs off with the visitor.

or

3. Finding his sister-in-law unendurable and a menace to his marriage, the husband drives her from his home.

Tennessee Williams chose something close to the last of these.

For the situation: "A portrait painter of international reputation both for her art and her Bohemian life is asked by the editor of a popular magazine to write her autobiography," a dramatist could have made, among others, these choices:

1. The painter, still nurturing a bitterness against her first lover, who is now running for political office, takes the opportunity to ruin his career by exposing him in her autobiography as a fraud.

or

2. She tries to blackmail him into marrying her now.

or

3. Realizing that she may harm his career, she decides not to publish her autobiography after all.

or

4. She falls in love with the editor of the magazine.

or

5. She realizes that the editor's motives in getting her to write her autobiography are those of vindictiveness against the world, and she therefore refuses to write it.

S. N. Behrman managed skillfully to incorporate the third, fourth, and fifth ideas in unity in *Biography*.

As we have said, if one were able to choose a point of departure for planning a play, the happiest choice would be situation. For that brings one almost at once to the consideration of plot. We *know* that this is the way Shakespeare worked, for (with the exception of *Love's Labour's Lost* and *The Tempest*) he always took the basis of his story from some already existing play, chronicle, tale, or romance; and we know, too, that he owed to his source almost nothing at all in the way of characterization or theme. It might be said that Shakespeare's point of departure was almost always a collection of situations (some accepted, some rejected from the source), and that from these he evolved his plot, characters, and theme. Such, too, was the case with the Greek tragedians, who were dealing with material drawn from popular mythology. (It is highly instructive to compare and contrast Aeschylus' *The Libation Pourers* and Sophocles' and Euripides' *Electra*—all three on the same legend—to

note how completely different they are.) Such, too, is the case
in our own century with anyone who undertakes to make a play
from actual historical material (for example, Maxwell Anderson's
Elizabeth the Queen and *Mary of Scotland;* Shaw's *Saint Joan*
and *Caesar and Cleopatra*)—no matter what liberties are taken
with fact.

CHARACTERS

A play may owe its inception to the dramatist's having become interested in a certain character or group of characters.
This must occur frequently enough: a writer is likely to be attentive and sensitive to the nuances of personal traits, habits, and
idiosyncrasies of the people he meets, reads of, or hears discussed.

Given an interesting character, a dramatist would be wise to
begin thinking at once of a situation in which to place him.

Suppose I should like to represent a woman of great compassion for others, a woman who believes it more important to
understand and to be generous toward others than to judge them.
I shall now wish to find another character with whom she will
have to deal, someone, perhaps, with a completely opposite set
of values—for that would be sure to make for drama—and to
make the contrast perfect, I wish this second character to be a
man. Among many possibilities I think of these situations:

1. The woman and man are husband and wife; the husband's
   father has shamefully neglected his children when they
   were young; now the old man is down on his luck, and
   his embittered son wants nothing to do with him.*

   or

2. The man, having power of life and death over his fellow
   citizens, has condemned a youth to death on a mere
   technicality. The woman is the condemned man's sister,
   and comes to plead for her brother's life. (This is the
   fundamental situation in Shakespeare's *Measure for Measure.*)

   or

* Wilde's *Lady Windermere's Fan* has some affinities with this situation, except that in that play it is the husband who is more generous and
the wife who is conventional-minded (rather than ungenerous); it is her
mother who has offended.

3. The man is in a position to bring about the death of the man he hates most in the world, by pressing charges against him. The woman undertakes to be the lawyer for the accused. (This is the fundamental situation in *The Merchant of Venice*.)

With any of these situations a dramatist would be well on the way in the planning of his play.

Suppose I wish to represent a man of incorruptible honesty who is utterly disgusted with human society's hypocrisies and pretenses. I could put him in a play with:

1. Another man whose integrity he has always believed to be as perfect as his own and who has his complete confidence in all matters. This friend proves to be a traitor, and he finds himself in the traitor's power.

or

2. Another man whose corruption and depravity the world well knows of and whom he despises. He discovers that he owes his very life to the secret kindness of this man.

or

3. A coquette who, despite her artifice and her love of flirtation and scandal, has inspired him with an enslaving passion for her. (This is the fundamental situation in Molière's *The Misanthrope*.)

or

4. A woman of great compassion, who has led an eventful and colorful life among the international set. Our incorruptible man, a magazine editor, embittered by a difficult life, contracts with the woman to write her autobiography, in the expectation that it will expose the shallowness of some public figures. (This is the fundamental situation in S. N. Behrman's *Biography*.)

Suppose I wish to show a lightheaded but beautiful chorus girl who has been living the life of a "gold digger." I could put her in a play with:

1. Another chorus girl, who invites her to go along on a blind date with two men who turn out to be gangsters. Our heroine becomes involved in a murder.

or

2. A scion of a wealthy and respectable family. Falling under the spell of her charms, he proposes to her and

marries her. This is the crucial situation in Anita Loos's hilarious novel *Gentlemen Prefer Blondes.*

or

3. A high-principled free-lance journalist who decides to accept the challenge of educating her to the serious issues of life. (This is the fundamental situation in Garson Kanin's *Born Yesterday.*) [5]

Thus, a dramatist's point of departure may be theme, situation, or character. He may be struck with the possibilities of one or the other of these by material drawn from personal experience, observation, reading. If he wishes to institute a search for material, he will find that the daily newspaper rarely fails to suggest something—not in the news which makes the headlines, but in the smaller items, particularly the "human interest" stories. Naturally, one cannot expect to find more than raw material—that is, material from which one must select and discard.

Here is a series of summaries from items culled from the news for a period of but two weeks:

A middle-aged man was brought to court and sued by his wife for desertion and non-support. Every time he tried to explain the circumstances of his case, he was pushed to the side by one of his three grown sons, who were accompanying their mother in court, and was unceremoniously told to "shut up." The judge, noting the father's treatment, ordered the others to be silent and asked the defendant to state his case. He said that he had been getting increasingly tired of the endless arguing and shouting in his house and the domination of his wife and sons. One day he took a walk in the outskirts of the city. Along the road he saw a sign announcing that a night watchman was wanted; it was an institution for the deaf-and-dumb. He took the job. Later his family traced him to his place of employment. The judge decreed that he was to keep his job and give his wife $1.25 a week. (For the purposes of drama, one would probably have to discard everything here except the basic relation of the man to his family; but that is good material.)

The police have found and released a man who had been kept prisoner in a dark room for eighteen years by his brother.

The victim was twelve years old when his mother died, leaving a legacy, which the elder brother kept to himself while he imprisoned the younger boy in a room in the house. The victim, though now thirty, looks fifty. The elder brother has been jailed. (Here is a situation and two characters with many possibilities.)

A prisoner in a state prison won the poetry contest sponsored by the prison authorities. When the winning poem turned out to be the work of Whittier, the winner was placed in solitary confinement. (Discarding the punishment visited upon the false poet, here is good comedy material. The setting could be changed from a prison to anywhere else.)

In Italy a man of no property and no means of earning a living fell desperately in love with a beautiful girl. When her family sternly refused to allow her to have anything to do with him, he captured her and carried her off to a hideout in the hills. In order to procure food for his mistress, he planned with another man to rob an old fruit vendor. When the old woman fought back and screamed, both men got into a panic, and one of them plunged a knife into her breast. In December 1923 the lover was sentenced to prison for life—on the day his sweetheart found she was pregnant. She bore a daughter, and eventually married someone else. Her brother, who was only a year old when she was carried off, fed on the tale of the wrong done her, though he knew her wronger only by photograph. Last year, a well-meaning lawyer was going through the records of the district (Calabria) and found that the wild youth of 1923 had been a model prisoner and was entitled to parole. He entered a plea of clemency with the President of Italy, and the man was released just before Christmas. He found his daughter, now a married woman, and the two were happily united. But his old sweetheart's younger brother heard of the other's release and learned where he was now visiting. He waited at a bus stop. When his intended victim appeared, he asked him his name, identified himself, and fired four shots that killed the other. No one of the district was able to tell police where the young avenger was hiding; though it took twenty-seven years, they approved of the revenge.

In a town in Germany some citizen, offended by a bronze sculpture of a nude woman beside the city's swimming pool, pasted the figure with glue and feathers one night and left a note: "One hundred frying pans could have been made out of this." (This is an interesting hint for a character. The situation might not prove very rewarding to use.)

During a party celebrating his tenth year in medical practice, a man was arrested by the authorities, who discovered that he had never been to medical school. (Discarding the party, one has a very good fundamental situation here.)

Within an hour of the wedding ceremony, a young bride was notified that her husband-to-be had died. He was killed by gas in his own flat. (If one decided not to have the death accidental, he might be started on a profitable train of thought, seeking first the motive for suicide.)

In a Swiss town two brothers, keeping watch beside their father's coffin, got into a row over his legacy. During the altercation, the old man rose up, in the best of health. His "death" had been a ruse to test his sons. (This is almost perfect material for a one-act comedy.)

In southern France a man, trying to end his wife's suffering as an incurable paralytic by killing her, succeeded in curing her. Two years earlier she had become bedridden with a mysterious paralysis. While she was asleep the other day, he slipped into her bedroom with a knife and aimed at her heart, but inflicted instead only a superficial wound on the side of her head. She leaped up from the bed and ran across the room screaming. It was the first time she had used her legs in two years. The husband tried, unsuccessfully, to hang himself. (If one omitted the attempted murder, he has good material for comedy here.)

A young heiress eloped with the family chauffeur after her social debut.

None of these is perhaps ideal material, but some are not bad, and all have possibilities for drama. In any event, the selection shows how much may be gleaned in the most casual of searches during a two-week period. An earnest dramatist need not limit himself this way, but rather should be forever alert to possible material when he comes upon it. Anything promising should be kept, with perhaps a notation upon what seemed, at first view, to be material in it.[6]

As a demonstration of how everything is grist to the dramatist's mill, it might be interesting at this point to list the materials Ibsen found he could use to good effect in a play that it is suggested you read, his masterful *Hedda Gabler:*

1. A young writer, a great admirer of Ibsen, one day sent him a parcel of Ibsen's letters and a photograph of the dramatist which Ibsen had given him. There had been no quarrel and there was no accompanying explanation. Ibsen investigated the matter and found that the package had been sent after the young writer had been drinking freely: he had intended to send back his sweetheart's letters and her photograph to her, and in an alcoholic muddle had returned Ibsen's instead. Ibsen also learned that the young writer had, under the influence of liquor, lost a completed manuscript too.

2. It was a widely publicized fact in Norway that the wife of a composer in a jealous fit burned the manuscript of a symphony he had just completed.

3. In Ibsen's circle of acquaintance it was well known that a brilliant man, a reformed alcoholic, at that time married to a beautiful and intelligent woman, had been the victim of a sudden whim of his wife. In order to test her power over him, she had brought into his study a small keg of brandy. When she came in, hours later, he had drunk so much that he lay unconscious on the floor.

From these three different sources were developed concepts for Hedda's character and Lovborg's, their dramatic relationship, and the climax of the play—after who is to say what mysterious workings of the creative imagination. The example is highly typical. The writer must keep all the avenues of his perception open, therefore, to what is going on around him.

CHAPTER THREE

Plot (1)

When we mean to build,
We first survey the plot.   *Henry IV, Part II*, i, iii

There are only two or three human stories, and they go on repeating
themselves as fiercely as if they had never happened before.
w. CATHER, *O Pioneers!*, II, 4

Don't trust that conventional idea.   DICKENS, *Hunted Down*

SITUATION AND INCIDENT

We have defined situation as "a state of affairs"—a concept
which is clearly a static one. But the very essence of drama (the
word itself comes from the Greek *dran*, "to do") is movement,
action. We move closer to the action which makes for drama
when situation becomes incident.

A man comes to visit a friend of his, unaware that his missing
cigarette case was left in this friend's flat. That is a situation.

Let us see how that situation can become dramatic incident.
This is an episode from one of the most brilliant of English
comedies (Algernon has just informed Jack that he refuses to
give his consent to Jack's marrying Gwendolen):

JACK

Your consent!

ALGERNON

My dear fellow, Gwendolen is my first cousin. And before I
allow you to marry her, you will have to clear up the whole
question of Cecily.

35

(Rings bell.)

JACK

Cecily! What on earth do you mean? What do you mean, Algy,
by Cecily? I don't know anyone of the name of Cecily.

(Enter LANE.)

ALGERNON

Bring me that cigarette case Mr. Worthing left in the smoking-
room the last time he dined here.

LANE

Yes, sir.

(LANE goes out.)

JACK

Do you mean to say you have had my cigarette case all this
time? I wish to goodness you had let me know. I have been
writing frantic letters to Scotland Yard about it. I was very
nearly offering a large reward.

ALGERNON

Well, I wish you would offer one. I happen to be more than
usually hard up.

JACK

There is no good offering a large reward now that the thing is
found.

                              (Enter LANE with the cigarette case on a
                              salver. ALGERNON takes it at once. LANE
                              goes out.)

ALGERNON

I think that is rather mean of you, Ernest, I must say.

(Opens case and examines it.)

However, it makes no matter, for, now that I look at the inscription, I find that the thing isn't yours after all.

JACK

Of course it's mine.

(Moving to him.)

You have seen me with it a hundred times, and you have no right whatsoever to read what is written inside. It's a very ungentlemanly thing to read a private cigarette case.

ALGERNON

Oh! it is absurd to have a hard-and-fast rule about what one should read and what one shouldn't. More than half of modern culture depends on what one shouldn't read.

JACK

I am quite aware of the fact, and I don't propose to discuss modern culture. It isn't the sort of thing one should talk of in private. I simply want my cigarette case back.

ALGERNON

Yes, but this isn't your cigarette case. This cigarette case is a present from someone of the name of Cecily, and you said you didn't know anyone by that name.

JACK

Well, if you want to know, Cecily happens to be my aunt.

ALGERNON

Your aunt!

JACK

Yes. Charming old lady she is, too. Lives at Tunbridge Wells. Just give it back to me, Algy.

ALGERNON

(Retreating to back of the sofa.)

But why does she call herself little Cecily if she is your aunt and lives at Tunbridge Wells?

(Reading.)

"From little Cecily, with her fondest love."

JACK

(Moving to sofa and kneeling upon it.)

My dear fellow, what on earth is there in that? Some aunts are tall, some aunts are not tall. That is a matter that surely an aunt may be allowed to decide for herself. You seem to think that every aunt should be exactly like your aunt! That is absurd! For heaven's sake give me back my cigarette case.

(Following ALGY round the room.)

ALGERNON

Yes. But why does your aunt call you her uncle? "From little Cecily, with her fondest love to her dear Uncle Jack." There is no objection, I admit, to an aunt being a small aunt, but why an aunt, no matter what her size may be, should call her nephew her uncle, I can't quite make out. Besides, your name isn't Jack at all; it is Ernest.

JACK

It isn't Ernest; it's Jack.

ALGERNON

You have always told me it was Ernest. I have introduced you to everyone as Ernest. You answer to the name of Ernest. You look as if your name was Ernest. You are the most earnest-looking person I ever saw in my life. It is perfectly absurd your saying that your name isn't Ernest. It's on your cards. Here is one of them.

(Taking it from case.)

"Mr. Ernest Worthing, B. 4, The Albany." I'll keep this as proof your name is Ernest if ever you attempt to deny it to me, or to Gwendolen, or to anyone else.

(Puts the card in his pocket.)

JACK

Well, my name is Ernest in town and Jack in the country, and the cigarette case was given to me in the country.

ALGERNON

Yes, but that does not account for the fact that your small Aunt Cecily, who lives at Tunbridge Wells, calls you her dear uncle. Come, old boy, you had much better have the thing out at once.

JACK

My dear Algy, you talk exactly as if you were a dentist. It is very vulgar to talk like a dentist when one isn't a dentist. It produces a false impression.

ALGERNON

Well, that is exactly what dentists always do. Now, go on! Tell me the whole thing. I may mention that I have always suspected you of being a confirmed and secret Bunburyist; and I am quite sure of it now.

JACK

Bunburyist? What on earth do you mean by a Bunburyist?

ALGERNON

I'll reveal to you the meaning of that incomparable expression as
soon as you are kind enough to inform me why you are Ernest
in town and Jack in the country.

JACK

Well, produce my cigarette case first.

ALGERNON

Here it is.

(Hands cigarette case.)

Now produce your explanation, and pray make it improbable.

(Sits on sofa.)

(from Wilde's *The Importance of Being Earnest*, 1)

Here we see that situation has become incident because there
is movement. *An incident is a happening.* The incident we have
quoted from *The Importance of Being Earnest* may be thus
briefly summarized: Algernon informs Jack that he is in possession of Jack's cigarette case. Jack asks to have it back. Algernon, after teasing him for a while, returns it.

We may note two facts concerning dramatic incident from
our example:

1. It presents a situation which is developed by action (that
   is, a happening which has consequences).
2. One of the characters figures more importantly than the
   others. (There were three characters: Algernon, Jack,
   and Lane. Though Jack is important, Algernon is the
   more important in this incident [not always elsewhere in
   the complete play]: it is Algernon who announces that
   he has the case, who retains it, and who eventually hands

it back to Jack.) *In any incident the doer is the important character.* (Jack in this incident [not always elsewhere in the play] is allotted the more passive role.)

Now, *not all incidents are dramatic incidents.* The mere presence of action does not inevitably make for drama. For example, this script, though it does contain movement and action, does not contain a happening of a dramatic kind (as we shall see) and is therefore not a dramatic incident:

> The scene is the lobby of a Broadway theater. At the left are the window and grille of the ticket office. The rear wall is made up entirely of double doors leading into the theater. At the right are two glass double doors leading to the street.
>
> As the curtain rises, a woman is seen tugging at one of the glass doors, R. When she opens it halfway, she keeps it in this position as she calls over her shoulder:

WOMAN

I won't be a moment, Marie! The man *is* in the box office.

> (She allows the door to shut after her as she comes into the lobby. She goes rapidly toward L., talking as she moves.)

Oh, I'm so glad you're open. We were in the neighborhood seeing a movie, and I said to Marie, "As long as we are here let's see if we can't get tickets." Marie was sure you'd be closed.

> (She has now reached the box-office counter.)

VOICE FROM THE BOX OFFICE

We are.

WOMAN

You are what?

VOICE

Closed, madam, closed. It's past ten o'clock.

WOMAN

I know it's late. But after all you *are* there.

VOICE

That's *my* business. Box office closes at nine.

WOMAN

Don't you have any tickets for this show?

VOICE

Plenty. Come around tomorrow. Open eleven A.M.

WOMAN

Couldn't you make an exception? Just this once?

VOICE

No. Good night, madam.

> (She looks at him wistfully, sighs, and
> walks slowly back toward doors R., and
> exit.)
> (The stage is empty for a few moments.
> The man in the box office is heard singing
> soulfully, *I'm sorry, dear*. Presently one
> of the rear doors opens, and ARTHUR, in
> evening clothes but looking quite di-
> sheveled, stumbles into the lobby.)

VOICE FROM THE BOX OFFICE

What's the matter, Mac? Can't take it?

ARTHUR

(Coming over to the box office.)

No, I can't.

VOICE

Is it that bad?

ARTHUR

It's worse than that.

VOICE

Say, you're Mr. Swinnerton! You're the author, aren't you?

ARTHUR

(Going R.)

I used to be.

VOICE

Aren't you going to wait for the curtain calls?

ARTHUR

(Approaching the glass doors.)

Not me. So long.

(Exit R.)

Here we have had plenty of physical movement—much more than in the episode from the Wilde play—the opening of the glass doors, the woman's moving across stage, her going back again, Arthur's entrance, his movement to the box office, and his exit. But the movement had no dramatic interest. We had, more-over, two incidents: (1) A woman tries to buy tickets for a show and fails. (2) The author of the play leaves the theater before the play is over. But neither incident is dramatic because the happening in each case is in no way developed; moreover, no character stands out as important in either incident. Most important of all, neither incident leads anywhere; when it ends, it leaves nothing to anticipate. In the case of the incident from Wilde's play, there is a great deal left to anticipate at the end of the episode: (1) How will Jack account for the inscription in the case? (2) Who is little Cecily? (3) Why is Ernest Jack in the country? (4) What is a Bunburyist? (5) What of Jack's desire to marry Gwendolen? The incident is connected with all these matters—and, as a reading of the complete play would show, a great many others.

The point, then, is that *the movement in a play is continuous until the end of the play: one dramatic incident leads to another.*

The movement and the happenings in our theater-lobby scene lead nowhere, offer nothing to anticipate. They also involve characters in no interesting way. It would, of course, be possible to rewrite the script so that both meaningless incidents become one meaningful (that is, dramatic) incident. Let us try it:

> As the curtain rises, a woman is seen tugging at one of the glass doors, R. When she opens it halfway, she keeps it in this position as she calls over her shoulder:

WOMAN

I won't be a moment, Marie! The man *is* in the box office.

> (She allows the door to shut after her as she comes into the lobby. She goes rapidly toward L., talking as she moves.)

Oh, I'm so glad you're open. We were in the neighborhood seeing a movie, and I said to Marie, "As long as we are here, let's see if we can't get tickets." Marie was sure you'd be closed.

> (She has now reached the box-office counter.)

VOICE FROM THE BOX OFFICE

We are.

> (One of the rear doors opens, and ARTHUR, in evening clothes but looking quite disheveled, stumbles into the lobby.)

WOMAN

> (To the man in the box office.)

You are what?

VOICE

Closed, madam, closed. It's past ten o'clock.

WOMAN

I know it's late. But after all you *are* there.

VOICE

That's *my* business. Box office closes at nine.

> (ARTHUR moves over quietly to the box office, not noticed by either of the others.)

WOMAN

Don't you have any tickets for this show?

ARTHUR

Madam, there'll be more tickets for this show than anybody will want. Take my advice, don't buy any.

> (ARTHUR is standing close to the wall L., and is therefore invisible to the man in the box office.)

VOICE

Say, who are you?

ARTHUR

(Ignoring him.)

There may not even be a performance tomorrow.

WOMAN

Oh, I'm sure you're wrong about that. It just opened tonight—

VOICE

(Angrily.)

Say, what fresh guy is out there? I'm coming out—

ARTHUR

(Making himself visible.)

Don't bother.

VOICE

Who sent for you—? Say! You're Mr. Swinnerton, aren't you?

ARTHUR

Yes.

VOICE

What are you doing out here? The show will be over in a few minutes.

ARTHUR

It's over already.

WOMAN

I don't understand—

VOICE

He's the author, lady—the man that wrote the play.

ARTHUR

Oh no I didn't!

VOICE

What's the matter, Mr. Swinnerton, aren't you feeling well?

ARTHUR

That is the wildest understatement in history.

WOMAN

(Opening her purse.)

I always carry aspirin in my bag—

ARTHUR

Thank you, madam, but never mind. Unless you happen to have some prussic acid—

VOICE

This is your first play, isn't it, Mr. Swinnerton? Authors usually get jittery before the final curtain—

ARTHUR

Authors are usually privileged to see their own last act.

VOICE

Well, whose last act have you been seeing?

ARTHUR

Not mine, not mine! You can bestow full credit on the star of
the show, on the juvenile lead, on the director, and even the
producer. *He* contributed a choice bit! That about sank the play.

VOICE

Everyone was praising the play out here during both intermissions.

ARTHUR

They loved it—up through the second-act curtain. You should
see them now.

WOMAN

I'm sure it's only the jitters, as the gentleman says, if you don't
mind my agreeing with him. Why, Marie and I are just dying
to see your play, Mr. Swinnerton. The advance publicity made
it sound so exciting!

ARTHUR

(To the man in the box office.)

Give the lady two orchestra seats and charge them to me.

VOICE

Very well, sir.

WOMAN

Oh, how can I ever thank you?

ARTHUR

(Beginning to move toward R.)

Don't. No, yes you can. Just promise to leave after the second
act.

WOMAN

Oh, I'm sure you're exaggerating, Mr. Swinnerton—

VOICE

(Impatiently.)

What day do you want them for, madam?

WOMAN

Would a week from Saturday night—?

ARTHUR

(Coming back a few steps.)

Make it tomorrow night. A week from Saturday the play won't
be here. Take my word for it.

(Exit R. quickly.)

WOMAN

Poor man! I'm sure he's quite wrong about his play, he's so
sweet.

VOICE

Well, madam? Here are two orchestra seats for tomorrow
night.

WOMAN

Are they in the front center?

(A glass door R. opens, and MARIE puts her head inside the lobby.)

MARIE

Gladys! Gladys!

GLADYS

(Turning around.)

What is it, Marie?

MARIE

Is anything wrong?

GLADYS

(Holding up the tickets triumphantly.)

Anything wrong? I should say not. Look! And they're for free!

In making the two incidents into one, it will be noted, we have managed to develop each of the two situations into dramatic incident. Arthur now emerges as the important person: he is the *doer*, and our interest is focused on him. Moreover, there are a number of things we may now anticipate: (1) The new play will be over and the audience will be coming through the rear doors in a minute; when we overhear their verdict, Arthur may be proved right or wrong. (2) Gladys might become involved in these opinions—she might even buttonhole a newspaper critic. (3) As a result of what she hears or says, she may determine to follow up her acquaintance with Arthur out of sympathy for him, or to bring him glad tidings. (4) Arthur might turn out, after all, to have had only a case of the jitters, and come back in time to hear the reactions of the audience; and so on.[7]

It will be noticed as well that both the episode from *The Importance of Being Earnest* and our revision of the lobby scene are much longer than the first version of the latter. This was inevitably the case. We may, indeed, pause here to state an important law of the theater: *in order to make an impression on the audience any given incident must have a certain extensiveness.* The audience can understand only as it sees and watches. An episode that comes and goes on the stage too briefly will not have had time to penetrate the audience's consciousness. In the first version of the lobby scene, each incident was over so quickly that it could not have left any significant impression upon the spectator.

This constitutes an important difference between the novel and short story on the one hand and the drama on the other. In the novel and short story, a writer may achieve powerful effects by severe condensation; what is most dramatic may be made more so by great brevity and terseness. Some short-story writers, like O. Henry, depend entirely upon the unexpectedness of their last sentence or short last paragraph for the major effect. The reader, coming upon the lightning stroke of such condensation, is free to sit and relish the shock he has received.

Not so in the theater. No leisure is permitted the audience to consider or digest what is happening on the stage. Comprehension must keep pace with what is occurring at every moment. Therefore, that which passes quickly on the stage has the effect upon the audience of being of only transitory importance. For example, these are the opening lines of *The Importance of Being Earnest:*

> The sound of a piano is heard in the adjoining room. LANE is arranging afternoon tea on the table, and after the music has ceased, ALGERNON enters.

ALGERNON

Did you hear what I was playing, Lane?

LANE

I didn't think it polite to listen, sir.

ALGERNON

I'm sorry for that, for your sake. I don't play accurately—
anyone can play accurately—but I play with wonderful expression. As far as the piano is concerned, sentiment is my forte.
I keep science for Life.

LANE

Yes, sir.

ALGERNON

And, speaking of the science of Life, have you got the cucumber sandwiches cut for Lady Bracknell?

LANE

Yes, sir.

(Hands them on a salver.)

ALGERNON

(Inspects them, takes two, and sits down
on the sofa.)

Oh!—by the way, Lane, I see from your book that on Thursday night, when Lord Shoreham and Mr. Worthing were
dining with me, eight bottles of champagne are entered as
having been consumed.

LANE

Yes, sir; eight bottles and a pint.

ALGERNON

Why is it that at a bachelor's establishment the servants in-
variably drink the champagne? I ask merely for information.

LANE

I attribute it to the superior quality of the wine, sir. I have often observed that in married households the champagne is rarely of a first-rate brand.

ALGERNON

Good heavens! Is marriage so demoralizing as that?

LANE

I believe it *is* a very pleasant state, sir. I have had very little experience of it myself up to the present. I have only been married once. That was in consequence of a misunderstanding between myself and a young person.

ALGERNON

(Languidly.)

I don't know that I am much interested in your family life, Lane.

LANE

No, sir; it is not a very interesting subject. I never think of it myself.

ALGERNON

Very natural, I am sure. That will do, Lane, thank you.

LANE

Thank you, sir.

(LANE goes out.)

It will be noted that in this brief passage, a number of matters are brought up: Algy's piano playing, the cucumber sand-wiches, the champagne drunk on Thursday night, Lane's way with the champagne, Lane's marital experience, Lane's philos-ophy of marriage. Of these only the cucumber sandwiches will be of account later.* (By contrast observe how much more ex-tended is the passage already quoted from this play, the episode dealing with the cigarette case.) As the play proceeds and other matters arise, the opening exchange between Algy and Lane is not likely to remain in the forefront of the audience's thoughts. (The incident concerning the cigarette case will remain with the audience for the rest of the play.) [8]

Let us take a closer look at the difference in this regard be-tween prose fiction and drama. The two paragraphs below are among the most dramatic in Thackeray's *Henry Esmond*. Colo-nel Henry Esmond and his cousin Frank, whose family has de-voted itself to the dangerous cause of the exiled Stuarts, at great personal risk have brought back into England from France the Stuart Prince, Pretender to the English throne; a licentious and self-willed young man, the Prince, they discover, has repaid their loyalty by attempting to seduce Frank's beautiful sister Beatrix, whom Henry has worshiped. They break into the Prince's bed-room, and find him asleep in his clothes on the bed. They awaken him:

> "If your Majesty will please to enter the next apartment," says Esmond, preserving his grave tone, "I have some papers there which I would gladly submit to you, and by your per-mission I will lead the way"; and, taking the taper up, and backing before the Prince with very great ceremony, Mr. Esmond passed into the little Chaplain's room, through which we had just entered into the house. "Please to set a chair for His Majesty, Frank," says the Colonel to his companion, who wondered almost as much at this scene, and was as much puzzled by it, as the other actor in it. Then going to the crypt over

* However, it is worth noting that these few speeches are not merely amusing chitchat with which to open a play. In them several basic matters are delivered parenthetically to the audience: Algy is a bachelor, Lady Bracknell is expected, a Mr. Worthing has been dining recently with Algy. They also perform another function admirably: they set the tone of the play.

the mantelpiece, the Colonel opened it, and drew out the papers
which so long had lain there.

"Here, may it please your Majesty," says he, "is the Patent
of Marquis sent over by your Royal Father at St. Germains to
Viscount Castlewood, my father: here is the witnessed cer-
tificate of my father's marriage to my mother, and of my birth
and christening; I was christened of that religion of which your
sainted sire gave all through life so shining an example. These are
my titles, dear Frank, and this is what I do with them: here go
Baptism and Marriage, and here go the Marquisate and the
August Sign-Manual, with which your predecessor was pleased
to honor our race." And as Esmond spoke he set the papers
burning in the brazier. "You will please, sir, to remember,"
he continued, "that our family has ruined itself by fidelity to
yours; that my grandfather spent his estate and gave his blood
and his son to die for your service; that my dear lord's grandfather (for lord you are now, Frank, by right and title too)
died for the same cause; that my poor kinswoman, my father's
second wife, after giving away her honor to your wicked
perjured race, sent all her wealth to the King; and got in return
that precious title that lies in ashes, and this inestimable yard
of blue riband. I lay this at your feet and stamp upon it: I
draw this sword, and break it and deny you; and, had you completed the wrong you designed us, by Heaven I would have
driven it through your heart, and no more pardoned you than
your father pardoned Monmouth."

                              (from Chapter XIII: "August 1st, 1714")

This highly dramatic passage, so thrilling to read, shows
Esmond, near the close of the novel, undertaking to break with
the Stuart cause, the cause in behalf of which his family has
sacrificed everything and for which he and Frank have jeopard-
ized their very lives. On a stage this important act could never be
presented this way in a single speech. It would have to be preceded by a passage which would lead up to the burning of the
papers. The speech itself would have to be rearranged into a
number of speeches, interrupted by the Prince and Frank; it
would even be more dramatic if a brief speech preceded the burning of each document, one at a time—with appropriate reaction
on the part of the Prince or Frank. The tearing off of Henry's

riband, the drawing of his sword, and the breaking of it would each make fine theater, and each give the Prince something to react to with words of his own. In this way, the scene would become more extensive—and achieve the importance it merits.[9]

Let us now examine this point from the opposite perspective. Suppose the plot of *Othello* as we find it in Shakespeare's play were, instead, the substance of a novel. Everything in the novel, of course, would lead up to the final pages, in which Othello comes into the bedchamber and kills Desdemona.

This last chapter might describe Othello's coming into the room with the lighted taper in his hand. It might (either by the author's direct narrative or by his casting it in terms of Othello's own thoughts) present the terrible conflict in Othello's heart: his still flourishing love for his wife, his awareness that to kill her is to kill himself, his sense of offering her life and his own on the altar of justice ("She must die or she'll betray more men"). He puts by the taper and approaches the bed. Desdemona is lying in tranquil sleep. He bends over and kisses her. Her fragrance, like that of a rose, overpowers his senses. If he will permit her loveliness to work upon him, he will never be able to do what he must do. He takes a pillow and lowers it swiftly over her face in his clutched hands. Our novelist might conclude his chapter with some such sentence as:

He could not smell the rose now.

Such a sentence—a better one would certainly occur to a first-rate novelist—might make a powerful ending.

In this way the killing of Desdemona could be shown in one brief dramatic sentence. Not so on the stage. There, to justify its position as the culminating action, it would have to be extended. If Othello entered, expressed in a speech the turmoil in his soul, went to the bed, kissed Desdemona, and smothered her at once (as in our novelist's version), the action would be much too brief, perhaps momentarily sensational, but not impressive, and too scantily proportioned for all that preceded. Let us see what Shakespeare did:

(A bedchamber in the castle: Desdemona in bed asleep.

Enter OTHELLO with a light.

OTHELLO

It is the cause, it is the cause, my soul,—
Let me not name it to you, you chaste stars!—
It is the cause. Yet I'll not shed her blood,
Nor scar that whiter skin of hers than snow,
And smooth as monumental alabaster.
Yet she must die, else she'll betray more men.
Put out the light, and then put out the light.
If I quench thee, thou flaming minister,
I can again thy former light restore,
Should I repent me: but once put out thy light,
Thou cunning'st pattern of excelling nature,
I know not where is that Promethean heat
That can thy light relume. When I have pluck'd the rose
I cannot give it vital growth again.
It needs must wither; I'll smell it on the tree.*

(Kisses her.)

Oh, balmy breath, that dost almost persuade
Justice to break her sword! One more, one more.
Be thus when thou art dead, and I will kill thee
And love thee after. One more, and that's the last;
So sweet was ne'er so fatal. I must weep,
But they are cruel tears. This sorrow's heavenly;
It strikes where it doth love. She wakes.

DESDEMONA

Who's there? Othello?

OTHELLO

Ay, Desdemona.

DESDEMONA

Will you come to bed, my lord?

* Othello here goes over to the bed.

OTHELLO

Have you pray'd tonight, Desdemona?

DESDEMONA

Ay, my Lord.

OTHELLO

If you bethink yourself of any crime
Unreconcil'd as yet to Heaven and grace,
Solicit for it straight.

DESDEMONA

Alack, my lord, what may you mean by that?

OTHELLO

Well, do it, and be brief; I will walk by.
I will not kill thy unprepared spirit;
No; heavens forfend! I would not kill thy soul.

DESDEMONA

Talk you of killing?

OTHELLO

Ay, I do.

DESDEMONA

Then Heaven
Have mercy on me!

OTHELLO

Amen, with all my heart!

DESDEMONA

If you say so, I hope you will not kill me.

OTHELLO

Hum!

DESDEMONA

And yet I fear you; for you're fatal then
When your eyes roll so. Why I should fear I know **not,**
Since guiltiness I know not; but yet I feel I fear.

OTHELLO

Think on thy sins.

DESDEMONA

They are loves I bear to you.

OTHELLO

Ay, and for that thou diest.

DESDEMONA

That death's unnatural that kills for loving.
Alas, why gnaw you so your nether lip?
Some bloody passion shakes your very frame.
These are portents; but yet I hope, I hope
They do not point on me.

OTHELLO

Peace, and be still!

DESDEMONA

I will so. What's the matter?

OTHELLO

That handkerchief which I so lov'd and gave thee
Thou gav'st to Cassio.

DESDEMONA

                    No, by my life and soul!
Send for the man, and ask him.

OTHELLO

                         Sweet soul, take heed,
Take heed of perjury; thou art on thy death-bed.

DESDEMONA

Ay, but not yet to die.

OTHELLO

                    Yes, presently: *
Therefore confess thee freely of thy sin;
For to deny each article with oath
Cannot remove nor choke the strong conception
That I do groan withal. Thou art to die.

DESDEMONA

O, Heaven, have mercy on me!

OTHELLO

                    I say, amen.

DESDEMONA

And have you mercy too! I never did
Offend you in my life; never lov'd Cassio
* at once.

But with such general warranty of heaven
As I might love; I never gave him token.

OTHELLO

By heaven, I saw my handkerchief in's hand.
O perjur'd woman! thou dost stone my heart,
And makes me call what I intend to do
A murder, which I thought a sacrifice.
I saw the handkerchief.

DESDEMONA

He found it then;
I never gave it him. Send for him hither;
Let him confess a truth.

OTHELLO

He hath confess'd.

DESDEMONA

What, my lord?

OTHELLO

That he hath us'd thee.

DESDEMONA

How? unlawfully?

OTHELLO

Ay.

DESDEMONA

He will not say so.

OTHELLO

No, his mouth is stopp'd;
Honest Iago hath ta'en order for't.

DESDEMONA

O! my fear interprets. What, is he dead?

OTHELLO

Had all his hairs been lives, my great revenge
Had stomach for them all.

DESDEMONA

Alas! he is betray'd and I undone.

OTHELLO

Out, strumpet! weep'st thou for him to my face?

DESDEMONA

O, banish me, my lord, but kill me not!

OTHELLO

Down, strumpet! *

DESDEMONA

Kill me tomorrow; let me live tonight!

OTHELLO

Nay, if you strive,—

* Othello forces her back in the bed as she tries to escape from it.

DESDEMONA

But half an hour!

OTHELLO

Being done, there is no pause.

DESDEMONA

But while I say one prayer!

OTHELLO

It is too late.

(He smothers her.)

No one who has once seen or read this scene will ever forget it.

Suppose a novelist wished to convey the information that a man, who was about to figure in a woman's life again after a separation of fifteen years, came to see her and was at first not recognized by her. It might very well be adequate to his purposes that he dispose of the matter in this summary manner:

> When Nolan suddenly appeared at Marion's studio, after a separation of fifteen years, she greeted him with her usual cordiality. But it was clear to him that she did not recognize him. After she had made several wild guesses as to who he might be, somewhat deflated he was forced to identify himself.

But in the theater this brevity would never do. See how S. N. Behrman, in his brilliant comedy *Biography*, writes the scene:

NOLAN

Hello, Marion.

MARION

(Doubtfully, feels she should remember
him.)

How do you do? Er—will you excuse me—just a second.

NOLAN

(Genially.)

Certainly.

(He moves right. MARION walks FEYDIE to
the hall door.)

FEYDAK

(Under his breath to her.)

Looks like a commission.

(She makes a gesture of silent prayer.)
. . .
(FEYDIE goes out. MARION turns to face
NOLAN, who is standing with his arms behind his back rather enjoying the surprise he is about to give her.)

NOLAN

How are you, Marion?

MARION

(Delicately.)

Er—do I know you?

NOLAN

Yes. You know me.

MARION

Oh, yes—of course!

NOLAN

About time!

MARION

(Brightly insecure.)

Lady Winchester's garden-party at Ascot—two summers ago—

NOLAN

Guess again!

MARION

No—I know you perfectly well—it's just that—no, don't tell me.

> (She covers her eyes with her hand, try-
> ing to conjure him out of the past.)

NOLAN

This is astonishing. If someone had said to me that I could walk
into a room in front of Marion Froude and she not know me
I'd have told 'em they were crazy.

MARION

(Desperate.)

I do know you. I know you perfectly well—it's just that—

NOLAN

You'll be awful sore at yourself—I warn you.

MARION

I can't forgive myself now—I know!

NOLAN

I don't believe it!

MARION

The American Embassy dinner in Rome on the Fourth of July
—last year—you sat on my right.

NOLAN

I did not!

MARION

(Miserably.)

Well, you sat somewhere. Where did you sit?

NOLAN

I wasn't there.

MARION

Well, I think it's very unkind of you to keep me in suspense
like this. I can't bear it another second!

NOLAN

I wouldn't have believed it!

MARION

Well, give me some hint, will you?

NOLAN

Think of home—think of Tennessee!

MARION

Oh!—

NOLAN

Little Mary Froude—

MARION

(A light breaking in on her.)

No! Oh, no!

NOLAN

Well, it's about time.

MARION

But—! You were—

NOLAN

Well, so were you!

MARION

But—Bunny—you aren't Bunny Nolan, are you? You're his
brother!

NOLAN

I have no brother.

MARION

But Bunny—Bunny dear—how important you've become!

NOLAN

I haven't done badly—no.

MARION

Here, give me your coat and hat.

> (MARION, taking his coat and hat, crosses
> upstage to piano, and leaves them there.
> Laughing, a little hysterical.)

You should have warned me. It's not fair of you. Bunny! Of all
people—I can scarcely believe it.

> (A moment's pause. He doesn't quite like
> her calling him Bunny but he doesn't
> know how to stop it. She sits on model
> stand looking up at him as she says:)

You look wonderful. You look like a—like a—Senator or something monumental like that.

(1)

The incident has been exploited for its full dramatic values. It
achieves its power because it is extended, not condensed (as in
the novel's passage). Note how every moment of this dialogue
is pulled out to sufficient length so that the audience may completely grasp what is at stake: even after Marion's "No! Oh, no!"
she does not immediately declare that she has remembered, until
six speeches later. (In the meantime, Mr. Behrman, skillful
dramatist that he is, is busily sketching Marion's character and
giving us a view of the kind of exciting, international life she
leads—a matter of utmost importance to the plot of the play.)

ACTION

As we have already implied, *physical movement may or may
not constitute dramatic action.* Non-professional theatrical per-

formances often overdo physical movement to the limits of absurdity, in the mistaken idea that it is bound "to keep the audience
interested." Members of the cast are seen forever whirling about
like so many dervishes—as though it were criminal for anyone
to sit or stand still for a few moments—getting up to take, offer,
or put out a cigarette and/or a light; going to fill up high-ball
glasses; bringing drinks; moving from sofas to chairs. So, too,
bad dramatists send someone out every few minutes to answer
the doorbell or the telephone. That kind of movement, when
not kept to a minimum, can be thoroughly disenchanting to an
audience: an excess of it is the stamp of the amateur.

Yet any of these actions could be a dramatic action, of
course, if it bore some significant relationship to the plot. Going
to fill a high-ball glass might be of dramatic import in the case
of a man who has recently joined Alcoholics Anonymous. It
would be a senseless piece of business for a woman to drop a
handkerchief and then pick it up (unless it were characteristic
of her to be dropping things), and equally senseless if someone
else returned it to her, and that were the end of the matter. But
in *Othello* Desdemona's dropping of her handkerchief figures as
a cardinal moment of the plot. What makes filling the high-ball
glass and Desdemona's dropping of the handkerchief a dramatic
action is that each of these actions has a consequence. In the case
of the woman dropping her handkerchief because it is characteristic of her, if no consequence ensues the act is a piece of
characterization rather than a dramatic action.

On the other hand, action need not be physical at all.
Dramatic movement may be the product of dialogue alone, if the
dialogue presents the evolution of an emotional involvement (or
the resolution of one) on the part of the persons speaking. That
can be dramatic action in the very best sense of the term. The
following quotation is from one of the greatest scenes in French
tragedy, from Racine's *Phèdre*. Queen Phaedra, having heard that
her husband Theseus is dead, has been talking to her stepson, the
young man Hippolytus, for whom she has been secretly nourish-
ing an all-consuming passion:

HIPPOLYTUS

My lady,
this is no time to agitate yourself.
Perhaps your husband still beholds the light;

perhaps the Heavens answering our tears
will give him back to us. For Neptune is
his guardian, and my father would not seek
in vain that god's protection.

PHAEDRA

                              Not twice—no man
can visit twice the banks where dwell the dead,
my lord. Since Theseus now inhabits those
sad somber shores, all hope is vain a god
can send him you again. For Acheron
is greedy and will never loose its prey.

                    (Her feelings mastering her.)

What say I? Theseus is *not* dead—he breathes
in you. Before my very eyes I seem
to see my spouse—I see him, speak to him—.
My heart—I'm lost, my lord!

                         (Looking away; more to herself than to
                         him.)

                              Despite myself
my foolish passion will unmask itself!

HIPPOLYTUS

                    (With pity.)

Astounding are the fruits of your devotion,
I see; and dead though Theseus is, he's here
before your eyes; your soul in love of him
must ever be a scorching fire.

PHAEDRA

                    Yes,
I long, I burn for Theseus, prince. I love
him, not as dwellers of the infernal shades
have seen him, fickle worshiper of myriad

successive loves, who vilified the couch
of Hades' deity himself—ah no!
but faithful, proud, yes even fiercely proud—
yet charming too, and young, attracting hearts
of all beholders, as only Gods are said
to do—or as I now behold in you.
He had your very bearing—yes, your eyes,
your trick of speech—he wore that noble blush
that colored his fair skin—when he traversed
the seas to Crete and by his worth aroused
my sister's love *—mine too, alas! Ah what
were you that time about? And why should he
have summoned all the finest heroes Greece
could boast—without Hippolytus? And why
were you too young then to have sailed aboard
the vessel when it brought him to our shores?
You might have been the one whose sword had slain
the Minotaur, despite the windings of
his vast retreat.†

(With increasing passion.)

That you might win your way
through its uncertain turns, my sister would
have armed your hand with that same fateful thread.**
But no! For I'd have been before her with
my help! It's I, not Ariadne, love
would first have taught that care of you!

(In a rush of passion.)

It's I,
my prince, I know it's I whose aid would out
that winding labyrinth have shown you the
escape! Solicitude for your dear head
had been my sought and cherished task! No thread
could then have satisfied your lover's fears;

* Ariadne's.
† the labyrinth where the Minotaur was housed.
** by means of which Ariadne helped Theseus find his way out
of the labyrinth after the hero had slain the Minotaur. Without that
aid Theseus would have wandered lost among its mazes until he perished.

a sharer of the peril you were doomed
to face, I would have walked before you to
encounter it myself. Within that maze
I would have penetrated by your side,
and chosen by your side to have emerged
or by your side within that maze to perish!

HIPPOLYTUS

(Shocked.)

Great Gods! What's this I hear? My lady, can
you have forgot that Theseus is my father?—
that Theseus is your husband?

PHAEDRA

(In confusion, trying to recover her dignity.)

Why do you
infer I have forgotten, prince? or that
I've lost all sense of caring for my honor?

HIPPOLYTUS

(Glad of an excuse to leave.)

My lady, pray forgive me. Though I blush
to own it, I had misconstrued your words
and all their innocence. My shame thereat
cannot sustain your glance another moment.
I go—

PHAEDRA

(Restraining him.)

Ah, cruel man! You understood
my words too well! I've said too much to draw
you into error! Alas, alas! Now hear

what Phaedra is and all her madness! I—
I love you.

> (HIPPOLYTUS tries to speak; she intercepts
> him, rapidly.)

Think not at the moment when
I love you that I fail to feel my guilt,
or that I like myself for loving you—
nor deem my weak compliance nourishes
the poison of this maddening love which so
unseats my reason! I, unhappy victim
of vengeful gods, abhor myself far more
than you could possibly detest me. I
can call upon the Gods to witness that!—
those Gods who lit the fatal fire in
my body, burning in my veins—those Gods
whose cruel sport it is to lead astray
a feeble woman's heart!

> (He turns from her in growing horror.)

Yourself, recall
to mind the past! It was not enough for me
to flee you, cruel one—I chased you from
the land! I sought to seem inhuman, hateful—
the better to resist you I besought
your hatred. What availed my idle efforts?
You hated me the more—I loved you none
the less. And my injustices to you
but lent you new enchantment. Languishing,
I withered—now in flames, and now in tears—
your eyes must sure persuade you this is truth—
if but your eyes one moment deigned to look
at me.

> (HIPPOLYTUS covers his ears with his
> hands, to hear no more.)

(II)*

* B. Grebanier, *Racine's Phaedra: An English Acting Version* (New York, 1958), pp. 37–42.

Here we see how, exclusively through dialogue, there may be powerful and intense movement—that is, dramatic action. The end of this piece of dialogue finds the two characters in a very different relation to each other from that which obtained when the dialogue opened. Before the lines where our quotation begins, Phaedra has been smothering her guilty passion; Hippolytus has had no slightest idea of it and has thought of her as a woman who hated him, a spiteful stepmother. At the conclusion of this passage the very lives of these two are at stake. Yet there has been absolutely no physical movement required for this action.

Naturally, we are not hinting that dramatic physical movement is not highly desirable in a play or that the absence of physical movement constitutes any kind of superiority. On the contrary, since the most powerful appeal in the theater is to the eye, dramatic physical action is characteristic of many of the world's finest plays. *Hamlet,* by general consent containing the subtlest psychological insight in all drama, runs over with physical action: the Ghost appears and vanishes, and later reappears to lead Hamlet on into the night; the King and Polonius hide behind a tapestry to eavesdrop on Hamlet and Ophelia; Hamlet presents a play before the King and Queen which drives the King in a panic from the chamber; Hamlet whips out his sword and nearly murders the King while the monarch is praying; Polonius hides in the Queen's chamber to spy on Hamlet; Hamlet runs Polonius through; the Ghost reappears while Hamlet is railing at his mother; a mob led by Laertes storms the royal palace; Ophelia in her madness distributes imaginary flowers to the King, Queen, and Laertes; Hamlet leaps into Ophelia's grave; Laertes and he grapple in the grave; Hamlet fights a fencing match; the Queen drinks the wine which the King has just poisoned; she dies; Hamlet is mortally wounded; he kills Laertes and the King. It would be hard for a play to have more physical action than this; yet every one of these actions is a dramatic action and is closely related to the plot.

The example of *Phèdre* merely shows that dramatic action can be achieved without physical movement. There are many such plays too. Any one of Ibsen's great plays would afford many a scene in illustration. (Read, for example, the last scene in the play, between Nora and her husband, in *A Doll's House.*)

This is the climactic scene in S. N. Behrman's comedy *The Second Man*. Kendall Frayne, a wealthy woman of thirty-five, is in love with the dilettante Clark Storey, and has decided to marry him against her better judgment; Austin Lowe, a brilliant chemist who is deficient in the art of self-expression, is madly in love with Monica Grey, a young, vibrant girl, who alternates between accepting him and rejecting him. Monica has a violent attraction to Storey, who for everyone's sake has been trying to keep her at a distance. The four have been drinking champagne, and are about to go up to a Harlem night club:

KENDALL

And now I really think we've talked enough nonsense. We'd better start.

STOREY

I'm just in the mood for a good jazz-band.

KENDALL

Who'll carry the champagne?

STOREY

Austin.

AUSTIN

I'll take it.

(He lifts hamper.)

Monica, I don't dance. Will you teach me?

MONICA

(Tensely.)

Before we go—there's something *I* want to say.

STOREY

You'll tell us in the taxi.

MONICA

No. Here.

KENDALL

Another revelation?

MONICA

Yes.

> (Her voice and manner are very strained,
> like one keyed up to accomplish an im-
> possible feat.)

STOREY

What's the matter, Monica? Aren't you well?

KENDALL

You would start this.

AUSTIN

> (Very concerned.)

Monica—!

MONICA

Since everybody's telling the truth—why shouldn't I?

STOREY

Don't say anything you'll be sorry for.

MONICA

Even if I *am* sorry—I'm going to say it.

KENDALL

I really think we ought to go out.

AUSTIN

The fresh air'll do her good.

MONICA

I'll say it if it—kills me.

AUSTIN

(Anxious.)

What *is* it, Monica?

STOREY

(Suspicious.)

Watch your step, child.

MONICA

I think you ought to know it, Mrs. Frayne. Austin, I think you ought to know it.

AUSTIN

I know more than I want to now.

(Picking up her wraps.)

There's been too much confession. Let's start.

MONICA

No, stop. All of you. I want you to know—that Storey—Storey
is the father of my child—my unborn child.

STOREY

(Amazed.)

Monica!

MONICA

There now, I've said it. I feel better.

(She takes a quick gulp of champagne.
KENDALL and AUSTIN stare accusingly at
STOREY. They are speechless.)

STOREY

She's ill. She's had too much champagne.

(II, ii)

Here again there is no significant physical action. But the scene
moves deftly to the moment when Monica makes her announcement, which has the effect of a bombshell. This is action in the
best sense of the word. (Note, too, how skillfully the dramatist
has extended the dialogue to achieve the maximum of effect.)

On the other hand, it is important to remember that nothing
is worse in a play than pointless dialogue—that is, dialogue which
has nothing to contribute to dramatic incident. For a sample of
such:

LUCY

I think I'll go downtown later this afternoon.

JOAN

Why?

LUCY

They're having linen sales in all the stores this week.

JOAN

They'll be mobbed.

LUCY

I know. If there's anything I hate it's crowds.

JOAN

Then why go?

LUCY

We're completely out of sheets and pillow slips.

JOAN

But you bought two dozen sheets last year. I was with you, remember?

LUCY

Yes. Our maid has been stealing them two at a time. There are only four of the two dozen left.

JOAN

I never heard of such a thing! Why don't you fire her?

LUCY

Oh, what's the use? They're all the same. Besides, they're the only things she takes. She's perfectly honest about money and jewelry.

JOAN

I keep everything under lock and key.

LUCY

I suppose I ought to, but you can't really lock up everything.

JOAN

I even keep the books that come from the book clubs locked in a clothes closet.

LUCY

Really?

JOAN

Yes. My maid is quite a reader.

LUCY

By the way, what's the current choice of the Masterpiece-of-the-Month Club?

JOAN

The Egg and They. Written by the same woman who wrote the other *Egg* books.

LUCY

I must get that. I enjoyed the others ever so much.

JOAN

I know what you mean. They made you wonder whether farmers' wives don't have the best of life.

I can just imagine my husband as a farmer. He has no use for animals—unless they come out of the oven.

Such dialogue, even if it were quite clever, can only militate against the soundness of a play, for it would not escape the audience that it is no more than mere padding.[10] It involves no kind of movement and it leads nowhere. There is no room in a play for talk for the sake of talk.

INCIDENT AND PLOT

Plot, Aristotle remarked a long time ago, is the soul of drama. Plot, of course, may be described superficially as a sequence of incidents, but that would be a very inaccurate definition, for *a plot*, as Aristotle went on to observe, must be "complete and whole. . . . A whole is that which *has a beginning, a middle, and an end*. A beginning is that which does not itself follow anything by causal necessity, but after which something naturally is or comes to be. An end, on the contrary, is that which itself naturally follows some other thing . . . but has nothing following it. A middle is that which follows something as some other thing follows it. A well-constructed plot, therefore, must neither begin nor end at haphazard."

If we may quote what we have said on this subject elsewhere:

Plot . . . is a matter of action—of the deeds that are done during the course of the story. . . . The characters of a play may be moved by subconscious processes which the audience is aware of; and these subconscious processes may lead to important actions. But such motivations are not part of the plot. Plot is made up of action. Thus, a modern writer might conceivably have chosen to explain Romeo's relationship with Juliet as a reaction from his frustration over Rosaline * (Shakespeare makes it the result of Romeo's being in love for the first

* The girl with whom Romeo imagines himself in love at the opening of the play.

time in his life); that frustration, though a motive for the plot, would not be part of the plot itself.

But action in itself does not necessarily constitute plot. A story detailing the many events occurring in the life of one individual may be totally lacking in plot: for example, a story which traced Romeo's life from birth, through his boyhood adventures, his experiences at school, his first attraction to a woman, his frustration over Rosaline, and so on through his meeting with Juliet and the consequences thereof. Romeo's boyhood adventures, his experiences at school, and his frustration over Rosaline do not coordinate into a plot because there exists no logical connection between the events preceding Romeo's meeting with Juliet and his actions in the play.

Action which constitutes plot is to be distinguished from a series of unrelated incidents in that *a plot contains a logical unity within itself:* it begins at a certain point; this beginning contains the roots of the middle; the middle gives rise to the question which the play must settle; the end answers the question, completing what was begun in the beginning.

In *Romeo and Juliet* what is pertinent to the play in the first act leads to the *beginning of the plot* (Act I, sc. 5):

1. Romeo, member of a family that is at feud with the family of Juliet, meets Juliet, and falls in love with her. What follows this happening leads to the *middle of the plot* (Act II, sc. 6):

2. Although their families are at feud, Romeo marries Juliet. This deed raises a question to be answered by the *end* of the play:

3. Will Romeo find happiness or catastrophe in his marriage with Juliet? *

Here the roots of the middle are in the beginning; the end follows as a result of what was done in the middle; and the whole contains a logical unity.

Again, a story detailing these matters: Othello's life as a young prince among his own people, the Moors; his resisting the infatuation of a Moorish woman; his fighting against the Venetian army; his capture by the Venetians; his life as a slave

* B. Grebanier and S. Reiter, *Introduction to Imaginative Literature* (New York, 1960), pp. 186–87.

in Venice; his rise in Venice as a man of valor; his service for Venice against various armies; his promotion to the generalship (several of these details, the play gives us to understand, were actually part of his life story); Desdemona's being left an orphan by the death of her mother; her devotion to her father; her brightness under the tutelage of her instructors; her being courted by various Venetian noblemen; Iago's being slighted by his mother in favor of a younger brother; his being rejected by the first woman he proposed to—all such possible incidents have nothing to do with the plot of *Othello*, which is concerned exclusively with the love between Othello and Desdemona. The beginning, middle, and end of that plot (as we shall later see) must be made up of incidents connected with that love.

Or, a story which recounts extensively: Marion Froude's early promise as an artist; her being attracted to Leander Nolan; their romantic walks in their native Nashville; her giving herself to him; her realization of their fundamental incompatibility and her need of a larger life; her suddenly leaving Nashville; her working hard at an art school in New York; her struggles to survive; her first important commission to paint a portrait; her going to Europe to try her fortunes there; her struggles there; her achieving recognition; her developing reputation and subsequent fame; her unconventional life; her love affairs with various celebrities; her love for Feydak; her career among the stars in Hollywood; Leander's shock at Marion's disappearance; his preparation for the law; his success as a lawyer; his earliest adventures into politics; his becoming engaged to Kinnicott's daughter; Kurt's impoverished boyhood as the son of a miner; his seeing his father shot down during a strike; his attempts to shift for himself; his tramping about the world; his working at odd jobs; his two years at Yale; his breaking into the magazine field—all such incidents, though they form the background of S. N. Behrman's *Biography*, are not part of its actual plot, which is concerned exclusively with the relationship of Marion and Kurt. The beginning, middle, and end of that plot (as we shall see later) must be made up of incidents connected with that relationship.

In constructing the plot of a play, therefore, one must first concentrate on those incidents which are to make up the plot. All other incidents in the play must be subordinate and contributory to the plot in the design of the play.

CHAPTER FOUR

Plot (2)

This blessed plot.   *Richard II*, ii, i

Nothing is law that is not reason.   SIR J. POWELL, *Coggs v. Bernard*

Perchance he whose plot is next to thine
Will see it, and mend his own.
                          E. R. CHARLES, *The Child on the Judgment Seat*

. . . If our elders break all reason's laws,
These fools demand not pardon but applause.   POPE, *Horace*, ii, i

If a good plot has its own inevitable logic, how is one to
describe that logic? Aristotle's analysis goes a long way toward
doing that: the beginning must contain the roots of the middle;
the middle must lead on to the end; the beginning must be a real
commencing; the end must complete what was begun in the
beginning.

But is it not possible to find an even more precise way of expressing this logic? William T. Price (1846–1920), a highly
educated, widely traveled attorney, who largely gave up his
profession to devote himself to his great love, the theater, thought
it was possible. For years he wrestled with the problem of discovering the logical equation in which any sound plot might be
stated. His model was the syllogism of formal logic, of which
the most familiar is probably:

> All men are mortal.
> Socrates is a man.
> Hence, Socrates is mortal.

He felt, quite correctly, that it ought to be possible to state a
plot with something like that same simplicity. If one could do

that, it would then be possible to shape one's material so that it would not violate that internal logic which a plot should have; it would also be possible to recognize what was wrong in any given play whose plot gave one the impression of being "not quite right."

Eventually Price was able to formulate his law of plot, the Proposition—which, we are quite willing to agree, is the one significant contribution to the science of playwriting since Aristotle's *Poetics*. This was the judgment of many of his students, among whom were the most successful American dramatists of their generation. It is a large remark, but, as we say, we do not dispute it—even though Price's very name seems unknown to the public or to the scholars these days. If we ourselves were asked to whom we are indebted for the basis of our ideas about playwriting, we should have to answer, "Aristotle and Price."

For a while Price practiced law in his native Kentucky, but he was soon more occupied with his avocation as drama critic. He came to New York, where he became drama editor on an important newspaper, as well as playreader and adviser to people of the theater. At the turn of our century, urged by many young dramatists whom he had helped, he founded the first school of playwriting ever established. This institution proved its value by the subsequent work of its students. Moreover, until the end of his days Price continued to act as play doctor for prominent producers like Belasco, who could depend upon him to find the flaws in a weak play and to mend them.

No doubt Price developed many valuable ideas about playwriting, which he must have communicated to those studying under him (his former pupils continued to consult him about each new work), but it is only the Proposition upon which he wrote significantly. Our gratitude for that would make us feel churlish if we were to elaborate upon our conviction that he did not investigate the corollaries of the Proposition—for example, the meaning of climax, the function of the central character (he speaks of Romeo and Juliet, for instance, as both being the central character in the play—a total impossibility), the choice of secondary characters. These corollary matters, and they are many, are so intimately connected with a correct stating of the Proposition that they render Price's formulation not quite adequate or precise. He himself never ceased to be dissatisfied with his formulation; had he investigated the implications of the Proposition, he must inevitably have restated it somewhat differently. We say this much to explain why we have had to recast his ideas concerning the Proposition and also greatly to expand upon its inevitable consequences, and not at all for the purpose of underlining the limitations of what he had to say. He was a pioneer, and a great one. Price's discovery of the Proposition is, indeed, an invaluable contribution. Above all, we wish to acknowledge gratefully our indebtedness to it for the groundwork of much of our own thinking on playwriting.

Now, the Proposition, which is the logical statement of a plot, must be understood to be:

1. An analysis of the *main action* only. It does not include subsidiary plots, if any. It has reference *only to action*, not to motives, psychological states, moral issues, or the theme, for plot is entirely a matter of action (though motives and characterization may be mentioned in a subordinate way).

2. An analysis of the action that is actually in the play— that is, from the rise of the first curtain to the fall of the last. It does not include material that precedes the rise of the first curtain, for that would be outside the *beginning* of the plot, and the Proposition must begin with that beginning. It does not include any material that might occur after the descent of the last curtain, for that would be outside the *end* of the plot, and the Proposition must conclude with matter dealing with that end.

Let us see if it is not possible to present the Proposition inductively. It will be more thoroughly understood if we do it that way. This will mean that our remarks about the Proposition will for a while have to be more or less tentative. We do not expect to arrive at a precise formulation of the Proposition for several pages. We have another reason for wishing to approach it by degrees, and that is that experience has proved that in applying the Proposition to any given play or to the material that one wishes to shape into a play, it is very wise practice to ask first:

What is this play about?
by which we mean:
What is the play's action about?

For example:

What is *Hamlet* about? The answer to this question can be only: Will Hamlet kill the King?

What is *The Importance of Being Earnest* about? Clearly: Will Jack be able to satisfy Lady Bracknell's requirements so he can marry Gwendolen?

What is *Romeo and Juliet* about? The answer: Will Romeo find happiness with Juliet?

The answer to each of these questions is, then, what Aristotle calls the *end* of the plot—and this is clearly the most important part of the action of the play, for it is what beginning and middle have been leading to. *What the play is about will be* therefore *dealt·with in the third step* of our three-step Proposition.

Now, the *middle* of the plot must contain an occurrence that in some way leads logically to the end of the plot. Let us see what these occurrences in the middle of the plot are in the same three plays:

What raises the question: Will Hamlet kill the King? This event: Hamlet, by presenting a little play before the King, proves to himself that the King is unquestionably guilty of the murder of Hamlet's father. (Now that Hamlet is certain, will he take vengeance?)

What raises the question: Will Jack be able to satisfy Lady Bracknell's requirements? This occurrence: Jack is forbidden by Lady Bracknell to marry Gwendolen unless he can acquire parents before the social season is over. (Now that he knows the conditions, will he be able to fulfill them?)

What raises the question: Will Romeo find happiness with Juliet? This fact: Romeo marries Juliet. (Now that they are married, will he find a way to avoid catastrophe?)

The occurrence in the middle of the plot that leads to the end of the plot will be the second step of our Proposition.

Now, the *beginning* of the plot contains an occurrence which forms the root of this middle action. Let us see what these beginning occurrences are:

What is the root of Hamlet's presenting his play before the King to test the King's guilt? Hamlet is told by the Ghost (who may or may not be speaking truthfully)

that the King has murdered Hamlet's father, and is
enjoined to avenge that murder.

What is the root of Jack's being forbidden to marry
Gwendolen by Lady Bracknell unless he can acquire
parents? Jack, having proposed marriage to Gwendolen, asks Lady Bracknell's consent.

What is the root of Romeo's marrying Juliet? Romeo meets
Juliet and falls in love with her at first sight.

*The occurrence in the beginning of the plot which contains the
root of the middle of the plot will be the first step* of our Proposition.

Let us now restate, still tentatively, the Propositions for
these three plays:

1. Hamlet is told by the Ghost (who may or may not be
   speaking truthfully) that the King has murdered Hamlet's father, and is enjoined to avenge that murder.
2. Hamlet, by presenting a little play before the King,
   proves that the King is really guilty of the murder.
3. Will Hamlet kill the King?

1. Jack, having proposed marriage to Gwendolen, asks
   Lady Bracknell's consent.
2. He is forbidden by Lady Bracknell to marry Gwendolen
   unless he can acquire parents.
3. Will Jack succeed in satisfying Lady Bracknell's requirements?

1. Romeo falls in love with Juliet at first sight.
2. He marries her.
3. Will he find happiness in his marriage with her? *

From this let us formulate the Proposition as it may be applied

---

* Price uses *Romeo and Juliet* as his example. But this is his final
way of stating the Proposition for that play:
1. "Romeo and Juliet, members of the houses of Montague and
   Capulet, in deadly strife, fall in love."
2. "They marry."
3. "Will it result happily and reunite their families?"
                    (from *The Analysis of Play Construction*, 1908)
To this one must make these serious objections:
1. Either Romeo or Juliet must be the central character. They
cannot both be. From our later discussion it will be clear that the climax
settles the question as to who is the central character. It is Romeo. The

to any sound plot. Like the syllogism of formal logic, our
Proposition is formulated in three steps:

    1. *The condition of the action.**
    2. *The cause of the action.*
    3. *The resulting action.*†

*The condition of the action is the first significant event of
the play, the event which holds the root of the cause of the action.*
For example (tentative), Romeo falls in love with Juliet at first
sight.

    *The cause of the action is the event which follows from the
condition of the action, and which raises a question which the
rest of the play must answer.* For example (tentative), Romeo
marries Juliet.

    *The resulting action will answer the question raised by the
cause of the action, the question which is the chief business of
the plot.* For example, Will Romeo find happiness with Juliet?

    It is to be noted that each of these three steps refers to *the
action*, to *the chief incidents of the plot.*

    It would be incorrect to say that the condition of the action
of *Romeo and Juliet* is that the families of Juliet and Romeo are
at feud with each other—incorrect for two vital reasons:

    1. Being at feud is a situation, not an event. It is static.
    2. This feud existed long before the play opens, and our
        Proposition must describe only what happens in the play.
        The feud existed *before* the beginning of the plot of this
        play.

    It is also to be noted that the condition of the action is the

---

Proposition must be stated in terms of the central character. The problem
with which the plot deals in *his* problem pre-eminently.

    2. The chief action of the play is certainly concerned with the
results of Romeo's marriage to Juliet. The question of the reunion of
the families, however, is a purely subsidiary one. The chief action of
the play—that is, the end of the plot—cannot be *two* different matters.

    * Price calls this "the conditions of the action." The plural is mis-
leading. This first step refers to *an action*, not a multiplicity of actions.

    † Price calls this "the result of the action." The phrasing implies
that this third step is mere situation—that is, static—and that the action
proper ends with Step 2. This third step, the *result*, is itself an action,
the most important part of the action of the play. Will Hamlet kill the
King? Will Jack be able to acquire parents? Will Romeo find happiness with Juliet? All questions that the play must answer, and can
answer, only in terms of action.

first *significant* event of the play, significant because it is the
event which begins the *plot*—that is, leads to the cause of the
action. The condition of the action is therefore not necessarily
the very first thing that happens in a play. For instance, Romeo
does not meet Juliet until the fifth scene of the first act; and it
is because he hopes to see Rosaline that he goes to the Capulet
ball, where by accident he meets Juliet. Before this encounter he
imagines himself in love with Rosaline, and the first thing that
Romeo does in the play is to tell Benvolio of his unrequited
passion for her. Suppose we mistook this first event to be the
condition of the action? Our Proposition would then read something like this:

1. Romeo informs Benvolio that he is hopelessly in love
   with Rosaline.
2. He is persuaded by Benvolio to go to the Capulet ball
   because Rosaline will be there.
3. Will he see Rosaline?

This would end the plot of the play before the conclusion of the
first act! Certainly, *Romeo and Juliet* does not concern itself
over the problem: Will Romeo see Rosaline? It would be hard
to imagine a more profoundly uninteresting plot than one which
would be concerned with the question: Will Mr. X see Miss Y? *

What of the episode of the cigarette case in *The Importance
of Being Earnest?* It is an episode that has important bearings on
what happens later in the play, but it nevertheless precedes the
condition of the action of the plot, which is, as we have said:
Jack, having proposed marriage to Gwendolen, asks Lady Bracknell's consent.

What of Horatio's seeing the Ghost in the first scene of
Hamlet? Dramatic it is, and important too, to the events which
follow. But it nevertheless precedes the condition of the action
of the plot (that is, it precedes the first step of the plot), which
is, as we have said: Hamlet is told by the Ghost that the King has
murdered Hamlet's father, and is enjoined to avenge that murder.

---

* *Romeo and Juliet* is an early work of Shakespeare's; possibly no
dramatic masterpiece of equal stature has so many flaws. It is safe to
assume, from a study of his later tragedies, that much of the business
of Act I would have been omitted as superfluous had he written the play
half a dozen years later, and that if he used the Romeo-Rosaline material
at all, he would have passed over it very quickly.

Is there any way in which we can recognize that an early event in a play may be not the condition of the action but only an event which precedes the beginning of the plot? Yes:

It will be noted that in our tentative statements of the Proposition for all three plays, *two* characters, the same two characters, appear in *each* of the three steps: Hamlet and the King; Jack and Lady Bracknell; Romeo and Juliet. Hamlet, Jack, and Romeo are each *the central character* of the play. The King, Lady Bracknell, and Juliet are each *the second character* of the play. *The Proposition always deals with events in which both the central and second characters are concerned.* Hence, an event involving Horatio, or Algernon, or Rosaline (whom, as a matter of fact, we do not ever meet in *Romeo and Juliet*) could not figure as one of the three steps which constitute the basis of the plot.

The fact that a plot concerns itself always with the relationship between the central character and the second character cannot be too much stressed. Here is an example of the kind of story which Hollywood movies have told a thousand times:

1. Geraldine, who is in love with Harold but cannot accept his affection because he is married to an invalid wife who is totally dependent upon him, takes final farewell of him and goes to Alaska.
2. Harold's neighbor, Boniface, starts a fire in his fireplace; during the night, the chimney catches fire; Boniface's house and all the nearby houses are burned to the ground; among the dozen victims of the fire is Harold's wife.
3. Free at last because of his wife's death, Harold boards the next plane for Nome, where he is joined in happy wedlock to Geraldine.

Now, although this story would seem to present one event following another, it does so only in the temporal sense (one thing happens *after* another) but not in the logical sense (one thing happens *because* of another). This is not a plot. In the first step, Geraldine is the central character and Harold the second. In the second, Boniface is the central character and Harold's wife the second. In the third step, Harold is the central character and Geraldine the second.

To be sure of his direction, therefore, the student should develop the habit of stating the Proposition so that the central character is always the *subject of the sentence*—for the simple reason that the central character is the subject of the plot. Note that we did not say: The Ghost informs Hamlet that . . . , but rather: Hamlet is informed by the Ghost that. . . . Note that in the second step we did not say: Lady Bracknell forbids Jack . . . , but: Jack is forbidden by Lady Bracknell. . . . Neither the Ghost nor Lady Bracknell is the central (the Ghost is not even the second) character; therefore neither should appear as the subject of the Proposition.[11]

It must be clearly understood that the attribution of the role of second character is in no way a product of the amount of interest attaching to any given person of the drama. Algernon is quite as interesting as Jack, perhaps more so; Cecily is quite as interesting as Lady Bracknell; Miss Prism is perhaps the most amusing governess in comedy. But the business of the plot involves Jack and Lady Bracknell, not Jack and Algernon. Hence it is Lady Bracknell who is the second character.

The basic business of the plot of *Othello* obviously involves Othello and Desdemona. The character of Iago looms very large in the play, and some performances (quite outrageously) have allowed him to dwarf even Othello in interest; he actually speaks a greater number of lines than Othello, and a great many more than Desdemona. But the plot deals fundamentally with the Moor and his wife, and hence it is Desdemona who is the second character.

Mercutio is perhaps the most fascinating character in *Romeo and Juliet*. But, although Shakespeare has managed to involve him brilliantly in a cardinal moment of the plot's unwinding, he is outside the most basic business of the story. The play does not especially concern itself with Romeo's relation to him.

To find the central character and the second character in a play, one has only to ask what the action of the play is about to find out *whom* the action of the play is about—Will Hamlet kill the King? Will Jack satisfy Lady Bracknell's requirements? Will Romeo find happiness with Juliet? This is one important reason why it is best to tackle the Proposition at the third step: one can thus positively identify the characters with whom the plot has to deal as soon as one can state *the resulting action*.

To find *the cause of the action*, as we have seen, one asks: What event *raises the question* which the rest of the play must answer—that is, what event involving the central and second characters raises this question? What event raises the question: Will Hamlet kill the King? (Clearly, Hamlet's presenting the play before the King and finding him guilty.) What raises the question: Will Romeo find happiness with Juliet? (Obviously, Romeo's marrying Juliet.)

To find *the condition of the action*, as we have seen, one asks: What event makes it follow logically that Romeo will marry Juliet? (Obviously, that Romeo meets her and falls in love with her.) What event makes it follow logically that Hamlet will present his play before the King? (Clearly, that he is informed of the murder by the Ghost—whose veracity is uncertain—and commanded to take vengeance.)

THE PROPOSITION FINALLY STATED

We have described our Propositions for *Romeo and Juliet*, *Hamlet*, and *The Importance of Being Earnest* as still tentative. Why? Because our statement of each has not paralleled the logic of the syllogism of formal logic:

> All men are mortal.
> Socrates is a man.
> Hence, Socrates is mortal.

Here we are able to arrive at a conclusion because there is a term common to each of the first two statements—namely, man. Similarly, what we need for a satisfactory Proposition is some element common to the condition of the action and the cause of the action (Steps 1 and 2), so that the resulting action (Step 3) is made a question that *needs* to be resolved.

Let us now revise our tentative statements of the three plays (see page 88) to formulate Propositions which will really show a procession of firm logic.

What is the common ground making for the dramatic interest between these two facts: Romeo falls in love with Juliet at first sight; Romeo marries her? Obviously, the family feud. It is the family feud which makes his falling in love with her and his marrying her dramatically significant. We can therefore state the Proposition for this play, at last, as:

1. Romeo, *scion of a family at feud with Juliet's family*, falls in love with Juliet at first sight.
2. *Although their families are at feud*, he marries her.

3. Will he find happiness in this marriage with her?

The common denominator in Steps 1 and 2 makes the question in Step 3 inevitable.

What is the common ground making for the dramatic interest between these two facts: Jack, having proposed marriage to Gwendolen, asks Lady Bracknell's consent; he is forbidden by Lady Bracknell to marry her unless he can acquire parents? Obviously, Gwendolen's acceptance of him. It is the fact that although she does accept him her mother puts impediments in their way which makes for the dramatic significance of their relationship. Our Proposition for this play will therefore be:

1. Jack, *having proposed marriage to Gwendolen and been accepted by her,* asks Lady Bracknell for her consent.
2. *Although Gwendolen has accepted him,* he is forbidden by Lady Bracknell to marry her unless he can acquire parents.
3. Will Jack succeed in acquiring parents so he can marry Gwendolen?

The common denominator in Steps 1 and 2 makes the question in Step 3 inevitable.

What is the common ground making for the dramatic interest between these two facts: Hamlet is told by the Ghost that the King has murdered Hamlet's father, and is enjoined to avenge that murder; Hamlet, by presenting a little play before the King, proves that the King is really guilty of the murder? Obviously, the Ghost's revelations. It is Hamlet's uncertainty about the reliability of the Ghost's revelations which makes the presentation of the little play before Claudius of dramatic moment.* Our Proposition for the play will therefore be:

1. *Hamlet is told by the Ghost* that the King has murdered Hamlet's father, and is enjoined to avenge that murder.
2. *Because Hamlet is unsure of the reliability of the Ghost's revelations,* he presents a little play before the King and through it proves that the King is really guilty of the murder.
3. Will Hamlet now kill the King?

The common denominator in Steps 1 and 2 makes the question in Step 3 inevitable.[12]

* See B. Grebanier, *The Heart of Hamlet: The Play Shakespeare Wrote* (New York, 1960), pp. 151–59, 165–83.

Let us now deduce the Proposition for several celebrated plays. We shall make our way, as already suggested, by asking questions pertinent to the heart of the plot. From the answers to these we shall be able to formulate the Proposition first tentatively, then finally:

Othello

What is the play about? Something to do with the love of Othello and Desdemona. Since he is the doer of the action,* this something concerns itself with his love for her much more than with her love for him. The play, fundamentally, deals with this question: Will Othello banish from his mind his unfounded jealousy of his wife and regain his untainted love for her? This, when properly stated, will be our third step, the resulting action of the play.

What event of the play raises the question of his regaining his untainted love for her? His allowing his mind to be poisoned against her by the insinuations of Iago. This will be the central fact of our second step, the cause of the action.

What event of the play preceding this cause of the action bears a logical relationship † to this cause? Othello's demonstrating to the world (Act I, scene iii) his complete confidence in his wife's love and in the soundness of their marriage. This is the action which constitutes the beginning of the plot, our first step, the condition of the action.

Now, what is the connecting link between the condition and the cause of the action here? The fact that Othello has every reason to be sure of Desdemona's loyalty. It is this which makes his succumbing to the machinations of Iago tragic.

Our Proposition for *Othello*, therefore, will be:

1. Othello, knowing Desdemona's complete love of him, defends his title to be her husband before the world.**

* Not at all because of the title of the play. The hero of *Julius Caesar* is not the man who gives the title to the play; the same is true of *Henry IV* (both parts) and many other plays.

† In our other plays the logical relationship has been one of cause and effect; in the case of *Othello*, the logical relationship is an adversative one.

** Scholars have long remarked that Shakespeare invented all the business of Act I before putting to use in Act II the material he found

2. Despite his knowledge of her complete love of him, he allows his mind to be poisoned against her by Iago's insinuations.
3. Will he regain his untainted love of her or will he not?

Hedda Gabler

What is the play about? It is clear that it has something to do with Hedda and Lovborg—more specifically, with Hedda, on the one hand, and with Lovborg and Thea's work, on the other. What Hedda would wish to do, in short, is to destroy Lovborg and Thea's work. That is the resulting action.

What event of the play raises the question as to whether or not Hedda will succeed in destroying Lovborg's work? When she succeeds in persuading him to go to the party where there is every likelihood that he will forfeit all he has accomplished in the way of rehabilitation and put an end to the bright future Thea's help has made possible. This is the cause of the action.

With what event of the play is this cause of the action in logical sequence? Hedda's learning that her old lover is in town and is being rehabilitated under the influence of a woman she has always hated. This is the condition of the action.

What is the common factor between condition and cause of the action? The truth that Lovborg, whom Hedda once rejected because she was too cowardly to throw in her lot with a man of his dissoluteness, has been able to reform and has begun to do great work.

Our Proposition for the play will therefore be:
1. Hedda, restless and trapped in a marriage to mediocrity, discovers that her old lover Lovborg, whom cowardice forced her to reject because of his dissoluteness, has done great work, is in town, and is well on the way to rehabilitation under the influence of Mrs. Elvsted.
2. Because Mrs. Elvsted, whom she has always detested, has

---

in the old Italian tale of Cinthio. But they have never asked why he did so. Clearly, because he needed the business he invented in Act I for the beginning of his plot. The whole play rests on the premise of the condition of the action—that Othello ought to know that he has reason to be sure of Desdemona's loyalty.

succeeded in helping him to work and to rehabilitate himself, Hedda persuades him to go to a party where he is fairly certain to destroy his work and his future.

3. Will she succeed in destroying Lovborg's work and his future?

The Wild Duck

What is the play about? Something to do with Gregers' intentions toward Hialmar—specifically, Gregers' determination to make of Hialmar's "false" marriage a "true" one.

What event raises the question as to whether or not Gregers will succeed in his missionary zeal? Gregers' telling Hialmar the facts about the arrangement of Hialmar's marriage.

With what event is this revelation of Gregers' in logical sequence? Gregers' learning that Werle married off Gina, Werle's former housekeeper and mistress, to Hialmar.

What is the common factor between the condition and cause of action here? Hialmar's living in ignorance of Gina's former relationship to Werle.

Our Proposition for the play will therefore be:

1. Gregers, returned after an absence to his father's home, discovers that Hialmar has married Gina without knowing that she was his father's mistress.

2. Because Hialmar is thus unaware that his marriage to Gina is built upon a lie, Gregers tells Hialmar the facts so that Hialmar may re-establish his marriage on the foundation of truth.

3. Will he succeed in transforming Hialmar's marriage to a fine one built on truth?

Cyrano de Bergerac

What is the play about? Cyrano's mad love for Roxane—more particularly, Cyrano's great need of expressing this love for her.

What event raises the question as to whether or not he will be able to express this love for her? His determination to speak to her through Christian.

With what event is this determination in logical sequence? Cyrano's being informed by Roxane that she loves Christian and wants Cyrano's aid in winning him.

What is the common factor between condition and cause of action? Cyrano's conviction that his long nose makes him too ugly ever to win Roxane's affection.

The Proposition for the play will then be:

1. Cyrano, madly in love with Roxane but unable to tell her so because he thinks his long nose makes him too hideous, is informed by her that she loves Christian and desires Cyrano's help in winning him.
2. Convinced that his physical ugliness will forever disqualify him from winning her ear for his love, he decides to find what satisfaction he can for his passion by writing Christian's letters to Roxane, thus also helping her to win the man she wants.
3. Will he ever succeed in letting Roxane know of his love for her?

The Cherry Orchard

1. (Condition of the action) Madame Ranevsky returns to her ancestral home after a long absence to discover from Lopakhin that her estate and her beloved cherry orchard are to be auctioned off to pay the debts of the estate unless she can raise the necessary funds in time.
2. (Cause of the action) She is assured by Lopakhin that her estate can be saved if she is willing to have her well-beloved cherry orchard cut down and the house and old buildings removed, by renting out the land to prospective home builders.
3. Will she save herself by agreeing to Lopakhin's plans, or will she prefer total ruin to the destruction of the things she loves?

STRINDBERG's The Father

1. Laura, the Captain's wife, a woman absolutely determined to have things her own way, is informed by the Captain that their child is to go to a boarding school.

2. In order to dominate the Captain once and for all, she insinuates to him that he has not the right to determine anything about the child's future since the child may not be his.
3. Will she succeed in dominating him?

SYNGE's *The Playboy of the Western World*

1. Christy discovers that, as a result of his having allegedly killed his father, a fine new life is opening for him and that he is taking on a new personality.
2. In the midst of his new successes with everyone, he sees his father again, whom he has not killed after all.
3. Will he be able to hold on to his new personality and the new life he has begun to make, or will he become a timid slave to his father again?

BEHRMAN's *Biography:*

1. Marion, a tolerant and humane woman, approached by Kurt, an editor with vindictive missionary zeal against society, to write her autobiography, with some doubt agrees to write it, partly because she is short of funds, partly because she is attracted by his brusque personality.
2. During the ensuing interviews with him, Marion, out of compassion for some secret hurt in him, falls in love with Kurt, who is already insanely jealous over her past love affairs.
3. Will Marion succeed in having a rewarding love for him?

HOWARD's *The Silver Cord*

1. Mrs. Phelps, a very possessive mother, learns, when her son David arrives with his new wife, that they are going to live and work in New York.
2. In order to keep her son with her, even if it means wrecking his marriage, she offers him an opportunity, which insures success, to do his work in her town.
3. Will she succeed in keeping her son with her? [13]

PROPORTIONS OF THE PLOT

We have said over and over again that a short cut to the third step, the resulting action, is finding "what the play is about." If we now look at the way full-length plays are proportioned, we shall have good reason to believe that the third step is indeed what the play is about.

For the three steps must not at all be thought to correspond to the three acts of a three-act play. In fact, that is almost never the case. In every good full-length play we know, *the third step, the resulting action, consumes the bulk of the play*—always more than a third, sometimes a half of the play or more.

Let us re-examine the three steps as they are proportioned in the plays which we have thus far analyzed:

Romeo and Juliet

1. Romeo meets Juliet and falls in love with her. (End of Act I)
2. He marries her. (End of Act II)
3. Will he find happiness with her? (Acts III, IV, and V)

The Importance of Being Earnest

1. Jack asks Lady Bracknell's consent to marry Gwendolen. (Act I)
2. Jack is forbidden by Lady Bracknell to marry Gwendolen unless he can acquire parents. (Later in Act I)
3. Will Jack succeed in acquiring parents? (Acts II and III)

Hamlet

1. Hamlet is enjoined by the Ghost to avenge the murder on Claudius. (End of Act I)
2. Hamlet gives the play before Claudius. (Act III, scene ii)
3. Will he kill Claudius? (Act III, scenes iii and iv; Acts IV and V)

Othello

1. Othello defends his title as Desdemona's husband. (End of Act I)
2. He allows his mind to be poisoned against her. (Act III, scene iii)
3. Will he regain his untainted love of her? (Act III, scene iv; Acts IV and V)

Hedda Gabler

1. Hedda learns that Lovborg is in town and is being rehabilitated. (End of Act I)
2. She persuades Lovborg to go to the party. (End of Act II)
3. Will she succeed in destroying his work and future? (Acts III and IV)

The Wild Duck

1. Gregers discovers that Hialmar's marriage is built on a lie. (Act I)
2. He tells Hialmar the facts. (End of Act III)
3. Will he succeed in transforming Hialmar's marriage? (Acts IV and V)

Cyrano de Bergerac

1. Cyrano is informed by Roxane that she loves Christian and is asked to help her. (Beginning of Act II)
2. He decides to write Christian's letters. (End of Act II)
3. Will he ever succeed in letting Roxane know of his love for her? (Acts III, IV, and V)

The Cherry Orchard

1. Madame Ranevsky learns that the estate is to be auctioned off. (Act I)

2. She is assured by Lopakhin that he can save her from ruin if she will lease the land. (Act II)
3. Will she accept Lopakhin's plans? (Acts III and IV)

The Father

1. Laura is informed by the Captain that their child is going to boarding school. (Beginning of Act I)
2. She insinuates that the Captain is not the child's father. (End of Act I)
3. Will she succeed in dominating the Captain? (Acts II and III)

The Playboy of the Western World

1. Christy begins to find a new life and a new personality because he has allegedly killed his father. (End of Act I)
2. He sees his father again. (Middle of Act II)
3. Will he be able to keep his new life and personality? (The rest of Act II, Act III)

Biography

1. Marion is approached by Kurt and agrees to write her autobiography. (Before the end of Act I)
2. Marion falls in love with Kurt, who is jealous over her past love affairs. (Before the end of Act II)
3. Will Marion succeed in having a rewarding love for him? (The rest of Act II, Act III)

The Silver Cord

1. Mrs. Phelps learns that David and his wife are going to live in New York. (Middle of Act I)
2. She offers David an opportunity, sure of success, to work in her town. (Later in Act I)
3. Will she succeed in keeping David with her? (Acts II and III)

It is thus clear that in the full-length play the plot is so proportioned that the bulk of the play is given over to the resulting action.*

    * It is in the proportioning of the plot that the most salient difference between the full-length play and the one-act play will be found. We have a number of pages to devote hereafter to the one-act play. At the moment let it suffice to remark that in the one-act play the third step, the resulting action, is the *briefest* part of the play; in this form, when the question is raised by the cause of the action, it is almost immediately answered.

CHAPTER FIVE

≈≈≈≈≈≈≈≈≈≈≈≈≈≈≈≈≈

Plot (3): Climax

The turning points of lives are not the great moments. The real crises are often concealed in occurrences so trivial in appearance that they pass unobserved.   W. E. WOODWARD, *George Washington*

There is a tide in the affairs of men
Which, taken at the flood, leads on to fortune;
Omitted, all the voyage of their life
Is bound in shallows and in miseries.   *Julius Caesar*, IV, iii

This hour's the very crisis of your fate.
    DRYDEN, *The Spanish Friar*, IV, ii

Always verging toward some climax . . . S. W. FOSS, *The Inventor*

    We have thus far constantly referred to the presence of the audience at a play as a never to be overlooked fact in determining the requirements of drama. However, it should be obvious by now that our discussion throughout this book is not from the point of view of the audience, but from that of the dramatist. The elements which make the Proposition need not ever be present to the consciousness of the spectator; there is no reason why he should identify the condition of the action, the cause of the action, or the resulting action. It is the dramatist who ought to be sure of these fundamental matters which constitute the basis of the plot.

    When a sculptor is preparing his clay model for a figure, he first makes an armature of pieces of metal and wire around which the clay can be wrapped and which will support the clay—a kind of skeleton for the body that is to come into being. When the figure is completed the spectator will, of course, be unaware of what the armature looked like; perhaps no one but another sculptor will even think of it. So too with the Proposition in drama. It is the armature of the play, and the audience need not be aware of it. But the dramatist must be certain that it is there if his play is to hold together. And the critic, viewing the finished play, may with advantage find the Proposition behind the play in order to certify his impression that it has a sound plot; if the play gives the impression of having fallen to pieces, he may account for its failure by discovering its lapse in logic—its lacking the correct steps that would make a sound Proposition.[14]

It is important never to forget that *the plot must stand as a logical unity quite independently of the ideas or concepts the play exhibits*. Unfortunately, during the political stress of the last decades many a potentially good play was wrecked on the rocks of the playwright's high-minded intentions. These plays often showed power over dialogue, characterization, and theatrical effects—but they collapsed because their authors were apparently so much exercised over the cruelties and barbarities of totalitarian governments that they ignored the logic of their dramas' plots. Their hatred and shock over the monstrous deeds of Fascist, Nazi, or Communist powers did them the greatest credit as human beings. But as dramatists it was their business to be sure that their rightness of sentiment did not result in wrongness of plot. An attack on Nazism, for instance, need not be inconsistent with a sound plot (as *Stalag 17* proved). In writing for the theater one must not permit the nobility of one's views to pervert the logic of the story.*

The Proposition must never be stated exclusively in terms of the ideas and/or emotions the play is to contain. This is one of the errors which beginners tend to make. As thus:

* We are reminded, in this connection, of an unforgettable experience in our childhood, on the occasion of our being taken to our first song recital in a concert hall. During World War I it was required that at all public performances the flag of the United States be in a conspicuous place on the platform. The soprano giving the recital was evidently so poor a singer that she was greeted throughout her first group of songs with only the thinnest and most perfunctory applause. At the end of the group she stood appalled at the indifference of her audience. Suddenly, she had an inspiration. She marched to the corner of the stage, and lifted the flag. The audience responded with wild and enthusiastic applause which lasted some ten minutes. After that, she was given a hearty hand after each piece. The analogy with the point we are making will not, we trust, escape the reader.

1. Henry is in love with Julia.
2. Henry knows she is indifferent to him.
3. Will he succeed in gaining her love?

This is not a plot, because there is no indication of any action here. If the material contained this matter:

1. Henry, whose love for Julia is unrequited, kidnaps her and takes her to his luxurious home on an island.
2. Although she continues to treat him with angry disdain, he entertains her with every delicate attention and service, and loads her with precious gifts.
3. Will he succeed in gaining her love?

—there would be the basis of a plot, because the condition and the cause are matters of action. Again, this is not a plot, because it states no action:

1. A woman, married to a mediocrity, is miserable because she doesn't know what to do with herself.
2. She is furious because another woman, whom she detests, is leading a useful life.
3. Will she find something to do?

But this is a plot:

1. A woman, restless and trapped in a marriage to a mediocrity, discovers that her old lover, whom cowardice forced her to reject because of his dissoluteness, has done great work, is in town, and is well on the way to rehabilitation under the influence of another woman.
2. Because this other woman, whom she has always detested, has succeeded in helping him to work and to rehabilitate himself, the first woman persuades him to go to a party where he is fairly certain to destroy his work and his future.
3. Will she succeed in destroying his work and his future?

The first woman is, of course, Hedda Gabler.

CLIMAX

But a sound Proposition alone is not enough for the shaping of a plot. There remains, in addition to the condition of the action, cause of the action, and resulting action, one more matter cardinal to our consideration of the structure of a plot: the climax.

The word itself is popularly used in many ways; in discussions of drama it is odd that it is most commonly used to designate the moment of greatest excitement or interest in the action of the play. We say "odd" because a moment that *is* of greatest excitement in a play will obviously be so to everyone; it therefore hardly needs to be singled out for identification, and, the fact of its being exciting having nothing to do with the structure of the plot, it scarcely calls—despite the hundreds of pages which have been expended on the topic—for any kind of comment. Thus, operating on the pointless definition of climax as the most exciting moment of the play, Professor J. D. Wilson has expended much ingenuity and dozens of pages to prove that the scene in which Hamlet presents his play before Claudius is the most exciting moment in the tragedy, hence the climax of the play. That that scene is in fact the most exciting, no one would wish to deny. But to recognize that it is illuminates nothing concerning the structure of the plot, and therefore nothing concerning the issues of the play.

Let us say at once that in a full-length play the climax is almost *never* the most exciting moment of the drama.*

When we were quite young we were taught at school that the climax of a story is "the highest point" of the action, and the teacher would draw on the blackboard a diagram like this:

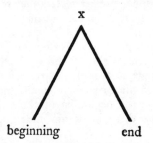

* If it were, it would thereby make the play sensational rather than dramatic, for which reason it is never the case in a true tragedy. Murder mysteries and melodramas which are purposely written in a sensational style tend, of course, to have a climax which is the most exciting moment. The same is often true of the one-act play, a form that is likely to be sensational rather than dramatic.

—*x* being the climax; up to *x* there was "rising action," after *x* "falling action." The expressions are so vague and so capable of diverse confused associations as to be wholly unserviceable. In point of fact, in our own youthful mind, nourished on the splendors of cowboy-and-Indian movies, the climax *x* marked the place where the hero and villain were struggling on the edge of a cliff; the villain fell off the cliff, and that, naturally, was the "falling action." We felt we understood perfectly.

Actually the climax of the play is the climax of the plot, and though of the utmost importance, it can very well be a moment that does not strike the audience with its importance at all. So it is often in life. As we have noted, a biographer of George Washington has said, "The turning points of lives are not the great moments. The real crises are often concealed in occurrences so trivial in appearance that they pass unobserved." *The climax of the plot is its turning point.* It is the point from which there is no return.

The climax of the plot determines more or less what the direction of the rest of the plot is to be. In a tragedy, this direction is firmly determined by the climax. In a play which is not a tragedy, this direction is indicated by the climax, but before the end some unexpected turn may change the direction. This is to say that in a tragedy the climax will make catastrophe for the hero inevitable; in a play which is not a tragedy, the climax will make either catastrophe or success seem inevitable—but in some such plays, toward the end some event may turn catastrophe or success to its opposite.*

The climax of a play may also be stated in terms of the relationship of the central and second characters—the relationship of whom, as we have seen, is part of the tissue of the Proposition. Between these two characters some sort of relationship is established in the beginning of the plot; in every play worthy of the name, this relationship undergoes some dynamic

---

* *Hedda Gabler* is an example of this type of plot. The question of the play is: Will Hedda succeed in destroying Lovburg's work and future? The climax of the plot seems to give an affirmative answer to this question, but before the end of the play events change it to a negative one. Of this, more presently. On the other hand, there are many plays which are not tragedies in which nothing occurs to alter the direction of the plot as fixed by the climax.

alteration.* *The climax of a play is the moment in which the most violent dislocation occurs in this relationship between the central and second characters.*

Let us find the climax in some of the plays whose Propositions have already been stated:

Romeo and Juliet

What is the point of no return here? The question raised in the play is: Will Romeo find happiness in his marriage to Juliet? This being a true tragedy, there is always the possibility—up to a certain moment—that he *will* find happiness with her. Shakespeare has been careful to make that quite clear. Despite the feud between the families, when Tybalt is raging at the discovery that Romeo has dared to appear without invitation at the Capulet ball, Capulet himself, head of the family and Juliet's father, says:

> Content thee, gentle coz, let him alone,
> 'A bears him like a portly † gentleman;
> And to say truth, Verona brags of him
> To be a virtuous and well-govern'd youth:
> I would not for the wealth of all this town
> Here in my house do him disparagement.
>
> (I, v)

Moreover, when Paris comes to him to sue for Juliet's hand, old Capulet tells him:

> But woo her, gentle Paris, get her heart;
> My will to her consent is but a part;

* This is one of the reasons why Plato's *Dialogues* are not plays (which they, of course, do not pretend to be). They have plenty of characterization, marvelous ideas, delightful dialogue, but though the *ideas* of the characters often undergo a complete transformation during the course of the dialogue, the *relationship* of the characters remains unchanged. This is also one of the reasons why those amiable containers from which Mr. Saroyan has been dispensing the milk of human kindness are usually not really plays either; the relationship between the leading characters tends to remain unchanged.

† well-bred.

An * she agree, within her scope of choice
Lies my consent . . .

(ɪ, ii)

Both of these incidents imply that if Romeo made the attempt
to procure the permission of Juliet's father, the lovers might live
in felicity together. The climax, then, will be the deed that makes
that felicity impossible. The killing of Mercutio by Tybalt is
probably the most exciting moment of the action, but it is not
the point of no return. Even though Romeo's good friend has
been killed partially because of Romeo, the latter, if his happiness with Juliet were the only consideration, could still make
peace with her family. But instead, overcome with remorse at
Mercutio's death, he fights Tybalt and kills him. Romeo's killing
of Tybalt is the climax of the play because with that deed he
forfeits all hope of acceptance by her family (Tybalt being a
chief member of it). Moreover, he has every reason to anticipate
death for himself when he kills Tybalt: the Prince has decreed
death to anyone who hereafter fights in the streets (I, i, 103–4);
this, Romeo is well aware of, for only a few minutes before he
fights Tybalt himself he has cried, attempting to end the duel
between Mercutio and Tybalt:

Tybalt, Mercutio, the prince expressly hath
Forbid this bandying in Verona's streets;
Hold, Tybalt! good Mercutio!

(ɪɪɪ, i)

Romeo's killing of Tybalt puts him at once under the probable
doom of death, murders the possibility of his enjoying felicity
with his wife, and disrupts the relationship between himself and
her in their utter need of living together.

The Importance of Being Earnest

The question raised in this play is: Will Jack succeed in
acquiring parents so that he can marry Gwendolen? The climax,
the deed which in this play makes inevitable the answer to that
question, is Jack's showing Miss Prism the handbag in which he

* if.

was found as a baby. Miss Prism has confessed leaving a hand-bag many years ago with a baby in it at the cloak room of Victoria Station, Brighton Line:

JACK

(Rushing over to MISS PRISM.)

Is this the handbag, Miss Prism? Examine it carefully before you speak. The happiness of more than one life depends on your answer.

MISS PRISM

(Calmly.)

It seems to be mine. . . . The bag is undoubtedly mine. I am delighted to have it so unexpectedly restored to me. It has been a great inconvenience being without it all these years.

JACK

(In a pathetic voice.)

Miss Prism, more is restored to you than this handbag. I was the baby you placed in it.

The immediate result of this action is that Jack discovers who his parents are, and that he, moreover, was christened with the highly desirable name of Ernest. The episode completely reverses the apparent impossibility of his marrying Gwendolen.

Hamlet

The question raised in the play is: Will Hamlet avenge his father's murder by killing Claudius? Before the climax Hamlet is well on the road to vengeance. When he presents his little play before the King, Claudius' conduct during its performance assures Hamlet that the King is certainly guilty. Hamlet has, moreover, caused the King to behave publicly in a way that would certainly fortify any charges he might bring against

Claudius. The play scene, the most exciting in the tragedy, is not, of course, the climax: nothing is *altered* in the relationship between the two chief characters. Ever since the Ghost's account of the murder, Hamlet has been the pursuer and Claudius the pursued. At the end of the play scene Hamlet is more the pursuer, the King more the pursued, than ever. What is the deed, then, that will violently upset this relationship? Hamlet's killing of Polonius (III, iv). With that deed Hamlet and the King exchange roles: the King becomes the pursuer of Hamlet, murderer of Polonius and now the pursued. And the King wastes no time in hurrying Hamlet out of the kingdom, where alone Hamlet can manage his revenge, and, further, is able to arrange for the Prince's death in England. Hamlet himself, before the scene in which he kills Polonius is quite over, realizes that he has forfeited everything. As he stands over Polonius' corpse, he says bitterly:

> This man shall set me packing.*
>
> (III, iv)

Othello

The question raised in the play is: Will Othello regain his untainted love of Desdemona or will he not? The play is a tragedy and the climax will therefore make the answer to this question inevitable. The answer will also involve Othello's own life. Once Othello believes his wife an adulteress, all the marrow empties from his bones: he knows he will never be able to fight again:

> O now forever
> Farewell the tranquil mind! farewell content!
> Farewell the plumed troops, and the big wars,
> That make ambition virtue! O, farewell!

---

* Because of the bewildering variety of interpretations on *Hamlet*, the reader may have some difficulty in following our analysis of this play. Part of the reason for the confusion of the commentators is their imperfect understanding of the meaning of climax and their consequent inability to identify it in this play. For an interpretation consistent with what has been here named as the climax and with that climax's revelation of the hero's character, see *The Heart of Hamlet*.

Farewell the neighing steed, and the shrill trump,
The spirit-stirring drum, th' ear-piercing fife,
The royal banner, and all quality,
Pride, pomp, and circumstance of glorious war!
And, O you mortal engines,* whose rude throats
Th' immortal Jove's dread clamours † counterfeit,
Farewell! Othello's occupation's gone!

(III, iii)

It is because he has made his love for her the center of his being;
his is a love, as he knows,

where I have garner'd up my heart,
Where either I must live, or bear no life,
The fountain from the which my current runs,
Or else dries up . . .

(IV, ii)

Once he makes a move against her life, he will be striking at his
own. Now, although Othello's mind has been poisoned against
Desdemona, he makes no such move until the climax. That occurs when, seeing the courtesan flinging back Desdemona's
handkerchief to Cassio, he concludes that Desdemona has given
Cassio that handkerchief and that her guilt is incontrovertibly
established. It is then that he decides to murder her:

I will chop her into messes.—Cuckold me!

(IV, i)

This is for him the point of no return. Even if the matter of the
handkerchief could thereafter have been cleared up, it is in-
conceivable that, having planned Desdemona's death, Othello
could live with himself.

Hedda Gabler

The question raised in this play is: Will Hedda succeed in
destroying Lovborg's work and future? The climax will be the
deed that will apparently make the answer to that question

* cannon.   † thunder.

inevitable. It occurs at the end of Act III, when Hedda burns
the manuscript of Lovborg's important book, the product of his
genius and Thea's encouragement and aid:

> Now I am burning your child, Thea!—Burning it, curly-locks!
>
>> (Throwing one or two more sheaves of
>> the manuscript into the stove.)
>
> Your child and Eilert Lovborg's.
>
>> (Throws in the rest.)
>
> I am burning—I am burning your child.

This deed appears to insure Hedda's evil triumph. But this play
is not a tragedy. It is therefore possible in such a play that some
event will change the course of the concluding action after the
climax. And so it is here. In the last act, it turns out that Thea
has kept all of Lovborg's notes, and she and Hedda's husband
at once engage feverishly upon the restoration of Lovborg's
burned masterpiece. Hedda, after all, has destroyed not Lovborg's work but herself.

The Wild Duck

The question raised in this play is: Will Gregers succeed in
transforming Hialmar's marriage to a fine one built on truth?
His revelation to Hialmar about Gina's past, instead of merely
destroying the lie, as he had hoped, and clearing the way for
newly erecting the marriage on a foundation of truth, has thus
far caused the sentimental and vacuous Hialmar only to become
sullen, mean, and to behave so much like the injured party that
he presently rejects even the daughter, Hedvig, whom he has
feigned to adore so much. The climax is the deed which will
seem to make inevitable the answer to the question as to whether
or not Gregers will finally succeed in transforming Hialmar's
marriage to a noble one built on truth. Convinced that a great
sacrifice is what is needed to bring Hialmar back to that godlike
nature with which Gregers has foolishly invested him, Gregers
persuades Hedvig to sacrifice the wild duck, her dearest possession, for Hialmar. This is the climax. Gregers is sure that

Hedvig's act will accomplish the miracle. Instead, Gregers' urging the deed upon the child only brings about general ruin. Hialmar can always be only his own egotistic, wretched, dishonest self. Hedvig's sacrifice avails nothing, and brings about her suicide. And her suicide drives Hialmar further and irrevocably into self-deception.

Cyrano de Bergerac

The question raised in this play is: Will Cyrano ever succeed in telling Roxane of his love for her? The climax, the deed which determines the course of the rest of the plot toward the answer to this question, is Cyrano's checkmating of De Guiche's attempt to prevent the marriage of Roxane and Christian. This move apparently ends the possibility of Cyrano's ever making known to Roxane his love. But this play, though sad, is not a tragedy: in the last act Cyrano is at last able to make his love known.

The Father

The question raised in the play is: Will Laura succeed in dominating the Captain? The climax, the act which provides the answer to that question, is Laura's provoking the Captain to throw a lamp at her, by showing him a letter that is in the hands of the Board of Lunacy. (In this letter there is a declaration by the Captain to a doctor that he fears for his sanity.) The violence Laura thereby provokes leads to the doctor's putting the Captain in a strait jacket and destines him for the asylum.

The Playboy of the Western World

The question raised in the play is: Will Christy be able to hold on to his new personality and the new life he has begun to make, or will he become a timid slave to his father again? The climax, which provides the inevitable answer to that question, is Christy's winning all the contests. (In the case of this play the answer indicated by the climax remains unchanged.) Christy will outface his father and will hold on to his new personality and his new life.

Biography

The question raised in the play is: Will Marion succeed in having a rewarding love for Kurt? The act which determines the answer is Marion's agreeing to have dinner with Kinnicott, allowing him to imagine that he can convince her not to publish her autobiography. This acceptance of an invitation to have dinner with Kinnicott at his lodgings precipitates a quarrel with Kurt, during which Marion realizes that she loves Kurt for the very qualities which make them utterly incompatible.

The Silver Cord

The question raised in the play is: Will Mrs. Phelps succeed in keeping her son David with her? The deed which determines the answer is her calling David back (when he is rushing out to save Hester from drowning) because he isn't wearing his coat and might catch pneumonia, and in indulging in this piece of callousness (masked as sentiment) in the presence of David's wife. This little act shakes David's belief in his mother, makes a showdown certain, and loses for Mrs. Phelps her influence over David. Nothing occurs thereafter in the action to alter the determinant nature of the climax.[15]

CLIMAX AND PROPOSITION

It is clear from everything we have said that the climax does not appear in any of the three steps of the Proposition. An error frequently made by beginners is to think of the second step, the cause of the action, as constituting the climax. But that step only *raises* the question: it does not determine the direction in which the answer to the question will lie. Thus, the fact that Romeo marries Juliet does not in any way indicate whether or not they will be happy, despite their love; the fact that Jack is forbidden by Lady Bracknell to marry Gwendolen unless he can acquire parents does not assure us that he will or will not acquire them; the fact that Hamlet is convinced by the little play that Claudius is guilty does not indicate whether or not he will achieve vengeance; the fact that Othello allows his mind to be poisoned against

Desdemona does not rule out the possibility of his learning the truth; the fact that Hedda can persuade Lovborg to go to the party does not establish the likelihood of her destroying his work; and so on.

It ought to be equally clear from all that has preceded that *the climax is part of the working out of the third step of the Proposition, the resulting action.* The third step is the question of the play; *the climax is the deed that begins to provide the answer.* Will Romeo find happiness in his marriage with Juliet? When he kills Tybalt he makes it inevitable that he will not find that happiness. Will Jack succeed in acquiring parents so he can marry Gwendolen? When he shows the handbag to Miss Prism he makes it possible to find out who his parents were. Will Hamlet kill Claudius and thus avenge his father's murder? When he kills Polonius he gives Claudius the opportunity to arrange for Hamlet's death. Will Othello regain his untainted love for his wife? When he decides that Desdemona must have given Cassio the handkerchief he chooses the path that leads to her destruction and his own. Will Hedda succeed in destroying Lovborg's work? When she burns the manuscript she seems to have insured the destruction of his work. Will Gregers succeed in transforming Hialmar's marriage to a fine one built on truth? When he persuades Hedvig to sacrifice her dearest possession, he feels assured of achieving his end. Will Cyrano ever succeed in expressing his love for Roxane to her? When he checkmates De Guiche he apparently surrenders all hope of that. Will Laura succeed in dominating the Captain? When she provokes him to throw a lamp at her she assures her ascendancy over him. Will Christy succeed in holding on to his new personality and his new life? When he wins all the contests he seems on the road to doing that. Will Marion succeed in having a rewarding love for Kurt? When she accepts Kinnicott's invitation to dinner, she precipitates the quarrel with Kurt which proves their incompatibility. Will Mrs. Phelps succeed in keeping her son David with her? When she calls David back from the rescue in the presence of David's wife she exposes herself for what she really is and is on the way to losing him.

Now, it is to be remarked that we have nowhere suggested that it is possible to summon a play into being just by contriving a Proposition out of the air. *Before there can be a Proposition*

there must be some raw material for the Proposition to shape.
It is for this reason that we had nothing to say about the Proposition until we had discussed the elements which constitute the raw materials of drama: theme, situation, incident, and characters. Time must be expended upon this raw material before one is ready to employ the shaping power of the Proposition. The energy used to investigate the possibilities of the raw material, with the full awareness that it continues to be only raw material, is energy well spent. A tentative outline of story (subject to any amount of later rearrangement and discarding) is highly useful; biographical sketches of the characters that one is thinking of using (subject, too, to enlargement and elimination later) are excellent exercises in becoming more familiar with the material; sometimes it is even worthwhile writing a tentative first act (with the full expectation of possibly being able to use little or none of it later on) in order to see what the material can unfold. With enough material thus at hand, one can use the Proposition fruitfully and creatively, finding out what to retain, what to reject, what needs rearranging, what needs amplification in the creator's mind. So employed, the Proposition can save one months, even years, of undirected writing.

But even so, patience and thought are required for the shaping of a sound plot.* As one begins to understand how to use the Proposition toward that end, he is usually plagued with a sense of the thinness of the material at hand. We have yet much to say that will help correct that limitation. The requirements of a good climax, for example, when thoroughly digested, help one immediately to understand how he may go about widening the perspectives of the story. What are the requirements of a good climax?

REQUIREMENTS OF A CLIMAX

Let us look over the climaxes we have already identified.

The first thing to be observed is that *the climax is always a deed performed by the central character.* Romeo kills Tybalt; Jack shows Miss Prism the handbag; Hamlet kills Polonius; Othello decides that the handkerchief in Cassio's possession was

---

* Ibsen is said usually to have spent two years planning a play, and only a matter of weeks in the actual writing of it!

a gift of Desdemona; Hedda burns the manuscript; Gregers persuades Hedvig to sacrifice the wild duck; Cyrano checkmates
De Guiche; Laura incites her husband to throw the lamp; Christy
wins the contests; Marion accepts Kinnicott's invitation to dinner;
Mrs. Phelps allows David's wife to hear her call David back from
the rescue.

Many a plot that might have been a sound one has been
ruined either by:

1. having a climax in which the central character is acted
upon, instead of being the doer of the climatic act, or (which is
sometimes the same thing)

2. assigning the crucial deed to some other character.

Suppose our plot went this way: Rudolph, member of a
family that is at feud with the family of Judith, meets Judith and
falls in love with her. (Condition of the action.) Although their
family is at feud, Rudolph marries Judith. (Cause of the action.)
Will Rudolph find happiness in his marriage to Judith? (Resulting action.) In the working out of the plot, this is what happens:
Old Krupp, Judith's father, having got wind of the elopement
and having organized a posse of family retainers, surprises Rudolph and Judith just as the pair are leaving the cell of Friar
Ludwig, right after the marriage ceremony. Old Krupp's men
seize Judith and whisk her away. Her father carries her off to a
convent and has the marriage annulled. Judith, brokenhearted,
becomes a novice at the nunnery. In despair, Rudolph commits
suicide. Now, the resulting action here certainly answers the
question raised: Rudolph does not find happiness in his marriage
to Judith. But like all such stories (and they have been legion),
this plot leaves us unsatisfied and unconvinced. A chief reason
for this is that the climax is wrong: Krupp's carrying off Judith
out of Rudolph's reach. And it is wrong for both reasons mentioned above: the central character, Rudolph, is not the doer of
the deed at the climax, but is only acted upon; also, the doer is
another character, old Krupp.

Suppose this were our story: Henri, who is uncertain about
the reliability of messages purported to be sent from the "spirit
world," agrees, for the sake of the experience, to go with two
friends (Hébert and Marius) to a medium's house for a séance.
There, the medium offers to come into contact with Henri's dead
father. A hollow voice begins to speak through the medium's

mouth, and Henri is informed from "beyond" that his father has been murdered by Charlot, the man now married to Henri's mother; he also hears a detailed account of how his father was murdered, and is enjoined to avenge the murder. (Condition of the action.) Because Henri is unsure of the realiability of messages from the spirit world, he arranges some private theatricals under the pretense of wishing to amuse Charlot. The piece presented faithfully mirrors the incidents outlined by the voice from beyond, and Henri is convinced, because of Charlot's behavior at the performance, that his stepfather is really his father's murderer. (Cause of the action.) Will Henri now kill Charlot and thus avenge his father's murder? (Resulting action.) In the working out of the plot, this is what happens: Charlot realizes from Henri's theatricals that his stepson knows the facts of the murder and that his own life is in jeopardy. That same night, while Henri is out celebrating the triumph of his experiment with Hébert and Marius, Charlot steals into Henri's bedchamber with a saw. He cuts a neat oblong out of the flooring near Henri's bed, covers it again with the carpeting, and hastens to the cellar, just below, where he places in a strategic position some stones, massive discarded andirons, and a couple of sacks of solidified cement. Henri returns home, eager for bed, steps on the fatal square, falls into the cellar, and breaks his back and both his legs. He is sent to the hospital. When he is released it is to spend the rest of his life in a wheel chair in the care of a nurse. It is sad to report that this is only an exaggeration of the kind of story which some writers have elected to present as a tragedy. There is no disputing that the question raised in the play is answered catastrophically for the hero, but the plot is, again, wholly unsatisfying.* A chief reason for this is that the climax, Charlot's sawing a square in the flooring, is wrong; the central character is not the doer of the deed, but is acted upon. The doer of the climax is here the second character.

Suppose this were our story—this time we shall not travesty any masterpiece: John, a poor artist of great ambition, is in love with Susan, a wealthy girl of seventeen, who is used to all the luxuries of life. She returns his love and has tried to persuade him to ingratiate himself with her family; she feels that they have

---

* In later pages on the subject of Tragedy, it will be made clear why such a climax is totally impossible for tragedy.

enough money to support them both until he can become famous. But John is too self-reliant to entertain the idea of such parasitism, and pleads with her to have the courage to throw in her lot with him and break with her family. If she will not, he is going away and she will never see him again. With this argument he persuades her to run away with him from Ohio to New York. (Condition of the action.) In New York he rents a one-room, cold-water studio, where he does all in his power to atone for the luxuries she was used to, and enthrones her as his queen in surroundings the sordidness of which he tries to obliterate. (Cause of the action.) Will he succeed in making her happy and contented despite her altered circumstances? (Resulting action.) In the working out of the plot, we observe that John, divinely happy with Susan at his side, works brilliantly and tirelessly at his painting. A well-known critic examines his paintings and offers to speak for John to an important art gallery. On a bitterly cold day, while John is out buying a present for the third month of their marriage, Susan is sitting in a shivering huddle before the little coal stove when her sister and a former suitor of Susan's appear. Her visitors are shocked at the conditions under which Susan is living, the sorry state of her clothes, the pathetic crudity of the furnishings. They speak of all the parties and gay times Susan has missed. The former suitor draws an exciting picture of all the pleasures waiting for them on their return. It is not hard to convince Susan that she ought to pack her bag and come back to Ohio with them. After all, Susan reflects, John still has his art, and no one can take that away from him. She leaves him a note saying that the marriage was all a mistake and that she is going to have it annulled as soon as she is back home. He had best forget her and think of his wonderful career. She departs with her friends. When John comes home with the present, purchased at so great a sacrifice, he finds her gone. Here again we have the sort of story which is only too common. Pathetic enough, and possible enough in actual life, it would have no dramatic impact upon the stage. Its faulty climax damages the plot's structure and could only ruin the total effect of the drama. The question as to whether or not John will succeed in making Susan happy and contented is certainly answered, but in a wrong way, for the answer is brought about by no deed of his. Since the climax involves Susan, her sister, and Susan's former beau,

John seems almost left out of the climax. To make the latter part of the story dramatically acceptable, it is John who must do or decide something which will determine the answer to the question of the play.[16]

Making sure that the climax is the deed of the central character is one of the important considerations which make for shaping a play. One's raw material, for instance, might concern itself with two people (or even three) about whom it becomes difficult to make the selection for the central character since they seem to have equal importance. One's choice in this cardinal matter may very well be settled by discovering which of the characters will be in the best position to be the doer of the best possible climax; that person will be the central character. Hence, it is possible to say, for example, that Romeo is the central character of *Romeo and Juliet,* even though Juliet shares an almost equal interest with him in the tragedy. (Some have argued the impossible position that in this particular play there are two central characters, just because their destinies are at one.) It is Romeo who is allotted the climactic deed that determines the ruin of their happiness, not Juliet. And therefore it must be Romeo, not Juliet, and not Romeo *and* Juliet, who must appear in each step of the correct Proposition as the subject of the sentence—that is, the central character.

Now, in addition to the requirement that the *climax* be a deed of the central character, it may have already been observed by the reader that it *is a deed which involves not the second character but a third person.*

Let us glance anew at the climaxes we have identified. Who figures at the climax in the deed of the central character?:

Not Juliet, but Tybalt.
Not Lady Bracknell, but Miss Prism.
Not Claudius, but Polonius.
Not Desdemona, but Cassio.
Not Lovborg, but his manuscript and Thea ("Now I am
      burning your child, Thea!")
Not Hialmar, but Hedvig.
Not Roxane, but De Guiche.
Not Christy's father, but the other contestants in the games.
Not Kurt, but Kinnicott.
Not David, but David's wife.

Why should this be so? Possibly for this reason: the condition and the cause of the action both involve the central and second characters; if the climax also involved the second character there would result indeed a deplorable thinness of dramatic material—the plot would lack scope and dimension. It would be like a serpent attempting to swallow its own tail. Drama must mirror the issues of life and afford an illusion of reality; and the essence of drama is conflict. If the conflict is limited exclusively to the talk of two people, the rest of the world is left out. We all know that there is no escaping contact with other people—or, failing that, at least with external objects outside one's own body; to exclude them is to sacrifice a sense of universal truth, and thereby the illusion of reality. If the issues of life and an illusion of reality are to radiate from a play, it is clear that people or else dramatic objects other than the central and second characters will have to be *brought into the story*—not merely talked about.

It is for this reason impossible to write a play which calls for only two characters, unless some dramatic object is used with the catalytic force of a third personality. Thus, William Gibson's *Two for the See-Saw* calls for a cast of only two people; but the play depends heavily upon a telephone—or rather, upon two telephones. In that clever drama the telephones are not only personalities in their own rights, but they represent other characters too. The hero's wife, for example, though she does not appear onstage, is an important person at the other end of the wire on one of these telephones. It is doubtful that anyone will try, as long as this play is remembered, to repeat the device—certainly, any dramatist should think twice before the public has the chance to brand him as a sedulous ape. The play must therefore be accounted an oddity, though a highly interesting one.

A strikingly original one-act play is Edward Albee's recent *The Zoo Story*. This, too, calls for only two characters. But as the play approaches its climax, a park bench suddenly becomes an object of extreme dramatic importance, a matter of vital issue between the two characters. Presently, the park bench gives way in importance to a knife, which becomes the equivalent of a third person at the climax and is the means of the play's achieving a highly exciting conclusion.

At the opening of *The Zoo Story*, Peter, a man in his early forties, is sitting on a bench in a park. He is smoking a pipe and reading a book. Jerry, a man in his late thirties, carelessly dressed, enters. Jerry starts talking to Peter by informing him that he has just been to the zoo. Peter, little inclined to conversation, tries to be polite. He is soon forced into listening to Jerry and into revealing that he himself is married, has two daughters and two parakeets, and makes eighteen thousand dollars a year as a textbook editor. Jerry, on his side, while moving restlessly about the stage, tells Peter that he lives in a rooming house in a poor neighborhood what is obviously a very lonely life; he has no permanent attachments in life; his parents are long since dead. He does love the ladies, but never, he confesses, for more than an hour. He also tells Peter of his vain efforts to win over the good will of the landlady's hostile dog. At last Jerry decides to sit down on the bench, and he explains that he has just visited the zoo to observe how people behave with the animals and how the animals behave with one another. Suddenly he pokes Peter on the arm:

JERRY

Move over.

PETER

(Friendly.)

I'm sorry, haven't you enough room?

(He shifts a little.)

JERRY

(Smiling slightly.)

Well, all the animals are there, and all the people are there, and it's Sunday and all the children are there.

(He pokes PETER again.)

Move over.

PETER

(Patiently, still friendly.)

All right.

(He moves some more, and JERRY has all
the room he might need.)

JERRY

And it's a hot day, so all the stench is there, too, and all the
balloon sellers, and all the ice cream sellers, and all the seals
are barking, and all the birds are screaming.

(Pokes PETER harder.)

Move over!

PETER

(Beginning to be annoyed.)

Look here, you have more than enough room!

(But he moves more, and is now fairly
cramped at one end of the bench.)

JERRY

And I am there, and it's feeding time at the lion's house, and
the lion keeper comes into the lion cage, one of the lion cages,
to feed one of the lions.

(Punches PETER on the arm, hard.)

MOVE OVER!

PETER

(Very annoyed.)

I can't move over any more and stop hitting me. What's the
matter with you?

JERRY

Do you want to hear the story?

(Punches PETER's arm again.)

PETER

(Flabbergasted.)

I'm not so sure! I certainly don't want to be punched on the arm.

JERRY

(Punches PETER's arm again.)

Like that?

PETER

Stop it! What's the matter with you?

JERRY

I'm crazy, you bastard.

PETER

That isn't funny.

JERRY

Listen to me, Peter. I want this bench. You go sit on the bench over there, and if you're good I'll tell you the rest of the story.

PETER

(Flustered.)

But . . . what ever for? What *is* the matter with you? Besides, I see no reason why I should give up this bench. I sit on this bench almost every Sunday afternoon, in good weather. It's secluded here; there's never anyone sitting here, so I have it all to myself.

JERRY

(Softly.)

Get off this bench, Peter; I want it.

PETER

(Almost whining.)

No.

JERRY

I said I want this bench, and I'm going to have it. Now get over there.

PETER

People can't have everything they want. You should know that; it's a rule; people can have some of the things they want, but they can't have everything.

JERRY

(Laughs.)

Imbecile! You're slow-witted!

PETER

Stop that!

JERRY

You're a vegetable! Go lie down on the ground.

PETER

(Intense.)

Now *you* listen to me. I've put up with you all afternoon.

JERRY

Not really.

PETER

LONG ENOUGH. I've put up with you long enough. I've listened to you because you seemed . . . well, because I thought you wanted to talk to somebody.

JERRY

You put things well; economically, and, yet . . . oh, what is the word I want to put justice to your . . . JESUS, you make me sick . . . get off here and give me my bench.

PETER

MY BENCH!

JERRY

(Pushes PETER, almost, but not quite off the bench.)

Get out of my sight.

PETER

(Regaining his position.)

God da . . . mn you. That's enough! I've had enough of you. I will not give up this bench; you can't have it, and that's that. Now, go away.

(JERRY snorts, but does not move.)

Go away, I said.

(JERRY does not move.)

Get away from here. If you don't move on . . . you're a bum . . . that's what you are . . . if you don't move on, I'll get a policeman here and make you go.

(JERRY laughs, stays.)

I warn you, I'll call a policeman.

JERRY

(Softly.)

You won't find a policeman around here; they're all over on the west side of the park chasing fairies down from trees or out of the bushes. That's all they do. That's their function. So scream your head off; it won't do you any good.

PETER

POLICE! I warn you, I'll have you arrested. POLICE!

(Pause.)

I said POLICE!

(Pause.)

I feel ridiculous.

JERRY

You look ridiculous: a grown man screaming for the police on a bright Sunday afternoon in the park with nobody harming you. If a policeman *did* fill his quota and come sludging over this way he'd probably take you in as a nut.

PETER

(With disgust and impotence.)

Great God, I just came here to read, and now you want me
to give up the bench. You're mad.

JERRY

Hey, I got news for you, as they say. I'm on your precious
bench, and you're never going to have it for yourself again.

PETER

(Furious.)

Look, you; get off my bench. I don't care if it makes any sense
or not. I want this bench to myself; I want you OFF IT!

JERRY

(Mocking.)

Aw . . . look who's mad.

PETER

GET OUT!

JERRY

No.

PETER

I WARN YOU!

JERRY

Do you know how ridiculous you look *now?*

PETER

(His fury and self-consciousness have
possessed him.)

It doesn't matter.

(He is almost crying.)

GET AWAY FROM MY BENCH!

JERRY

Why? You have everything in the world you want; you've told me about your home, and your family, and *your own* little zoo. You have everything, and now you want this bench. Are these the things men fight for? Tell me, Peter, is this bench, this iron and this wood, is this your honor? Is this the thing in the world you'd fight for? Can you think of anything more absurd?

PETER

Absurd? Look, I'm not going to talk to you about honor, or even try to explain it to you. Besides, it isn't a question of honor; but even if it were you wouldn't understand.

JERRY

(Contemptuously.)

You don't even know what you're saying, do you? This is probably the first time in your life you've had anything more trying to face than changing your cats' toilet box. Stupid! Don't you have any idea, not even the slightest, what other people *need?*

PETER

Oh, boy, listen to you; well, you don't need this bench. That's for sure.

JERRY

Yes; yes, I do.

PETER

(Quivering.)

I've come here for years; I have hours of great pleasure, great satisfaction, right here. And that's important to a man. I'm a responsible person, and I'm a GROWN-UP. This is my bench, and you have no right to take it away from me.

JERRY

Fight for it, then. Defend yourself; defend your bench.

PETER

You've *pushed* me to it. Get up and fight.

JERRY

Like a man?

PETER

(Still angry.)

Yes, like a man, if you insist on mocking me even further.

JERRY

I'll have to give you credit for one thing: you *are* a vegetable, and a slightly near-sighted one, I think . . .

PETER

THAT'S ENOUGH . . .

JERRY

. . . but, you know, as they say on TV all the time—you know —and I mean this, Peter, you have a certain dignity; it surprises me. . . .

> PETER

STOP.

> JERRY
>
> (Rises lazily.)

Very well, Peter, we'll battle for the bench, but we're not evenly matched; I was a commando, once.

> (He takes out and clicks open an ugly-looking knife.)

> PETER
>
> (Suddenly awakening to the reality of the situation.)

You *are* mad! You're stark raving mad! YOU'RE GOING TO KILL ME!

> (But before PETER has time to think what to do, JERRY tosses the knife at PETER's feet.)

> JERRY

There you go. Pick it up. You have the knife and we'll be more evenly matched.

> PETER
>
> (Horrified.)

No!

> JERRY
>
> (Rushes over to PETER, grabs him by the collar; PETER rises; their faces almost touch.)

Now you pick up that knife and you fight with me. You fight for your self-respect; you fight for that god-damned bench.

PETER

(Struggling.)

No! Let . . . let go of me! He . . . help!

JERRY

(Slaps PETER on each "fight.")

You fight, you miserable bastard; fight for that bench; fight for your parakeets; fight for your cats, fight for your two daughters; fight for your wife; fight for your manhood, you pathetic little vegetable.

(Spits in PETER's face.)

You couldn't even get your wife with a male child.

PETER

(Breaks away, enraged.)

It's a matter of genetics, not manhood, you . . . you monster.

(He darts down, picks up the knife and backs off a little; he is breathing heavily.)

I'll give you one last chance; get out of here and leave me alone!

(He holds the knife with a firm arm, but far in front of him, not to attack, but to defend.)

JERRY

(Sighs heavily.)

So be it!

(With a rush he charges Peter and impales himself on the knife. Tableau: For just a moment, complete silence, Jerry impaled on the knife at the end of PETER's still firm arm. Then PETER screams, pulls away, leaving the knife in JERRY. JERRY is motionless, on point. Then he, too, screams, and it must be the sound of an infuriated and fatally wounded animal. With the knife in him, he stumbles back to the bench that PETER had vacated. He crumbles there, sitting, facing PETER, his eyes wide in agony, his mouth open.)

PETER

(Whispering.)

Oh my God, oh my God, oh my God . . .

(He repeats these words many times, very rapidly.)

JERRY

(JERRY is dying; but now his expression seems to change. His features relax, and while his voice varies, sometimes wrenched with pain, for the most part he seems removed from his dying. He smiles.)

Thank you, Peter. I mean that, now; thank you very much.

(PETER's mouth drops open. He cannot move; he is transfixed.)

Oh, Peter, I was so afraid I'd drive you away.

(He laughs as best he can.)

You don't know how afraid I was you'd go away and leave me. And now I'll tell you what happened at the zoo. I think . . . I think this is what happened at the zoo . . . I think. I think that while I was at the zoo I decided that I would . . .

would . . . walk . . . north . . . or, northerly, until I . . . until I . . . found . . . you. Or . . . somebody. And . . . I decided that I would talk to you . . . I would tell you things . . . and things that I would tell you would . . . Well, here we are. You see? Here we *are*. But . . . I don't know . . . could I have planned all this? No . . . no, I couldn't have. But I think I did. And now I've told you what you wanted to know, haven't I? And now you know all about what happened at the zoo. And now you know what you'll see in your TV, and the face I told you about . . . you remember . . . the face I told you about . . . my face, the face you see right now. Peter . . . Peter? . . . Peter . . . thank you. I came unto you

                (He laughs, so faintly.)

and you have comforted me. Dear Peter.

                    PETER

                (Almost fainting.)

Oh my God!

                    JERRY

You'd better go now. Somebody might come by, and you don't want to be here when anyone comes.

                    PETER

        (Does not move, but begins to weep.)

Oh my God, oh my God.

                    JERRY

      (Most faintly, now; he is very near death.)

You won't be coming back here any more, Peter; you've been dispossessed. You've lost your bench, but you've defended your honor. And Peter, I'll tell you something now; you're not really a vegetable; it's all right, you're an animal. You're an animal, too. But you'd better hurry now, Peter. Hurry, you'd better go . . . see?

> (JERRY takes a handkerchief and with great effort and pain wipes the knife handle clean of fingerprints.)

Hurry away, Peter.

> (PETER begins to stagger way.)

Wait . . . wait, Peter. Take your book . . . book. Right here . . . beside me . . . on your bench . . . my bench, rather. Come . . . take your book.

> (PETER starts for the book, but retreats.)

Hurry . . . Peter.

> (PETER rushes to the bench, grabs the book, retreats.)

Very good, Peter . . . very good. Now . . . hurry away.

> (PETER hesitates for a moment, then flees, stage-left.)

Hurry away . . .

> (His eyes are closed now.)

Hurry away, your parakeets are making the dinner . . . the cats . . . are setting the table . . .

PETER

> (Off stage. A pitiful howl.)

OH MY GOD!

JERRY

> (His eyes still closed, he shakes his head and speaks; a combination of scornful mimicry and supplication.)

Oh . . . my . . . God.

> (He is dead.)

Here the knife has eloquently taken the place of a third character. Without some such device, however, no two-character piece can manage to have a proper plot. *It is utterly impossible to write a play in which the dramatic problem becomes resolved merely through the talk of only two people.* The Four-Poster was a piece for the theater containing only two characters. But this was not a play at all. It made no pretence to having a plot; it was merely a panorama of the married life of two people. Another piece, *The Voice of the Turtle,* tried valiantly to dispense with a third character, but eventually its author wisely succumbed to the inevitable and brought the third person onstage.

De Musset and Schnitzler (e.g. *Anatol*) each wrote a number of highly agreeable little dialogues which cannot be called one-act plays; the talk between the two characters is charming and does little more than capture a mood; there is no plot; and, in any event, the dialogues are far more delightful to read than to see in the theater. Recently Samuel Beckett's *Krapp's Last Tape* was presented as a "one-act play." It contains but one character and a tape-recorder; the voice on the tape-recorder is, of course, a second character; but the piece is merely an incident without plot, a presentation of a mood.

Such pieces belong to a species that used to be common to musical reviews and vaudeville, and were known by type as a *sketch. A sketch,* not pretending to be a play, *is the presentation of an interesting incident*—a beginning without middle or end, a sort of vignette.

As for the use of a dramatic object instead of a person at crucial moments of the play, even a work with a number of characters may have recourse to such a method. In the climax of *Hedda Gabler,* it has already been noted, it is a manuscript which takes the place of a third character. This manuscript stands for Thea's influence on Lovborg; it is Thea and Lovborg's "child" which Hedda is conscious of destroying. In the climax of *The Father,* again, it is a letter and a lamp which do in lieu of the third character normally figuring in the climax.

CHAPTER SIX

Plot (4): Proportioning the Full-Length Play

Trifles make perfection, and perfection is no trifle.   MICHELANGELO

None but an author knows an author's cares,
Or Fancy's fondness for the child she bears.
                                        COWPER, *The Progress of Error*

Saepe stilum vertas, iterum quae digna legi sint
Scripturus.*   HORACE, *Satires*, I, X,

                        How sour sweet music is,
When time is broke and no proportion kept!   *Richard II*, V, V

Entre esprit et talent il y a la proportion du tout à sa partie.†
                                        LA BRUYÈRE

Let him be kept from paper, pen, and ink,
So he may cease to write and learn to think.
                            PRIOR, *To a Person Who Wrote Ill*

We have already seen (pages 100–103) that in a full-length play the resulting action takes up the bulk of the play. Since the climax is part of this resulting action, we naturally expect to find it somewhere in the latter part of the drama. Let us note where it occurs in some of the plays already analyzed:

Romeo and Juliet (5 acts), Romeo kills Tybalt in Act III, scene i.

*Correct often and carefully if you expect to write anything worth being read twice.
† Between intelligence and genius there is the same proportion as between the whole and its parts.

The Importance of Being Earnest (3 acts), Jack shows Miss
   Prism the handbag toward the close of Act III.
Hamlet (5 acts), Hamlet kills Polonius in Act III, scene iv.
Othello (5 acts), Othello sees the handkerchief and decides
   to kill his wife in Act IV, scene i.
Hedda Gabler (4 acts), Hedda burns the manuscript at the
   curtain of Act III.
The Wild Duck (5 acts), Gregers persuades Hedvig to
   sacrifice the wild duck at the end of Act IV.
Cyrano de Bergerac (5 acts), Cyrano checkmates De Guiche
   toward the close of Act III.
The Father (3 acts), the Captain hurls the lamp when the
   curtain falls on Act II.
The Playboy of the Western World (3 acts), Christy goes
   out to win the contests at the curtain of Act II.
Biography (3 acts), Marion accepts Kinnicott's invitation
   to a private dinner in the middle of Act III.
The Silver Cord (3 acts), Mrs. Phelps calls to David in his
   wife's presence at the curtain of Act II.

With the exception of only one of these plays, *The Importance of Being Earnest*, the *climax*, it is clear, though it occurs
in the latter part of the play, *never occurs during the last moments of a full-length play*. If it did occur near the conclusion
of the play, the effect would be sensational rather than dramatic.
That is why the only kinds of plays which are free from this
stricture are farces and melodramas; their tone is sensational
rather than dramatic. *The Importance of Being Earnest* was
subtitled a farce by its author, though it is a very elegant farce
indeed; it is therefore not extraordinary that its climax occurs
so near the conclusion of the play as it does.*

Some of these plays are in five acts, one is in four, the rest
are in three. The five-act form is the oldest and dates back to
the tragedies of ancient Greece. For a long time it was almost
the only form in which dramatists wrote. With few exceptions
the greatest dramatists up to the nineteenth century used it exclusively: Shakespeare, Beaumont and Fletcher, Jonson, Webster, Dekker, Heywood, Massinger, Ford, Corneille, Racine,

---

* For relevant observations on the attributes of farce and melodrama, see the chapter on Tragedy and Comedy, below.

Molière (who experimented more than any of these others with shorter forms of the drama), Congreve, and Sheridan.

In the five-act play, the climax occurs either in Act III or in Act IV.*

In the nineteenth century the four-act play and the three-act play became gradually more common, though the five-act form continued to flourish (*Cyrano de Bergerac*, Turgenev's *A Month in the Country*, Gogol's *The Inspector-General*). Ibsen and Chekhov were fond of the four-act play, though Ibsen wrote a number of plays in five acts (*Brand, Peer Gynt, The Lady from the Sea*, and *The Wild Duck*) and in three acts (*A Doll's House, Ghosts*, and *The Master Builder*).

In a four-act play the climax occurs in Act III.

By the end of the nineteenth century, the three-act play had become the most common of all dramatic forms, and so it has continued to be in the twentieth century. So much is this, indeed, the case that when five-act and four-act plays are written nowadays, they usually masquerade as three-act plays. If one's program at the theater reads:

> Act I: Scene 1.
>   Scene 2.
> Act II: Scene 1.
>   Scene 2.
> Act III

—one is about to see what is, after all, a five-act play with two intermissions mercifully omitted. If the program reads:

> Act I: Scene 1.
>   Scene 2.
> Act II.
> Act III.

or

> Act I:

* *Romeo and Juliet* is perhaps the earliest of Shakespeare's masterpieces—though it was preceded by many works from his hand. It certainly has more irrelevant material in it than any other of his great plays. It is interesting to note that the climax occurs earlier in Act III than in any other of his masterworks with a third-act climax; and in this play it must be admitted that, if we take a view of what follows the climax, it occurs a little too early.

                        Act II: Scene 1.
                                 Scene 2.
                        Act III.

or

                        Act I: Scene 1.
                                 Scene 2.
                        Act II: Scene 1.
                                 Scene 2.

—one is about to see what is really a four-act play with one or two intermissions omitted.*

In the three-act play the usual (but not inevitable) *place for the climax is at the end of Act II*, as it is in the examples of *The Playboy of the Western World* and *The Silver Cord*. This is the logical locus for the climax, for there it provides just enough suspense before the last act to keep the audience during the second intermission eager for the rest of the play and anxious to know how matters will turn out in the end.†

(Ibsen's four-act plays are actually fairly close to the three-act form, for normally Ibsen covers in the first two acts the ground which would be covered in the first act of a twentieth-century three-act play. His first act often does little more than paint the characters—most powerfully—and present the opening situation. It is not surprising that he has his climax at the end of Act III of the four-act *Hedda Gabler*, for that would correspond to the end of Act II in a three-act play.)

Taking as our norm, then, the three-act play, let us see how the Proposition arranges itself within that form. The climax comes at the end of Act II. That leaves the rest of the resulting action for Act III. Act II, then, concluding with some of the resulting action, will have begun with part of the cause of the

---

* In Elizabethan five-act drama, with its multiplicity of scenes, the division into acts is more or less arbitrary—in Shakespeare's case, largely the work of editors later. On the Elizabethan stage there were no intermissions allowed the audience; scene followed scene without interruption. Once intermissions between acts began to be the vogue, however, the tendency was to have one scene (that is, one place and one continuity of time) per act. Recently, some dramatists have allowed themselves the laxity of having the stage set represent several rooms at once.

† In recent years there have been a few plays written in two acts—that is, plays which have only two scenes. In such plays the climax will have to occur, naturally, in the second act.

action. Act I, thus, will have contained the condition of the action, and also the beginning of the cause of the action. Often, then, this is the proportioning of a three-act play:

Act I.   The condition of the action.
          Beginning of the cause of the action.
Act. II. Continuation of the cause of the action.
          Beginning of the resulting action.
          Climax.
Act III. Remainder of the resulting action.

HOW MANY ACTS SHALL I HAVE?

Those who are familiar with the details of Shakespeare's career as a dramatist will assure you that he was the last of writers to turn his back upon current vogues in the theater.* It is therefore likely that if he had been working in the twentieth-century theater he would have used the three-act form in some of his works.

Would he have been able to cast *Romeo and Juliet* into three acts? Maintaining as our ideal, for the sake of the severity of the experiment, that each act must contain no more than one scene, we are able to concede that it would be quite possible to plan the story without the multiplicity of scenes common to the Elizabethan theater. This play is unique among Shakespeare's masterpieces in having a good many flaws. Without a sigh we should be able to discard in the modern theater whatever is superfluous or inept in the play: the jokes with which the play opens, Romeo's confession of his sufferings over Rosaline to Benvolio, the preparations for Juliet's marriage to Paris, the pointless jests of the musicians when Juliet is found apparently dead. Some of the material could quite adequately be brought in parenthetically, without being presented on the stage before the audience's eyes: the fighting in the streets in the first scene, the Prince's prohibition of any further fighting in the streets, the feud between the two families, much of the Romeo-Rosaline material.

If what we chose to retain of the material were to be attempted in a three-act play, we should try to place the climax,

---

* The remark must stand even with those (we believe, misguided) enthusiasts who are positive his plays were authored by Bacon, Marlowe, Oxford, Burton, Queen Elizabeth, or a committee of authors.

the killing of Tybalt, at the end of the second act. With a little ingenuity it would seem, at first, as though we could manage the first two acts well enough. The first act would contain the condition of the action and the beginning of the cause of the action, as thus:

Act I.   The Capulet ball. All the material connected with the feud between the families, the Prince's prohibition of fighting in the streets, Romeo's callow attachment to Rosaline, must be brought in parenthetically. (Possible methods of bringing it in: the talk of Romeo, Benvolio, and Mercutio; the talk of Capulet and his guests; the talk between Romeo and Juliet—all interspersed throughout the act.) In this act Paris asks Capulet for Juliet's hand and is encouraged in his suit. Lady Capulet urges Juliet to marry Paris; Juliet promises to consider the matter. Romeo and his friends come in. Tybalt recognizes Romeo, is incensed, and vows vengeance. Romeo and Juliet meet and fall in love. They arrange to marry the next morning.

So far, good enough (from the standpoint of plot). We are sacrificing the incomparable balcony scene. But then! Shakespeare has the genius to write poetry of as exalted an order for the first act which we have outlined for him! In the second act we shall have the continuation of the cause of the action, the beginning of the resulting action, and the climax, as thus:

Act II.   A street. We see the lovers right after they have been hastily married by Friar Laurence. (In Shakespeare's play we see them just *before* that event.) Juliet, anxious not to be missed at home, takes leave of Romeo (leading to the resulting action). Romeo is joined by his friends. Tybalt comes in, tries to pick a quarrel with Romeo. Mercutio, furious at his friend's seeming cowardice, compels Tybalt to fight with him. Romeo, in trying to stop the duel, makes it possible for Tybalt to kill Mercutio. Romeo, in despair, fights Tybalt and kills him (climax).

So far, good enough again. But ah! What of the ground still to cover? We can bring in the banishment of Romeo parenthetically (in a conversation between Juliet and the Nurse, similar to the scene in Shakespeare's play). But we must then show that her parents force Juliet into agreeing to a marriage with Paris. We can change Juliet's running to Friar Laurence for help, by having him come to her (as soon as he has heard the news of the new marriage arrangements). But we must see him give the potion, hear his plans for reuniting the lovers, and then see her, alone, taking the potion. All this could be managed in a third act in Juliet's chamber.

But what remains to be told of the story cannot be fitted into that third act, for there must be left an interval of time during which Friar Laurence sends a letter to Romeo explaining what he has done, time for the letter to be held up while Friar Lawrence's messenger is in quarantine, time for Romeo to return from exile. This much could all be brought in parenthetically in a fourth act, but a fourth act, because of the absolute necessity of the interval of time, there would have to be.

We might conclude, then, that *Romeo and Juliet* could be told in a four-act play—if we were hasty in our conclusions. For what of the climax now? It stands at the end of Act II—too far from the end of the play. The result would be to make Acts III and IV long-winded. Shakespeare, then, writing in the twentieth century would doubtless still have used the five-act form (even if he allowed himself only one scene per act) and kept the basic disposition he has given his plot:

Act I.   The lovers meet.
Act II.   They marry.
Act III.   Romeo kills Tybalt.
Act IV.   The marriage with Paris is arranged, and Juliet drinks the potion.
Act V.   Romeo returns. The lovers die.

If he had elected to use the three-act form, the story he would have told would have by necessity been quite different in its details.

From this unconventional excursion of ours, we may conclude that *the number of acts to be used will depend upon the material, and also that the material to be used will depend upon the number of acts.*

In the juggling of the possibilities afforded by these alternatives, *content will be found to be a matter inseparable from form, and form a matter inseparable from content: each conditions the other.*[17]

Our excursion may also have demonstrated the wisdom of following this procedure: Since the three-act play is the norm today, first try the possibilities of the three-act form with your material (after, of course, you have your Proposition and know your climax). Begin with locating your climax at the end of Act II. Then sketch in the parts of the story to be covered in Acts I, II, and III. You will quickly find out whether or not you need a longer form (because of an *inevitable* need of the passage of time or separation in space).*

If after first trying your climax at the end of Act II you now find that there is more of the essential material of your story than can be reasonably covered in the first two acts, you may require a four-act or a five-act play. For a four-act play try the climax at the end of Act III, for a five-act play at the end of Act IV. If you are afraid of appearing old-fashioned with a four-act play, you have only to list your first two acts as the first two scenes of Act I—if with a five-act play, you have only to list both Acts I and II as having two scenes each—and your play will be accepted as a three-act play and everyone will be happy. (See pages 141–142.)

If, on the other hand, you find that the climax at the end of Act II would leave you with more of the essential material of the story than can be reasonably covered in a final third act, then deciding on a four-act play or a five-act play will not right the difficulty; for now, a second-act climax would mean a highly disproportioned play. When this dilemma arises (assuming that you have a foolproof Proposition and climax) your error is prob-

* We italicize *inevitable* because every dramatist runs into problems of time and space intervals; these often are not inevitable, and when they are not, must be manipulated so as to fall within the possibilities of a single scene. The beginner and the aesthetically indolent are ready to drop a curtain every time such a problem presents itself. But the real craftsman does not allow himself the destructive easiness of such laziness, for he knows that *in the solution of just such problems the best dramatic results often come into being.* We shall explain more fully later what we mean by this. By an inevitable interval, we mean one that is absolutely necessary to the story's essentials, as in the case cited from *Romeo and Juliet.*

ably that you are planning to begin your play either too early or too late in the turn of your story.* (We illustrate what is "too early or too late" in what immediately follows.)

WHERE DO I BEGIN MY PLAY?

Before writing your first act, it is very useful to list all the relevant facts of the story you are about to tell, and to put them down in chronological order. In the case of *Hamlet,* for instance, the list would begin something like this:

1. The elder Hamlet and his wife are rulers of Denmark.
2. Gertrude gives birth to a son, who is named after his father, on the same day that the Gravedigger begins his profession.
3. During young Hamlet's childhood he is a favorite with Yorick, the court jester.
4. Yorick dies.
5. The King's brother, Claudius, and the Queen are irresistibly drawn into an adulterous relationship.
6. Claudius, so enamored of Gertrude that he must have her for himself, and equally eager to possess the crown, plans, without Gertrude's knowledge, to murder his brother.
7. Claudius murders the elder Hamlet. At the time, Prince Hamlet is away at the University.
8. Sometime before this, Prince Hamlet has been given a seal of the royal house of Denmark.
9. Learning of his father's death, Hamlet at once returns to Denmark.
10. Two months after the murder, Claudius marries Gertrude.

* Until the closing pages of this book we everywhere assume that our dramatist-to-be will be refraining from experiments with such techniques as call for multiplicity of scenes and/or a variety of blackouts —until he has tried his hand for some time at the much more difficult and more basic challenge of managing one long uninterrupted scene per act. Indeed, we strongly urge that he begin with a few one-act plays (a form soon to be discussed). After he has become familiar with the less pliable forms of dramaturgy, he will find techniques requiring multiplicity of scenes extremely easy—perhaps too easy to bother with!

11. Horatio, Prince Hamlet's closest friend, leaves the University too and goes to Denmark.
12. At about this time an apparition garbed in the armor of the late King is seen walking on the battlements after midnight.
13. Immediately upon Horatio's arrival the soldiers who have seen the apparition inform him of its appearance.
14. Horatio, skeptical, agrees to join the guard that very night to see if the report of the soldiers is true.
15. Horatio joins the guard and the apparition does appear.
16. Horatio informs Prince Hamlet about the Ghost later that morning.
17. Hamlet decides to join the men himself that night.
18. He sees the Ghost and follows it.
19. The Ghost tells of the murder and bids the Prince avenge it.
20. Hamlet swears the men to secrecy concerning what they have seen that night.
21. Some weeks later, a company of players arrives in town.
22. Hamlet conceives of the idea of having the players present a play before Claudius to test his guilt.
23. Hamlet observes the King during the performance of the play, and so on.

Now, it is obvious that no one in his right mind would have written *Hamlet* so that it began with Point 1 and proceeded with what follows on our list, in strict chronological order; to do so would be never to reach the chief business of the tragedy, which is the question of Hamlet's killing Claudius. As a matter of fact, Shakespeare begins his play with Point 15. All that precedes that is brought in later: Point 1 in I, v; Points 2, 3, and 4 in V, i; Point 5 in I, v; Point 6 partially in I, v, and more emphatically in III, iii; Point 7 in I, v; Point 8 in V, ii; Points 9, 10, and 11 in I, ii; Points 12, 13, and 14 in I, i.

But if Shakespeare had had no more experience than he had at the time of writing *Romeo and Juliet* (which takes a little too long in getting started), he might have been tempted to begin *Hamlet* with Point 6. After all, the planning and execution of a murder is exciting stuff for drama. But it would have been an unwise choice, because it would have left far too much story to present before he could arrive at the condition of the action, which does not occur until Point 19. This would have constituted the mistake of beginning the play at far too early a turn in the story. Therefore, all *the facts of the story preceding the opening incident* (Point 15) *are brought in* parenthetically, but *not haphazardly*—not thrown at the audience all at once—but introduced *where they are dramatically pertinent.* It is not important for us to know precisely on what day Horatio has arrived at court (Point 11) until he greets Prince Hamlet (Point 16); it is then we realize that it must have been on the night before. The murder of Hamlet's father need not be indicated until the Ghost reveals it (Point 19), since, however exciting, it is still subordinate to the matter of Hamlet's revenge; and even the murder itself, so far as Claudius' motives go, need not be fully explained until a more suitable time—that is, when Claudius is on his knees, trying to pray (III, iii). Hamlet must have been given a duplicate of the royal seal of Denmark before his father's death; but it is not necessary even to mention it—important though it proves to Hamlet's life—until the last scene of the play, when Hamlet is telling Horatio of his changing the documents while aboard the ship bound for England (V, ii).

The list of relevant facts in *Biography* would begin like this:

1. Marion and Leander Nolan take walks together in their native Nashville, Tennessee.
2. They have a love affair.
3. Marion suddenly leaves Nashville in pursuit of a career.
4. She develops an international reputation as a portrait painter, painting heads of governments and leading personalities all over Europe.
5. She has a successful period painting the stars in Hollywood too.
6. She is a guest at Lady Winchester's garden party at Ascot.
7. The next year she is a guest at a Fourth of July dinner at the American Embassy in Rome.
8. For some years she has a very close relationship with Feydak, a distinguished Austrian composer.
9. She is a good friend of Feydak's brother, also a composer, but a less successful one.

10. The celebrated Feydak dies.
11. Feydak's brother is offered a contract for Hollywood and comes to America.
12. Nolan becomes engaged to marry the daughter of an influential publisher.
13. Kurt, a magazine editor, decides that Marion's life would make a sensational book.
14. Nolan decides to look Marion up in order to assume the blame for the Bohemian life she has been leading.

It is at this point that Mr. Behrman has begun his play. All these facts are brought in parenthetically, one at a time.

If it is an error to begin a play too early in the story, it is an equally grave mistake to begin it too late. For instance, suppose Shakespeare had begun *Hamlet* with Point 21, where the Players come to town. Might he have not brought in parenthetically all that preceded this event, in the manner we have indicated—especially considering all the story that was yet to be told? Well, had he done so, the play would have lacked the condition of the action, Step 1 of the Proposition. The interview with the Ghost reveals the beginning and basis of the plot; to relegate it among the matters which would precede the opening of the play would be to exclude it from the play's plot. A play which excludes the beginning of the plot will seem, as it proceeds, to lack foundation, to be insecure. To begin a play *after* the condition of the action has occurred is to begin at a fatally late turn of the story.

In this connection it is worthwhile repeating the substance of an earlier footnote. It is a fact familiar to Shakespearean scholars that in *Othello* all the business of Act I was invented by Shakespeare to precede the material from the old Italian tale which he began to put to use in Act II, but they have never asked why Shakespeare was moved to invent it. The answer quite plainly is that this new material contains the beginning of the plot, the condition of the action. Unless Shakespeare had shown Othello's certainty of Desdemona's love and of his title as her husband, the rest of the story would have had no foundation. To have begun (as the libretto for Verdi's opera *Otello* does begin) with Shakespeare's second act would have been to begin too late.

There is another serious blunder that some dramatists have made. It is possible to make the error, while not excluding the beginning of the plot, of passing over it so rapidly—that is, going almost immediately from condition of the action to cause of the action—that the condition of the action leaves absolutely no impression upon the audience. When the beginning of the action (the condition) is hurried over in this way, the play again will not seem to have its proper foundations. The reason? We have already expatiated upon the principle that what is of significance on the stage must have a certain extensiveness (see pages 54– 68). The beginning of the plot is one of the most significant parts of the plot, and therefore cannot be shown in a kind of lightning flash. It is to be noted that Points 15, 16, 17, and 18 in our list for *Hamlet*—scenes in I, i, ii, and iv—all lead to the condition of the action, Point 19 (I, v), and thereby give that scene even greater emphasis. Thus, too, much of what occurs in I, i, of *Othello* and all of what occurs in I, ii, lead to (and add to the extensiveness of) the great scene in I, iii, the condition of the action.

This error of making short shrift of the condition of the action was largely responsible for the weakness in plot of two American plays, each of which was a dramatization of a novel and each of which could easily have been powerfully organized with the story at hand: McCullers' *The Member of the Wedding* and Capote's *The Grass Harp*. There is all the more regret over this weakness in view of the wonderful possibilities of each play and the exquisitely poetic quality of the material.

In *The Member of the Wedding*, as the story is first to be met with in Mrs. McCullers' novel by that name, the heroine, Frankie Adams, is a lonely girl going through the difficult transition from childhood to adolescence. She is too old to play any longer with very little children and too young to be accepted as yet by the adolescents in the neighborhood. Her brother is away in the Army, and her only companions are Bernice, the Negro servant of the house, and a precocious little boy much younger than herself, and from Bernice she receives, more often than not, ridicule. She yearns to become a member of a club of adolescents, but she continues to be rejected by them. Because of a misunderstanding she misses the opportunity to acquire a friend of her own age. Dejected, wretched in her desire to "belong," she hears the overwhelming news that her brother has become engaged to be married and is coming home. She concentrates all her romantic imagination on his home-coming and succeeds in turning it into a compensation for her rejection by others. Her brother comes home with his bride-to-be, and suddenly Frankie is living in a dream world of delight. How beautiful and wonderful the young couple seem to her! Now, as though it were a great revelation, she realizes that she can participate in all this beauty and wonder by becoming a member of the wedding, by going away with them to the regions of enchantment for which they must surely be destined. All her efforts are now bent toward the great event, the wedding of which she is determined to be a part. She buys herself an outrageous dress—to her eyes, the last word in magnificence—and that gets her involved in some highly dramatic experiences with a soldier. At last the wedding party is ready to move on to its glorious future. Frankie finds to her dismay that she is not allowed to go along. After this, the novel concerns itself, as a novel may do, with the aftermath of Frankie's disappointment, and how she thereafter does make a friend, and how she finds herself "accepted" at last.

When we attended the theater to see the dramatization of this utterly charming novel, we were dismayed to read on the program the following outline of scenes:

> Act I.
>
> Act II.
>
> Act III: Scene 1.
>
> Scene 2.
>
> Scene 3.

This augured very ill for the last act. And so it turned out, for the last act was a kind of mad scramble to get in too much material: the aftermath of Frankie's failure to become a member of the wedding party, her making a friend after all, her finding herself belonging—not to mention matter relative to Bernice and Bernice's brother which had nothing to do with the business of the play at all. The play that Mrs. McCullers undertook to write raised the question: Will Frankie succeed in becoming a member of the wedding or not? Once that question was answered, the plot had reached its end, and the play should have been over soon thereafter.

But it turned out that the beginning of the play was even weaker in its structure. If the question of the play was: Will Frankie succeed in becoming a member of the wedding?—then the cause of the action must have been Frankie's decision to become a member of the wedding. The condition of the action must therefore have been Frankie's learning of her brother's return and the forthcoming wedding. Or, to state the Proposition from which a well-constructed plot might have been made with materials selected from the novel:

1. Frankie, a lonely girl, rejected by her contemporaries and having rejected a possible friend, is suddenly shocked and then elated to hear of her brother's imminent return and his forthcoming wedding.

2. Because of her rejection and her intense need to become a member of something, she falls in love with the idea of the wedding when she sees her brother and his fiancée, and decides to become a member of it.

3. Will Frankie succeed in becoming a member of the wedding or not?

When the curtain went up on Mrs. McCullers' play Frankie's brother and his bride-to-be had already arrived, were on stage, and Frankie sat at their feet worshiping them. Behind this, unless one had read the novel (which the play had no right to count upon), there was no way for the audience to know of Frankie's long loneliness and her rejection and longing to be a member of something. At the end of Act I, the cause of the action was introduced: Frankie decided to become a member of the wedding. For a play which was not a farce,* this left an enormous stretch of four more scenes in which to answer the question (the resulting action). At the end of Act II the plot had not advanced an inch: Frankie simply exulted anew in her decision to become a member of the wedding! Act II was, therefore, an act without any development of the plot at all—which meant there was no dramatic movement for about one-third of the entire play. This unfortunate construction was a direct result of the dramatist's having begun her play at too late a turn of the story. The plot thus lacked a firm foundation, the importance of Frankie's elation over her brother's return not having been in any way led up to; the condition of the action was presented at the rise of the curtain, and since it was over and done with in a matter of minutes, it lacked

---

* In a farce the plot is more often than not a mere excuse for stringing together a collection of funny situations. Consequently, in a farce there is often a great distance between the cause of the action and the final curtain.

any dimension, and therefore could not have impressed the audience as forming the base of the story. Had the first act shown Frankie's loneliness, her rejecting a possible friendship because of her fear that the girl would reject her, her great need of belonging to something, her learning of her brother's return and imminent marriage and her excitement over that, there would have been enough content in this for Act I. That would have allotted to Act II the arrival of the bridal pair, her falling in love with the idea of the wedding and her deciding to become a member of it, and (the climax) her rushing off to the bridal pair's carriage to join them. Act III would be the rest of the resulting action. The play thus proportioned would have shown a steady, unhalting progress of the plot. As the play now stands, Act II is hopelessly static.

Something similar happened in Capote's dramatization of his enchanting novel *The Grass Harp*. Here the story is of a boy; a sweet-tempered, timid old maid, who is a relative of his; and the house's Negro servant—all leading an intense and close life in the kitchen of the house and keeping as much as possible out of the way of the mistress of the house, the old maid's sister, a brittle, efficient, successful, unloving businesswoman. The center of life for the three waifs in the kitchen is a patent medicine brewed by the old maid, the recipe for which she learned from the gypsies as a girl. At the right time of the year the three of them go into the fields and woods gathering the herbs needed for the concoction, though some of the ingredients are known only to the old maid. That is her secret and the other two respect it. They have great fun helping her brew the medicine and bottle it. She sells some fifty bottles of it a year at a dollar a bottle. But the best of all is the elaborate correspondence she conducts with her various clients, and in which they come to make her their confidante in all the transactions of their family life. All three looked forward to these letters as a chief source of interest. Suddenly, the brittle sister is awakened by a promoter from the North to the possible financial success of the medicine. In anticipation of putting the product on the market, she orders large numbers of bottles and labels. But then she encounters an unforeseen obstacle: when she asks for the recipe, the old maid refuses! Gentle, always bending to the will of her clever sister, she nevertheless exhibits a strange stubbornness on this one matter: the recipe is the only thing in the world that is really hers, and she thinks it not fair to be asked to part with it. The sister reminds her that everything the three have is owing to her bounty: the house, their very food. The old maid admits that this is true enough, and since their having kept house for the sister has apparently not been enough compensation, it is only just that the three of them move out. They, in fact, do so, and take up their lodging in a tree house that the boy has used in his playing. We need not, for the sake of the point we have in view, outline the rest of the story. We hope that we have sufficiently incited the interest of the reader to peruse this delightful book himself.

Now, it must be clear from our summary that the outstanding dramatic event, as far as we have gone into the story, is the sister's demand of the recipe and the old maid's refusal. Its effect is striking in the extreme when one comes upon it in the novel. But the play of the same name opens with the three hastily laying the table in the dining room of the house for a dinner at which the promoter is to be the sister's guest. Within some ten minutes of the rising curtain, the request for the recipe is made and refused. Unless one knew the novel, the importance of the recipe to the old maid and the other two could not possibly be clear to the audience. The recipe is demanded, refused, and then forgotten; it is talked of, in fact, before the audience has even a chance to learn who the three are, what their relationship to one another and to the medicine is. What should have been the cardinal matter in Act I was over and done with after about the first quarter of an hour—instead of being led up to and itself given sufficient extensiveness for the audience to be impressed with it. This beginning at too late a turn of the story, again, leaves nothing for Act II—which in the play is an unfortunate hodgepodge of odds and ends obviously introduced to fill in the act because it must be traversed to make up a full-length play. The drama as compared with the novel is a pathetic waste of wonderful material.

These errors should be enough to speak anew for the merits of not beginning to write until one has a sound Proposition and climax, and then designing the play in terms of them.

To summarize: *Arrange to have your condition of the action in a prominent position in Act I. Lead up to it so as to give it the importance it bears as the foundation of the plot. When you arrive at it, do not treat it with too much brevity, but give it sufficient extensiveness.* (It would do no harm at this point to reread the pertinent scenes in the plays we have analyzed—Hamlet's interview with the Ghost, Othello's scene before the Duke of Venice, Cyrano's scene with Roxane, Hedda's long dialogue with Thea establishing the facts about Lovborg—to see how in each case the dramatist has given the condition of the action the double emphasis of being led up to and being allotted an impressive number of lines.)

THE EXPOSITION

Intimately connected with the problem of where to begin the play is the problem of managing the exposition. Wherever one begins, there is always a certain amount of information constituting the background of the action, with which the audience must become acquainted so that the play can proceed. The imparting of this information is known as the exposition. In dramaturgical discussion it is a time-honored (and highly exaggerated) platitude that the exposition is very hard to manipulate. There was a period, now happily nevermore to return, when the approved method of opening a play was to have two maids with feather dusters appear in the living room or main foyer of the house and indulge in a conversation something like this (going through the motions, meanwhile, of dusting the premises):

MAGGIE

I hear that Master Ronald is returning tomorrow after ten long years at sea.

MOLLIE

Yes, indeed, and what a shock it will be for him when he learns that his fiancée, Miss Arbutus, is going to marry his uncle, Lord Winterbottom, next week!

MAGGIE

Enough to break the poor young master's heart.

MOLLIE

Still, what was the young master to do when his uncle, Lord Winterbottom, who had full control over his education and the purse strings, ordered him to make a man of himself before he would give his consent to the marriage?

MAGGIE

Nothing but what he did. How was he to know that while he was away Lord Winterbottom was going to encourage Miss Arbutus' father, Mr. Pothlethwaite, to get deeper and deeper in debt to him, so that now there's no way out but that the poor girl had to agree to marry him to keep her father from absolute ruin?

MOLLIE

Exactly. The wedding is to take place in this very room this coming Thursday.

MAGGIE

Today's Sunday, isn't it? That's in just four days.

MOLLIE

Of course the young master has now come of age, so far as his inheritance is concerned, and may do as he pleases from now on.

MAGGIE

That's if he has any money to do anything with.

MOLLIE

What do you mean?

MAGGIE

Well, one day, not so long ago, I overheard Mr. Abercrombie
—that's Lord Winterbottom's attorney, you know—discussing
financial matters, and I wouldn't be the least surprised if the
poor young master finds out that Lord Winterbottom has specu-
lated with the money he had in trust for the young master until
none of it is left.

MOLLIE

Sh-sh! Here comes Lord Winterbottom and Miss Arbutus.

One is happy to report that such openings have disappeared
with feather dusters. Not only was it absurd that for no reason
under the sun two maids should be discussing what they both
already knew, but it was also a burden to the audience to be
required to digest all of the information at once and to remember
who were Master Ronald, Lord Winterbottom, Miss Arbutus,
Mr. Pothlethwaite, Mr. Abercrombie—and to bear all that in
mind in what followed.

Perhaps in no play in the world is exposition more brilliantly
managed than in Sophocles' *Oedipus Tyrannus*.[18] It is a play that
will richly repay patient analysis; no single fact connected with
the background of the action is brought in until it can be of
maximum dramatic service to the action itself. The exposition is
distributed, fact by fact, throughout the tragedy, and always
with the supremest science of where to place it.

We have already shown in our listing of the chronologically
earliest facts connected with the story of *Hamlet*, how Shakespeare distributed the first fourteen throughout the play, and how
some of them do not appear until the last act because they are of
no dramatic pertinency until then. This kind of procedure will
be found in all the plays we have analyzed (with the possible exception of *Romeo and Juliet*). Thus, in *Othello* we do not learn

that the handkerchief was Othello's first gift to Desdemona during their courtship until Emilia tells us so (III, iii, 290), precisely when it is important for us to know that fact—just after Desdemona has lost it; we do not learn the importance Othello attaches to it until after that (III, iv, 55–68), when it is most important for us to understand—when Othello is asking Desdemona for it; yet because of the significance the handkerchief bears in the climax, a beginner might have made the mistake of eagerly introducing these pieces of information very early in the play— just to be sure, perhaps, that he had got that over and done with. Again, in *Hedda Gabler* we do not have the answer to the puzzling question as to how a woman like Hedda could have married a man like Tesman until after a third of Act II, in Hedda's conversation with Brack; the unfortunate alliance began with Hedda's thoughtlessly remarking, just to break the silence during a walk with Tesman, that she would like to live in the villa they were at the moment passing.

We recommend that, in order to manage the exposition efficiently, first a list be made in chronological order of the relevant facts to be brought in during the course of the play—a list such as we began to make for *Hamlet;* the list, of course, should include all the facts of which you are reasonably sure, down to the final curtain. When you have decided where your opening situation is to be, you can then, at least tentatively, decide upon the likeliest place to bring in each of the preceding points. These matters antecedent to the play are highly unlikely to be brought in in the same order of the list; * in the case of *Hamlet,* for ex-

* The grand exception to this is *The Tempest*, the last play Shakespeare wrote. As though to prove that he could manage the impossible, in the second scene of the play he did the one thing that cannot be done: gave a straight account, in chronological order, of all the events that had preceded the opening of the play, down to the moment in which the speaker, Prospero, is making the narration. It was a daring feat and brought about triumphantly only through the brilliance of the characterizations and the dialogue during the course of the narration. Nevertheless, to safeguard audience interest, Shakespeare had used a clever trick in the preceding (the first) scene of the play. All that occurs in that scene is a general hullabaloo during which a ship is apparently sinking, people are jumping overboard, passengers are shrieking in panic—without our being able to discover who is who or what their relationship to one another is. It is all over in a very few minutes. After that, Shakespeare knew, the audience will listen with the greatest attention to any explanation that

ample, the earliest to be introduced were Points 12, 13, and 14; Points 9, 10, and 11 were next; Point 1 next; Point 5 next; Point 6 (partially) next; Point 7 next; Point 6 (more fully) next; Points 2, 3, and 4 next; Point 8 last of all.

Naturally, we mean in no way to imply that the mechanics we have recommended in determining the position of the various parts of the·exposition are absolutely indispensable. A practiced writer may feel he can carry the information in his head and know by instinct when to bring it in to the best advantage. Nor do we imply that whatever position one may have first determined upon may not, in the heat of writing, inevitably give way to another one. The creative imagination is capable of wiser decisions than can be made by the strict use of a precise outline. At best our suggestions for managing the exposition are meant to be no more than rules of thumb—roughly practical measures rather than (like the principles of Proposition and climax) infallible scientific ones. For the creative imagination, we do not forget,

turns

Bodies to spirit by sublimation strange,

As fire converts to fire the things it burns.

Nevertheless, the creative imagination is not always ready to come at a summons. And everyone must learn to crawl before he can walk, and to walk before he can run. Even a Beethoven cannot compose until he has mastered the laws of harmony and counterpoint. If later he chooses to break them, he then does so for good artistic reasons, not out of ignorance or frivolous impulse.

---

is likely to follow. By this device Shakespeare fortified his experiment in flying in the face of good dramaturgical practice, and felt the safer in treating the audience to the long exposition of the second scene.

CHAPTER SEVEN

Plot and Character

Such a plot must have a woman in it.
RICHARDSON, *Sir Charles Grandison*

A character, or that which distinguishes one man from all others, cannot be supposed to consist of one particular virtue, or vice, or passion only; but it is a composition of qualities which are not contrary to one another in the same person. DRYDEN, *Criticism in Tragedy*

When a man loses his estate, his health, his strength, he is still the same person, and has lost nothing of his personality. . . . A person is something indivisible. REID, *Intellectual Powers*

It is impossible to think of people, or to deal with them, as members of a class, a mass or a community. Class, mass, and community are but fictions employed to mask a man's distaste for other human beings. The world is populated only by individuals.
REINABERG, *Hither and Yon*

"Society" in this representative town of the Pacific Coast is somewhat difficult of characterization. BOWLES, *In Merriam*

Elsewhere we have attempted to answer the question "What does the writer write about?" in this way: "About life as it is, as it has been, as he feels it should be—about other people, about his relationship to them, about himself, about his God, about Nature, and about the things Man himself has created. The degree to which he can illuminate these relationships will always be a criterion of his greatness." *

In the case of the dramatist the emphasis must be upon "about other people," for no matter how philosophical or intel-

* B. Grebanier and S. Reiter, *Introduction to Imaginative Literature* (New York, 1960), p. 3.

lectual a playwright's purposes may be, he can achieve them only through the agency of the persons of his drama. How far philosophy can make good theater may be pleasurably investigated in a study of one of the twentieth century's greatest dramatists, Luigi Pirandello, whose *Six Characters in Search of an Author, Naked, Right You Are, As You Desire Me, Each in His Own Way*, and *The Pleasure of Honesty*—to mention only a few plays of this prolific writer—all pose tantalizing philosophic questions; but they do so strictly in terms of dramatic composition. In the plays of Pirandello the philosophic question is not baldly expressed, as in some pretentious twentieth-century American plays, by having various characters step up to the footlights and deliver a series of not so profound harangues about Life and Society; it emanates from the plot and the character relationships.

Certainly, in drama,* more than in any other form of literature, the *audience*, during the progress of the story, concerns itself above all other elements with the characters of the play, the persons of the drama. It is safe to say that the better the play, the more the audience is intent upon the characters, rather than on the plot or the theme.

This, at first, might seem to be contradictory to everything we have thus far said. We have insisted with Aristotle that plot is the soul of drama, and we continue to insist that considerations of plot are the cardinal considerations in drama. But when we say this, we are talking from the point of view of the *dramatist*, not the audience. For when characters in a good play prove absorbing, it is always because of what they *do*, not because of what people say about them. In a novel the author can step forward and deliver some telling strokes of characterization while he narrates; he can have other characters in the story "discuss" the character traits of his men and women. In a play the dramatist has no opportunity to address the audience with observations on his characters; and there is no weaker device in the theater than employing as a chief means of characterization one group of characters to "discuss" other persons of the drama. Such discussions are static and therefore (the very nature of drama being an

---

* Drama, that is, exclusive of farce and melodrama, in which characterization is likely to be kept to a minimum and the interest attaches itself chiefly to a succession of hilarious or gripping situations.

unceasing movement from point to point) highly undramatic. They may do well enough on a printed page, where they may be lingered over, but they can be only dull on the boards. *In a play the characterization must be revealed basically through the action of the characters.* It is for this reason that to a dramatist, during the creation of his play, the characters must be subordinate to the plot, for their revelation of personal traits is dependent upon the workings of the plot.

In the modern theater this fact has been sometimes forgotten. However notable in fiction have been some results of the twentieth-century preoccupation with psychological analysis of motivation and character (as in the novels of D. H. Lawrence, for example), the theater has unquestionably suffered from a remorseless delving into psychological factors.* Just because an audience is likely to be more absorbed in the characters of a play than in the plot, many dramatists of our time have attempted to depict characters without benefit of plot; in such plays whatever action is present seems to have been invented to "illustrate" the characterization.† This is like attempting to decorate the walls of a living room in an apartment house before the foundations have been laid and the supporting walls have been constructed.

An example of such procedure came to our attention the other day when a student discussed with us his plans for a one-act play. This was his material: His hero is a college lad torn by multiple interests (he has some gifts as an actor, a writer, and a musician) who cannot focus upon any one of them and make a success of it. He envies his roommate friend, a boy who knows just what he wants, concentrates on his goal, and is making good

---

* It was against the psychologizing out of existence of all dramatic values in the theater that the French Existentialist movement in literature, with its emphasis on the *deeds* of men and its insistence that a man's character is simply the sum total of his acts, was directed. Existentialism has therefore, whatever may be said for or against it as a philosophy, provided an excellent point of view for dramatists, and the movement has produced some plays of considerable quality (for example, Sartre's *The Flies* and *No Exit*).

† A few reviewers, indeed, have come to speak patronizingly of a well-constructed plot—because of the recent scarcity of good plots—as though the conception of plot were a kind of antediluvian inheritance no longer required by the theater.

at it. Our hero is failing in his studies, and postpones facing responsibility by going out with friends for a good time when he should be working. His sweetheart, convinced that he will never change, comes to his room and gives him back his ring, telling him that their engagement is off, and leaves. His roommate comes in and lectures him on the necessity of coming to grips with his studies; because of his envy, he quarrels with his roommate, who rushes out to find another place to live. He is left alone. He begins to make an effort, despite his despair, to study; his misery makes it impossible. "Now," said our student-author, "I can end the play in one of two ways: I can have him turn on the gas and commit suicide; or I can have the phone ring—it is some friends who wish him to go to a movie, and he eagerly agrees to meet them and go. Which do you recommend?" Naturally, we answered, "Neither."

This summary of the story, of course, contained no plot and no climax (though our young author thought turning on the gas or going to the movies would make a suitable climax [19]). All that the material held was a series of episodes illustrative of the weakness in the hero's character. Such a dilemma came, obviously, from beginning to write a play the wrong way—by trying to invent action that would show character. He had three people: the hero, the girl, the roommate, but he had not involved them in a plot.

As we have said long ago, it is perfectly reasonable to start one's thinking about a play by desiring to represent a certain character or certain characters. It is perfectly reasonable to wish to write a play about such a young man as the would-be author conceived his hero as being. But, as we have also said, given the characters (the boy, the girl, the roommate, in this case), one must then start thinking of the action and, as soon as possible, tentatively at least, arrive at a plot relationship of the characters. No such plot relationship existed in this student's material; the girl and the roommate just wandered in and out of the story to show the kind of human being the hero was. However, it would be easy enough to involve these three people in a plot. The roommate, successful in all things, could, for instance, steal the affection of the girl from the boy—with several possible consequences to all three (depending on who became the central character). Or, the girl, in order to make the boy wake up, could play up to the roommate and evoke the boy's jealousy—with, again, several possible consequences to all three. A plot evolved from either of these basic situations would exhibit far more effectively (in terms of drama) the character of the boy (and of the girl and the roommate as well) than a series of episodes unconnected with a plot and which merely illustrated the fact that the boy was weak.

This is the kind of error, so enfeebling to the life of any play, which has caused havoc in the structure of many contemporary works. It results from coming to the false conclusion that just because an audience will be likely to find its greatest interest in the characters of a good play, the action can be allowed to take care of itself—that the action can be trusted to take some sort of shape from the characterization (instead of vice versa, which is actually the case)—that the action can be treated as a kind of by-product of the characterization. One could not indulge such an attitude toward action even when writing in the looser form of the novel. To recur to our trope, it would be like concluding that because one lives *inside* individual rooms of a house, there is no need of a basic structure outside for the building itself.

When approaching the creation of one's characters, therefore, one must begin with the requirements of the plot. From the viewpoint of the dramatist, character exists because of the plot, not plot because of character. It is to get nowhere, for example, to begin by sketching the character traits of, say, ten people—each highly individualized, for the sake of variety—and then decide, "Now that I have my characters I'll put them into some sort of play."

Concerning the characters, *the first question to be asked is: "Which are the characters I need for the plot?"*

WHAT CHARACTERS DO I NEED FOR THE PLOT?

Proceed this way, and your work at once takes on dimension.

Let us imagine ourselves in Shakespeare's place when he came to write his *Romeo and Juliet*. As the central and second characters he would, of course, require Romeo and Juliet. Next, Tybalt becomes necessary because the climax is to be Romeo's killing of him.

The central character, the second character, and a third character required for the climax are the three indispensable characters in every play.

Now, *Romeo and Juliet* is a tragedy; and the climax of a tragedy must be an act consciously performed by the hero, not an accidental one.* Shakespeare therefore needs a motivation for Romeo's killing of Tybalt. (In his source for the play, Romeo's killing of Tybalt was accidental.) The dramatist therefore invents the character of Mercutio (not to be found in the original story). Mercutio is a close friend of Romeo's; to motivate the climax, Shakespeare invents the scene in which Romeo's intervention in the duel between Mercutio and Tybalt becomes the reason for Mercutio's death. Because he feels guilty for the slaying of his good friend, Romeo will in a fit of desperation fight Tybalt to the death.

It must have been through some such kind of planning that Shakespeare discovered the need of Mercutio—a most lucky discovery, for Mercutio turns out to be one of the most fascinating people in the play. To provide motivation for the climax, Mercutio thus becomes one of the next most essential characters in the play—more essential, indeed, than even Juliet's parents or Romeo's parents. For though the elder Capulets and Montagues are part of the story, because of the family feud, it is at least conceivable that the story might have been told without their ever being represented before our eyes on the stage. Not so with Mercutio.

After the three indispensable characters the next most necessary characters are those required or suggested either by the Proposition or the climax. Mercutio was required by the climax.

In *Hamlet*, Hamlet (as central character), Claudius (as second character), and Polonius (as the third character needed in the climax) are indispensable. Next, since the first step of the Proposition requires him (see page 94), the Ghost becomes a necessary character. Also, since the second step of the Proposition involves Hamlet's presenting a play before Claudius, the Players become essential too.

In *Othello*, Othello (as central character), Desdemona (as second character), and Cassio (as the third character needed in

* The reasons for this will be discussed in the chapter on Tragedy.

the climax) are indispensable. Next, since the second step of the Proposition requires him (see page 96), Iago becomes essential. Also, since it is necessary for the climax that Desdemona's handkerchief be stolen (see page 113), Emilia becomes vital too: it is Emilia who appropriates the handkerchief and then gives it to Iago.

In *The Importance of Being Earnest*, Jack (as central character), Lady Bracknell (as second character), and Miss Prism (as third character needed in the climax) are indispensable. Since Gwendolen figures in the first two steps of the Proposition (for it is she whom Jack wishes to marry, and since the whole plot hinges on his desire to marry her), she is certainly a necessary character.

In *Hedda Gabler*, Hedda (as central character), Lovborg (as second character), and Thea (as third character needed in the climax) are indispensable. Since Hedda is to be defeated in her desire to destroy Lovborg's work, and since, moreover, it is part of the plot that Hedda is now married to someone other than Lovborg, Tesman becomes a necessary character.

In *Biography*, Marion (as central character), Kurt (as second character), and Kinnicott (as third character needed in the climax) are indispensable. Since Kinnicott's concern is over his daughter's betrothed, Nolan is necessary too. Naturally Kinnicott's daughter Slade can be used with advantage too, though Nolan is more essential than she.

In each of these plays the dramatist, having proceeded thus far in his choice of characters, would have had a handful of necessary persons of the drama with whom he was in a position to work out his play in fuller detail. In the instance of *Hedda Gabler*, Ibsen, in fact, would have had nearly his entire cast. Neither Brack nor Tesman's aunt was absolutely essential, although Brack has been used significantly by the playwright, and Tesman's aunt has also been powerfully integrated into the play.[20]

THE OTHER CHARACTERS

When the dramatist has discovered the characters required by the Proposition and the climax (Hamlet, Claudius, Polonius, the Ghost, the Players), he must now consider the incidents of the action.* This will mean, of course, that the action, at this point of the planning of the play, will possibly suggest other characters and that the characters may very well suggest parts of the action. Also, the characters already determined upon may suggest additional characters who may profitably be used in the action.

Thus, in the case of *Hamlet*:

1. Since it was to possess Gertrude that Claudius originally murdered Hamlet's father, her presence becomes a dramatic addition to the cast.

2. Since Hamlet is to kill Polonius, a son to Polonius, Laertes, as eager to avenge *his* father's death as is Hamlet to avenge the late King's, becomes a valuable addition. Claudius can use this Laertes as a pawn in the King's final conflict with Hamlet.

3. Since Hamlet's fatal killing of Polonius will give Claudius the opportunity to hurry Hamlet out of Denmark, an agency to supervise the Prince's getting to England for his own execution becomes advisable. To supply this turn of the plot Guildenstern and Rosencrantz are invented.

4. Since the beginning action will require that someone trusted by Hamlet must induce Hamlet to meet the Ghost without Claudius' hearing of it, Horatio is invented. The fact that the Ghost is seen by others makes it plain, too, that the apparition is not a hallucination of Hamlet's.

5. Since Claudius and Laertes' plot against Hamlet's life will require that the unbated and envenomed rapier be presented to the duelists in such a way that that weapon will fall into Laertes', not Hamlet's, hands, Osric is invented.

And so on. Naturally, once their roles in the action are fixed, the dramatist is free to enlarge on the relationship of each of the characters to the other persons of the play. The more inter-

---

* It is extremely useful to write a summary or outline of these incidents in the order in which they are to appear in the play. Naturally, such a summary is subject to constant revision during the planning and even the writing of the play. But it forms a solid basis on which to work.

related and interdependent the characters become, the better. So, Gertrude's relationship to her son becomes a source of interest, as does her relationship to Ophelia; Laertes' relationship to the King and to his sister becomes equally so; the same may be said of Guildenstern and Rosencrantz's relationship to Hamlet, of Horatio's role during the presentation of the play before the King, of Osric's encounter with Hamlet.[21]

IN WHAT ORDER DO I PROCEED?

The reader now has a considerable amount of information concerning situation, incident, plot, Proposition, climax, and the choice of characters. We have already said that whether his first thoughts for his play are of a theme, character, or situation, he had better proceed quickly to a formulation of the plot. It is also clear, by this time, that he cannot be content with his plot unless it yields him a sound Proposition and a right climax.

But we have nowhere implied that the very first step in planning a play is to "think up" a Proposition. That would presuppose that one could conjure a play into being out of thin air, as thus:

1. A, convinced that his friend B is having an affair with A's wife, persuades B to go on a hunting trip with him.
2. When they are alone in the woods, A, aiming his gun at B, wrings a confession of guilt out of B.
3. Will A avenge himself on B?

Now, after the Proposition one tries to find a climax, and, lacking everything but the above Proposition, he might spend endless unprofitable hours in search of a correct climax and the appropriate third person. Why? Because one really has not yet any material for a play when he has no more than such a Proposition.

The Proposition and the climax must emerge from one's material.

Instead of attempting at the outset to form a Proposition, it would be much wiser to take the situation as it is set down in the first step above, and then proceed to consider the possibilities of the interrelationship of the three persons involved. What are their feelings about one another? Does A love B still or does he now hate him? Does A still love his wife or does he hate her now?

Does the wife dislike her husband or actually love him deeply? Has she yielded to B out of love, out of jealousy over A, out of momentary weakness?

Out of such questions, new and interesting possibilities may evolve. After this procedure, instead of attempting a Proposition as yet, it would be better to try making a roughly tentative summary of a story—with the full expectation of later drastically revising it. If thereafter one attempted a Proposition, it would be in the better position of having material with which to form a good one.[22]

There is, naturally, no *one* way of proceeding. We have known instances where a dramatist, unable to decide conclusively the direction of the plot or who (indeed) ought to be the central character, wrote the first act of a three-act play with the intention of using that act simply as his raw material. The procedure justified itself. Out of that tentative first act he became acquainted with his chief characters and their interrelationship, and also saw looming ahead various possibilities of plot. He was now in a position to weigh the merits of X, Y, or Z as central and second characters; to ponder the various plots which might emerge from what he already knew about the relationship of his characters; to consider the dramatic value of each of these possible plots; to discover which of the possibilities led him to a satisfactory climax and which did not. Eventually, he was able to evolve a sound Proposition and climax. After that, in most cases, the original first act was entirely discarded. But it had served its purpose well. Such a method of composition is, in the long run, a far greater saving of time and effort than a directionless writing and rewriting guided by only a vague notion of what might be done with the material.[23]

CHAPTER EIGHT

The One-Act Play;
The Television Play

Ab uno disce omnes.*   VIRGIL, *Aeneid*, II, 65

Brief words, when actions wait, are well.
    BRET HARTE, Address at the Opening of the California Theater

Every man feels instinctively that all the beautiful sentiments in the
world weigh less than a single lovely action.
    JAMES RUSSELL LOWELL, *Rousseau and the Sentimentalists*

When one is past, another care we have.
    HERRICK, *Sorrows Succeed*

    Theoretically, this is not the place to deal with the one-act
play. If the reader's love of logic finds itself too much offended,
he may skip this chapter and read it after he has read the chapters
on Characterization and Dialogue. But our purposes are exclusively practical. This is not a book on the theory of drama; it
is a book on how to write plays. And we feel that it is now time
for our reader to be writing a play: experience has taught that
he will be wise to begin with a one-acter.
    It is chiefly as an invaluable discipline in playwriting that we
recommend the one-act play. There was indeed a period, earlier
in our century, when the one-acter flourished on the boards;
Broadway audiences went willingly to see a program of three or
four one-act plays as an evening's entertainment. Very clever
writers like Lord Dunsany, brilliant ones like Pirandello and
Schnitzler, turned out a number of them; Eugene O'Neill's

    * From one learn all.

earliest successes were in this form, and there are those who
are of the opinion that he never again did better as a dramatist.
There were even companies whose talents were devoted exclusively to the presentation of the one-act play. But its day of glory
has passed, and although leading dramatists continue to write in
this form occasionally and no doubt will continue to do so, its
vogue is now chiefly among college and amateur acting companies. The limitations which the one-act play imposes upon the
writer are such as to make it less inviting than the full-length
play. On the other hand, it is these very limitations which make
the one-acter so excellent a discipline for the creation of more
ambitious works.

Before we discuss the characteristics of the one-act play, we
should like to suggest a few highly selected readings in the one-
acter. The reader will do well to read most or all of them: [24]

J.-P. Sartre, *No Exit*
E. O'Neill, *In the Zone*
    The Long Journey Home
    Ile
    Moon of the Caribbees
J. M. Barrie, *The Twelve-Pound Look*
Lord Dunsany, *The Lost Silk Hat*
    A Night at an Inn
H. Hall and R. Middlemass, *The Valiant*
S. Glaspell, *Trifles*
T. Rattigan, *The Browning Version*
A. Strindberg, *Miss Julie*

CHARACTERISTICS OF THE ONE-ACT PLAY

*The playing time in the theater of a one-act play varies
from about twenty minutes to a little over an hour.*

*The one-act play is an elaboration of a single, significant
incident.*

Clearly, in such a play the dramatist is not allowed the
scope which the full-length play affords. The multiplicity of incidents in *Romeo and Juliet* permits the dramatist to let his
characters blossom and expand before our eyes as the play
progresses. Romeo, when we first meet him, is a callow youth, in
love with love, and something of a bore; after he falls in love

with Juliet, he rapidly develops into an exciting, richly poetic adult. Juliet is at first a colorless, obedient child; love converts her into an imaginative, passionate young woman. In a masterpiece like *Hamlet*, we see new facets in the make-up of Hamlet, Claudius, Gertrude, Laertes, Horatio, every time they reappear upon the stage.

The dramatization of a single significant incident does not allow the author of the one-act play to realize human beings in this kind of full dimension. *There is not time enough for the author to acquaint us with more concerning his characters than the single incident demands that we know.* In O'Neill's *In the Zone*, for example, only Smitty has been given any striking distinguishing traits; the other men are only barely differentiated— and this is true even of the central character, Driscoll. The story of this play renders it superfluous that anyone but Smitty stand out clearly as an individual. If the other men did, the play would be only overburdened by unnecessary characterizations, and would thus lose its concentrated power.

Indeed, *there is likely to be a small cast of characters in the one-act play.** Here again the reason is that there is not time enough during the progress of the action for the audience to become familiar with more than a few persons.

Since a one-act play contains action, though centered upon a single act, like all plays it necessarily contains a plot. And since it contains a plot, a good one-act play will make possible the formulation of a sound Proposition for its plot and will contain an identifiable climax. But *the proportioning of the action in terms of the Proposition and the location of the climax are* both *notably different in the one-act play* from what they are in the full-length play.

PROPORTION AND CLIMAX IN THE ONE-ACTER

This is a summary of the action of O'Neill's *In the Zone:*

The scene is the forecastle of the British tramp steamer *Glencairn*, ten minutes before midnight in the fall of 1915—

---

* *In the Zone* is in this respect quite exceptional. The presence of nine persons makes it all the more imperative that O'Neill not reveal most of them as distinct individuals.

during World War I. The characters are all seamen of the ship. When the curtain goes up, Scotty, Ivan, Swanson, Smitty, and Paul are all in their bunks, apparently asleep. Smitty slowly turns around, looks about to be sure the others are asleep, climbs softly out of his bunk, and stands cautiously in his stockinged feet. He now bends down and carefully pulls out a valise from under a bunk. Just then Davis appears in the doorway with a large steaming pot of coffee. Puzzled and suspicious, he retreats into the alleyway to observe Smitty, who is plainly anxious not to be observed. Smitty takes out some keys and unlocks the valise. The slight noise awakens Scotty, who peers at Smitty from his bunk. Smitty opens the valise, takes out a small tin box, which he hides under his mattress, replaces the valise, climbs back into his bunk, closes his eyes, and pretends to snore. Davis comes in again and awakens the sleeping men.

They tumble out of their bunks and begin to have their coffee. Jack, Driscoll, and another man saunter in. Davis gets excited because someone has opened a porthole. They are in the war zone now, and are frightened because of the danger of meeting submarines. Scotty is of the opinion that it's not only the submarines they have to fear; he looks significantly at Smitty. There is always, he adds, the danger of German spies. And the ship is carrying a cargo of dynamite! Smitty and Scotty go out to report to the bosun.

Scotty returns in a minute with the information that Smitty is "out on the hatch starin' at the moon" like a man half daft. While Scotty keeps watch at the doorway to alert the others if Smitty should reappear, Davis recounts Smitty's mysterious behavior in extracting the tin box. Scotty is able to certify the truth of Davis' report. Jack makes for Smitty's mattress, but is prevented from touching the revealed box by Driscoll. Driscoll, though chagrined that grown men can be "shiverin' loike childer at a bit av a black box," nevertheless admits that there is something queer about all this.

They discuss what might be in the box. What can the contents be to make Smitty behave so strangely? Then, Davis reminds them, there is that open porthole—it would have been like a lighthouse to any submarine in the vicinity. Smitty must have opened it to give signals to the enemy. What's Smitty's nationality anyway? English? Smitty, whose educated speech has given him the nickname "the Duke" among the men, could easily be a German spy educated in England for the purposes of espionage. He's never said where he comes from and he has never confided in his shipmates. He has a "sly air" about him, as though he were hiding something.

Scotty warns that Smitty is coming back. Smitty is unaware of the black looks of his shipmates as he stealthily feels under his mattress to make sure his box is still there. He suddenly becomes aware of the resentment of the others, sighs, and walks out of the doorway again. The men are now convinced that he is a spy. The sudden thud of a piece of driftwood against the ship almost raises a panic among them.

Driscoll, who can no longer bear the tension, wants to throw Smitty's box out of a porthole. The others warn him: it may be a box of explosives. While Scotty watches again for Smitty's return, the men fetch a bucket of water. Very gingerly Driscoll extracts the box from under the mattress, and drops it into the pail of water. They are now prepared to throw Smitty overboard and later report him as missing, but Jack protests that they have no proof yet of Smitty's guilt. Driscoll decides that they must open the box; if Smitty's villainy is proved by the contents, they will kill him and tomorrow pretend it was a suicide.

When Smitty comes back he is seized. They show him the box plunged in the water. He becomes anguished and enraged. What right had they to tamper with his private belongings? Driscoll demands he tell them what is in the box. Smitty refuses to answer. Despite Smitty's resistance, at Driscoll's direction the men take his keys from him. Driscoll selects what seems to be the right key and reaches for the box in the water. "Don't open that box, Driscoll!" Smitty cries. "If you do, so help me God, I'll kill you." Driscoll accuses him of being a spy, as he starts to open the box. To silence Smitty's enraged protests, Driscoll gags him with a wad of waste. Smitty is tied, hand and foot, while the men cluster around the box, but they draw away as Driscoll opens it. Inside is a rubber bag. Driscoll unties the string and takes out a small packet of letters. At first the men are surprised. "On'y letters!" But Davis reminds them that these may be orders to the spy: a spy order might be worse than a bomb. Despite Smitty's muffled protests, Driscoll reads one letter aloud; it is a sad love letter from a girl. Still not convinced, after glancing through the other letters, Driscoll reads the last of them: a letter in which the girl renounces Smitty for having wrecked her life, as he has his own, with his drunkenness. As he finishes, Smitty is heard to be sobbing behind his gag. Driscoll restores the letters to the bag and the bag to the box, locks it, and puts it back under the mattress.

Then he steps quietly over to Smitty, cuts the ropes, and unties the gag. Smitty turns his face away, shaken with grief. No man among them can find a word to say. At last Driscoll explodes, "God stiffen us, are we never goin' to turn in fur a wink av sleep?" They all, except Smitty, return to their bunks, as Driscoll turns down the light.

Obviously Smitty is the focus of interest in this play. It is with him that we identify. But during the course of the action he *does* nothing; it is he who is *acted upon*. The doer of the action is Driscoll.

It is Driscoll who takes all the decisive steps. It is he who appropriates the box, he who throws it into the water, he who opens it with the key, he who reads the first and last letters, he who has the last word and the last action.

The Proposition for this play is:

Condition of the action: Driscoll, under the instigation of the other men, convinced that Smitty's box contains an explosive or other treasonable matter, appropriates the box.

Cause of the action: Despite Smitty's insistence on the private nature of the contents, Driscoll opens the box with the key seized from Smitty.

Resulting action: Will Driscoll find that the contents of the box prove Smitty to be a spy?

It will be remembered that in the full-length play the third step of the Proposition is allotted the largest portion of the play. From our summary of the action of *In the Zone* it will be seen that, as is characteristic of the one-act play, the third step is here allotted the smallest portion of the play.

Unlike the full-length play, *in the one-act play the resulting action is the shortest part of the play: the cause of the action raises the question of the play and the question is answered fairly rapidly.*

The climax of *In the Zone* is Driscoll's reading of Smitty's sweetheart's last letter. It will be noted that, as is characteristic of the one-acter, this climax occurs near the final curtain.

In the one-act play, unlike most full-length plays, *the climax comes near the final curtain*. That is to say, the cause of the action raises the question of the resulting action, and shortly thereafter the climax evokes the answer to that question.

This proximity of the climax to the conclusion of the play is one reason why the one-act play is likely to be more or less sensational or "theatrical" in its effect. In the full-length play there is more room for the events following the climax, thus permitting the climax a fuller dramatic impact. There is not time or space in the one-acter to prepare a richly full, noble, or deeply moving conclusion. Hence, nothing is more difficult than to achieve a grand tragic effect in this form.

It is precisely these considerations which must determine whether one's material is suitable to the longer or shorter dramatic form. On pages 31–33, at the conclusion of Chapter Two, we have listed a number of news items which we offered as suggestive of dramatic material. Let us re-examine them in the light of our recent remarks:

> The middle-aged man sued by his wife for non-support. The story value of this account centers upon the man's washing his hands of his family—a single incident, striking rather than dramatic in effect, and hence suitable for a one-acter.
>
> The man kept prisoner in a dark room for eighteen years by his brother. The situation and the relationship of the brothers invite a more extended treatment. This would be better as basic material for a full-length play.
>
> The prisoner who won the poetry contest. Again, it is the revelation of the true authorship of the winning poem which provides the interest—a single, striking incident. Material for a one-acter.
>
> The Italian released through the efforts of a well-meaning lawyer. If the point of the story is the young man's vengeance—material for a one-acter. However, if one wished to dwell on the lawyer's efforts, there would be material for a full-length play with an ironic end.

The offended German citizen. Here, we agreed, we had little more than an interesting character. Decision as to the form to be employed would have to be conditioned by the material invented for the action.

The doctor who had never been to medical school. The mere exposé of the man is not interesting enough. His long career, probably overshadowed by fear of exposure, is more valuable for dramatic purposes. Material for a full-length play.

The suicide of the bridegroom. An invention of his motives would lead one to material for a full-length play. Such a suicide would be too melodramatic in a one-acter.

The father rising from his coffin. This is perfect one-act-play material.

The cured paralytic. One-act-play material.

The eloping heiress. If the elopment became the chief business of the play, a one-acter is called for. However, if the dramatist wished to elaborate the girl's relationship to her family, friends, and the chauffeur, there could easily emerge material for a full-length play.[25]

HINTS FOR THE ONE-ACT PLAY

Clearly, the paramount conditioning factor in this form is the comparative brevity of the play itself. Therefore, ways and means may be studied of achieving the maximum of effect with the minimum of time. For, again, it must be recollected that the audience in a theater can feel and understand no more than it can absorb, moment by moment. In the one-act play the audience must be made to become involved in the drama even more quickly than is necessary in the full-length form.

Now, it is a fact that of the two channels of communication with the audience, the visual and the auditory, the visual is the more powerful of the two in the theater. Thus, wise directors and actors know that the gesture will capture the audience before the word. If one character is sitting at a desk and is to summon the second character to him, the line "Come here!" will suggest to a director that the former in summoning the latter will wave his hand toward himself. But the best way for the man at the desk to do this is to wave his hand, *not while* he is saying "Come here!" *nor after* he has said it, *but before* he says it. The gesture so rendered, the audience will understand his intent even before he speaks. Within limits, the stronger the visual appeal, the better the effect.

Now, *many one-act plays capitalize on this basic truth by opening with some pantomime before the dialogue begins.* This is the case with *In the Zone*. There is all that business, as recounted in the first paragraph of our summary, of Smitty's looking around, creeping out of his bunk, going to the valise, extracting the box, hiding it under his mattress—while Davis looks on—and crawling back into his bunk, before a word is spoken in the play. Similarly, there is action unaccompanied by words in the opening of *The Twelve-Pound Look*, *The Lost Silk Hat*, and *Krapp's Last Tape*. Opening a one-act play with pantomime is not a law, but it is a good device as a means of involving the audience at once.* Of course, the material of the play does not always make such pantomimic effects feasible.[26]

In the one-acter there is not a moment to spare in making the persons of the drama familiar to the audience. Now, since it is essential that the audience be able to identify by name the important people in a play, a wise choice of names for the characters may itself provide an efficient saving of everyone's time. These two suggestions deserve some thought on the dramatist's part:

1. Be sure that the names of the persons of the drama are conspicuously different from one another. If a cast of four is made up of Mary, Tom, Julia, and Victor, their identities will be grasped at once, as soon as each is named on the stage. On the other hand, audiences are hard put to it for a while if in the same play they are expected to distinguish Robert from Roderick,

---

* Full-length plays sometimes use this device too. It is quite traditional with thrillers: for example, in an unlit library, the shadowy form of a man is seen entering the room through the french windows; he rushes to the bookshelves, takes down first one book and then another, feverishly searching through the pages for something concealed in a volume; he finds it—or doesn't; footsteps or voices approach; exit swiftly through the french windows. Shakespeare himself did not disdain to use similar effects. The leading example is the first brief scene of *The Tempest*, where nothing is made clear beyond the specific and vivid impression that a ship is sinking. In *Hamlet* the Ghost is used in the opening scene in a somewhat similar manner—shown and withdrawn without explanation.

Jim from Jack, Harriet from Henrietta, Mr. Samuelson from Mr. Sorensen. The dramatist is wiser not to introduce people with similar names in the same play.

2. Avail yourself of likely associations with certain names. Jackson and James both suggest a butler or chauffeur; Maggie, a maidservant; Bob, a lively boy or young man; Priscilla, a prim girl. And since the audience will associate certain temperamental traits with various parts of the globe, even if the characters in question are English-speaking, the audience can be invited to make the correct temperamental association with such names as Camille, Pierre, Monique; Angus, Bruce; Sean, Deirdre, Cathleen; Pasquale, Luigi, Concetta, Giacomo; Dolores, Maria Concepcion.

There is no reason, in fact, why both these suggestions should not be used to advantage in a full-length play as well.[27]

"ONE-ACT PLAYS" WHICH AREN'T

It should be obvious from our discussion in this chapter that we do not consider plays which call for a curtain or a blackout once, twice, or more often before the play is over, true one-act plays, no matter how labeled by their authors (for example, Noel Coward's *Fumed Oak*, Clifford Odets' *Waiting for Lefty*, Irwin Shaw's *Bury the Dead*, and Anatole France's *The Man Who Married a Dumb Wife*). Such curtains or blackouts are required because there are two or more incidents; and such plays, if we are to keep our notions straight, should be considered abbreviated forms of the full-length play. They are to the full-length play as the novelette is to the novel. The distinction between the one-acter and the full-length play is more than a matter of the amount of time involved in the presentation of the play. Some such abbreviated full-length plays are shorter than a number of existing one-act plays.

The beginning dramatist owes it to himself to write a one-acter requiring only one set and containing only one sequence of time. In the managing of both these limitations he will learn a great deal about playwriting. Nothing is to be learned if the beginner allows himself to drop a curtain or call for a blackout every time he faces a problem of sequence in time or place.

A student-dramatist recently submitted a one-act play in

which his story, as he conceived it, required a passage of time for the resolution of his plot. In the middle of his script there appeared this stage direction:

DAVID and RUTH go out.

The logs in the fireplace have been burning merrily. By degrees the wood is consumed. When the logs have been reduced to ashes RUTH and DAVID come in again.

That was enough to disqualify the piece as a one-acter. It signified immediately that the episode concluded and the one about to begin were completely detached from each other. The break shattered the continuity that is to be expected of the true one-acter. (We say nothing of the absurdity of asking the audience to wait patiently, twiddling their thumbs, while the logs, burning merrily or otherwise, are being reduced to ashes.)

When this play was refused as unacceptable, the author (who had a perfectly good plot to work with) was forced to tackle the script again with the object of managing an uninterrupted sequence of time. In order to incorporate the required lapse of time, it eventually became necessary for him to rearrange all the incidents of his play. And that, in turn, meant that he had to bring his characters into more complicated conjunction with one another—so that he was now employing with dramatic effect certain characters whom, in his first version, he had used quite perfunctorily. The revision resulted, characteristically, in a play far superior to the first version. In short, the very challenge of managing one uninterrupted sequence of time, when met, afforded the dramatist a fresh vision of his material. It is not too much to say that the truly creative man or woman never thinks of walking around an obstacle when one suddenly appears in his work; he prefers to accept it as a challenge to be met and overcome. It is precisely these obstacles which invite to a widening of the dimensions of a creator's work.

Of course, there are in existence one-act plays which successfully employ the use of blackouts for varying the scene and bringing before the eyes moments anterior in time to the plot of the play. This is basically the technique of the cinema, and it is largely by contagion from that medium that it has found its way on the stage. This fading in and fading out of various scenes from the main scene requires very little mastery to manage, and that is perhaps the reason why the technique has recently been more popular.

Thus, had O'Neill chosen to write *In the Zone* this way, he might have interpolated by a fade-in such scenes as these:

1. When Smitty lifts the tin box out of the valise. Blackout: A scene in which a drunken Smitty, duffel bag in hand, is leaving his lodgings. He tells his landlady that he wishes to leave no forwarding address, that all his mail is to be returned to the sender.

2. When the men are discussing Smitty's nationality. Blackout: A scene on the deck of the ship in which the men ask leading questions of Smitty. He is evasive.

3. When the men are talking of the danger of spies. Blackout: A scene in a saloon where men are excitedly poring over a newspaper recounting the latest sinking of a ship by German submarines. Among those present, Smitty is indifferent. And so on.

It would have been easier to project the dramatic ideas this way than in the concentrated manner employed by O'Neill. Whatever the effect of such a technique could have been in the individual scenes, it is exceedingly doubtful that the total effect by the end of the play would have had more power than the severer, traditional technique he has actually used.

In any case, whatever the technique, the one-act play should present no more than *one significant* incident.

It should be remarked, however, that the presentation of a single incident which is not part of a plot does not constitute a play. Such a piece is called a *sketch*, and we have commented upon the sketch in connection with Beckett's *Krapp's Last Tape* (see p. 138).

TELEVISION PLAYS

Experimenting with the one-act play is especially to be recommended for those who wish to write television dramas. With the exception of only a very few, most television plays run for under a half hour; some run for just under an hour.* This

---

* At the present writing only "The Play of the Week" regularly presents a play that runs for nearly two hours; occasionally a special

clearly implies that a television script ought to be conceived as a one-act play, and the writer can safely organize his material as though he were going to write in that form.

But the medium of television favors, of course, a certain shifting of scene. For example, the camera may wish to follow a character out of a room into the hallway, to the doors of the elevator, and into the elevator itself—provided that there is a dramatic reason for so doing. About such effects, when they are incidental, the writer need not trouble himself, for the director will add them if he chooses. However, because of the medium, a television script should not be conceived as taking place on a single set—and this is perhaps the only significant difference between a one-act play for the stage and a half-hour or full-hour television script. Here the fade-in technique is appropriate— indeed, is more or less called for.

To the writer who has mastered the composition of a one-set one-act play, therefore, the writing of television drama should come easily. Instead of confronting the problem of how to bridge time and place, he now simply calls for a blackout when such a problem arises, and places the new scene in another set. Such a work is far easier to write than a one-set play, and that may account for the rather appalling inferiority of the run-of-the-mill television play. Where there is little challenge there is little opportunity for developing mastery.

Of course, producers of television plays do not wish a script to call for more than a few different sets (usually, from three to five), because of the expense involved.

As for the form in which a television manuscript is to be presented, it is identical with that of a stage play. A three-set television drama should be written as though it were a three-scene play.* Television directors prefer to have the script typed only on the right half of a page, so that the directions for production may be recorded by them on the left-hand side.

---

program will offer that much time for a play. For these programs, of course, the analogy must be the full-length play.

* In the earlier days, television scripts called for special directions for the camera and sound effects. These are no longer wanted.

CHAPTER NINE

Characterization

I am not a politician, and my other habits are good.
ARTEMUS WARD, Fourth of July Oration

Men, some to business, some to pleasure take;
But every woman is at heart a rake.
POPE, *Moral Epistle* II

Women may be whole oceans deeper than we are, but they are also a whole paradise better.
J. O. HOBBES, *The Ambassador,* III

Those who always speak well of women do not know them sufficiently; those who always speak ill of them do not know them at all.
G. PIGAULT-LEBRUN

A self-made man? Yes—and worships his creator.
H. CLAPP

Men are but children of a larger growth.
DRYDEN, *All for Love,* IV, i

Every man is odd.
Troilus and Cressida, IV, v

Man is of soul and body formed for deeds
Of high resolve.
SHELLEY, *Queen Mab,* IV

Humani nihil a me alienum puto.*
TERENCE, *Heauton Timoroumenos,* I, i

I wish the bald eagle had not been chosen as the Representative of our country; he is a bird of bad moral character; like those among men who live by sharping and robbing, he is generally poor, and often very lousy. The turkey is a much more respectable bird.
B. FRANKLIN, *Letter to Sarah Bache*

* I consider nothing that is human alien to me.

It should be superfluous to say that a dramatist must know his characters intimately before he begins to write his play. It will not do to become familiar with them during the process of the writing itself, for endowing them with traits as each emergency arises can result only in their becoming pasteboard figures. In this matter, as in all others connected with playwriting, the more the preparation before actually writing, the less the expenditure of time in the writing itself. One must know everything about the characters before they can be introduced into the play.

Naturally, one first concentrates on the main characters. When one has the main outlines of the plot established, the first problem is to choose wisely the kind of people who are to figure in it.

Obviously, the thing most to be avoided is writing a play which the audience will brand as "old hat." The effect of staleness is rarely a product of insufficient novelty in the plot,* for the number of basic situations available to a storyteller are not infinite. Gozzi, author of *Turandot*, proved to his own satisfaction that there were only thirty-six, and Schiller insisted that there were fewer than that; Gérard de Nerval reduced the number to only twenty-four. In any case, it is plain that the number is a limited one. Triteness, therefore, must be not a matter of the plot so much as of the characters' relationship to the plot. For though there are certain universals in human behavior—and great literature has always been concerned with exhibiting them —every human being is himself and no one else. In the composition of men and women the variations are indeed infinite. And every honest writer has, in consequence, the possibility of creating an "original" work. Aeschylus, Sophocles, Euripides, von

---

* When it is, it is usually because of the use of some trite device in the resolution: for example, the whole affair turns out to have been a dream, and the dreamer wakes up with nothing requiring solution or resolution; or, the author having involved his story in an apparently inextricable knot, he kills off the character standing in the way of an ending; or, the author having brought a character to a situation in a dead end from which no acceptable exit presents itself, he causes that person to commit suicide (though, of course, such a resolution could be made acceptable in the study of a neurotic or psychopath who had worked *himself* into such a situation). To a discriminating audience, nothing is quite so irritating as recourse to tricks as unconvincing as these.

Hofmannsthal, and Sartre have all written plays on the vengeance of Electra against her mother, yet each is completely original (though the story was ancient even when Aeschylus wrote it), because the relationship of the characters to the plot in each play is new.

Similarly, Euripides' *Hippolytus* and Racine's *Phèdre* deal with the same story; their differences are more remarkable than their resemblances. The contrast between the two is the more striking in that Racine was plainly indebted to Euripides for a number of lines and some telling dramatic effects. Nevertheless, it is equally plain that Racine was a dramatist and poet of such originality as will be found in the possession of only consummate genius. Both dramatists conceived the identical story from quite different points of view. Here are a few of their basic dissimilarities:

Euripides' *Hippolytus*	Racine's *Phèdre*
1. Hippolytus is the central character.	1. Phaedra is the central character.
2. Phaedra disappears from the play by committing suicide at the end of the third act. (The play has five acts.)	2. Phaedra commits suicide (through totally different means) and dies just before the final curtain. (The play has five acts.)
3. Hippolytus dies in the last act just before the final lines.	3. Hippolytus is killed offstage after the end of the fourth act.
4. There is no scene in which Phaedra confesses her love to Hippolytus. She confesses the passion to her Nurse, and it is the Nurse who tells Hippolytus of Phaedra's obsession, offstage.	4. The scene in which Phaedra avows her love to Hippolytus (see pp. 69–74) was inevitable, since she is the central character. It is one of the great scenes of the play.
5. The Nurse's revelation provides the occasion for a great scene (see below), in	5. Hippolytus makes almost no attempt to upbraid Phaedra for her love for

which Hippolytus upbraids the Nurse and Phaedra for the latter's illicit passion. This scene was inevitable since he is the central character.

6. Hippolytus is firm against the love of all women.

7. Theseus is informed of the innocence of Hippolytus, after he has sent his son to his death, by the goddess Artemis.

him. He cannot stand up against the violence of her feelings, and takes refuge by concentrating on his love for Aricia.

6. Hippolytus is deeply in love with Aricia, enemy to his father's line. This not only makes for an interesting dramatic complication, but also is the cause for his innocently underestimating the danger in which he stands from the rejected Phaedra.

7. No goddess intervenes. Phaedra, just before her death, confesses the truth to Theseus, and clears Hippolytus' name.

These are some of the more obvious differences between the two plays. Euripides, because of his conception of the story, wrote the scene below, rather than such a one as that from which we have quoted on pp. 69–74 (see point 4 above). It is interesting to compare the two (translation by Gilbert Murray):

HIPPOLYTUS enters, closely followed by the NURSE. PHAEDRA cowers aside.)

HIPPOLYTUS

O Mother Earth, O Sun that makest clean,
What poison have I heard, what speechless sin!

NURSE

Hush, O my Prince, lest others mark, and guess—

HIPPOLYTUS

I have heard horrors! Shall I hold my peace?

NURSE

Yea, by this fair right arm, Son, by thy pledge—

HIPPOLYTUS

Down with that hand! Touch not my garment's edge!

NURSE

Oh, by thy knees, be silent or I die!

HIPPOLYTUS

Why, when thy speech was all so guiltless? * Why?

NURSE

It is not meet, fair Son, for every ear!

HIPPOLYTUS

Good words can bravely forth, and have no fear.

NURSE

Thine oath, thine oath! I took thine oath before!

HIPPOLYTUS

'Twas but my tongue, 'twas not my soul that swore.

NURSE

O Son, what wilt thou? Wilt thou slay thy kin?

* This line is meant, of course, ironically.

HIPPOLYTUS

I own no kindred with the spawn of sin!

(He flings her from him.)

NURSE

Nay, spare me! Man was born to err; oh, spare!

HIPPOLYTUS

O God, why hast Thou made this gleaming snare,
Woman, to dog us on the happy earth?
Was it Thy will to make Man, why his birth
Through Love and Woman? . . .
Why do we let their handmaids pass the gate?
Wild beasts were best, voiceless and fanged, to wait
About their rooms, that they might speak with none,
Nor ever hear one answering human tone!
But now dark women in still chambers lay
Plans that creep out into light of day
On handmaids' lips—

(Turning to the NURSE.)

As thine accursèd head
Braved the high honor of my Father's bed,
And came to traffic—. Our white torrent's spray
Shall drench mine ears to wash those words away!
And couldst thou dream that *I*—? I feel impure
Still at the very hearing! Know for sure,
Woman, naught but mine honor saves ye both.
Hadst thou not trapped me with that guileful oath,
No power had held me secret till the King
Knew all! But now, while he is journeying,
I too will go my ways and make no sound.
And when he comes again, I shall be found
Beside him, silent, watching with what grace
Thou and thy mistress shall greet him face to face!
Then shall I have the taste of it, and know

What woman's guile is. Woe upon you, woe!
How can I too much hate you, while the ill
Ye work upon the world grows deadlier still?
Too much? Make woman pure, and wild Love tame,
Or let me cry for ever on their shame!

> (He goes off in fury. PHAEDRA still cower-
> ing in her place begins to sob.)

The mere presence of scenes so opposite in effect would be enough to indicate the vast differences between the two plays.

This study in contrasts should furnish a hint why the stories of mythology and those of the Bible can never be stale: they are capable of an almost endless variety of treatments within the limits of the accepted story, because they are capable of an almost endless variety of relationships and motivations of the characters to that story. (They can never be stale for another reason too, of course: the good stories they have to tell are archetypal human experience to which there will always be universal response.)

SELECTING THE CHARACTER TRAITS

A thing is trite when it has become so common as to provoke no interest. Not unnaturally, one's first thoughts about characters suitable to a plot are likely to be commonplace. So long as one does not compound at once with one's first thoughts on this head, their triteness may be all to the good—if one thereupon decides, "Very well, then; I'm certainly not going to use you," and starts steering at once in another direction.

Suppose I wished to write a tragedy about a man who destroys himself because of jealousy concerning his wife's apparent unfaithfulness. The first thoughts likely to occur would be of a man very suspicious by nature and of a woman highly flirtatious. Though these notions are not impossible material, they give promise of the commonplace.

Now, there is no concept in dramaturgy more important for the playwright to bear constantly in mind than this: *the quintessence of drama is conflict or opposition*. The principle has generally been understood to be true of the action: it is well known that a good quarrel onstage, for example, makes good theater.* But the element of conflict or opposition permeates every aspect of drama. It is the stuff of which drama is made. The traits of the different characters in a play, for instance, must not only be varied; they must be in each character in a certain opposition to those of another person of the drama. Thus, note the contrasts between Romeo and Paris, Romeo and Mercutio, Romeo and Tybalt, Mercutio and Tybalt, Mercutio and Benvolio, Juliet and the Nurse; Hamlet and Claudius, Hamlet and Laertes, Hamlet and Horatio, Hamlet and Polonius, Claudius and Polonius, Claudius and Laertes, Claudius and Gertrude; Algernon and Jack, Algernon and Lady Bracknell, Gwendolen and Lady Bracknell, Gwendolen and Cecily.

But more than this, *the best plays often show the character traits of the persons of the drama in a certain opposition to the situations in which the persons find themselves.* Thus, in *Othello* Shakespeare avoided the clichés we have suggested for husband and wife; the husband is not a man suspicious by nature, the wife is not a flirt. He chose exact opposites of these. There would be little tragedy involved in the ruin of a usually suspicious man through jealousy, for such a man has the daily experience of jealousy. If he falls through jealousy it will not be very far. Shakespeare's hero, on the contrary, is a man to whom jealousy is an unfamiliar passion.† Desdemona knows this to be true of him, and she answers Emilia's query as to whether or not Othello is a suspicious man with:

Who? he? I think the sun, where he was born
Drew all such humors from him.

(III, iv)

* But it is not always remembered that a good play cannot be made up of quarrels. That can be as dull as a succession of quarrels are in life. There are dramatists whose characters never exchange words with one another except in tones of hostility or tartness, and these people become great bores.

† We are aware that this remark will come as a shock to people who have accepted too glibly such tag phrases as "the jealous Moor"—a first cousin to the equally false "the mad Hamlet."

That is why it never occurs to her that he could be jealous. Othello knows himself well enough at first; he can honestly disclaim any kinship with the man who is temperamentally jealous:

> 'Tis not to make me jealous,*
> To say my wife is fair, feeds well, loves company,
> Is free of speech, sings, plays, and dances well;
> Where virtue is, these are more virtuous.
>
> (III, iii)

Iago, too, knows that this is the truth; he speaks gleefully of Othello's "unbookish jealousy" (IV, i)—proof that he estimates the Moor to be one unlearned in the meaning of suspicion. It is the quintessence of the dramatic that it should be Othello, a man who has never in his life known what it is to be suspicious of anyone, who is to fall when the poisons generated by the unfamiliar passion of jealousy have done their work in him.

Desdemona, on her part, is a quiet, refined, exquisite woman, who never gives her husband the slightest excuse for distrust. How much more dramatic than a flirt such a woman, as the victim of her husband's suspicions!

Thus we see that Shakespeare has chosen for his two chief characters in this play a man and a woman temperamentally in opposition to the situation in which they will find themselves.

Again, suppose I wished to write a play in which, when an innocent girl seems by overwhelming evidence to be proved a whore and even her father, her betrothed, and her relatives renounce her—only her cousin (with more reason than any of the others to doubt her too) refuses to believe in her guilt. The first thoughts likely to occur for that cousin would be a gentle, sweet, trusting girl, a kind of Pollyanna or Rebecca of Sunnybrook Farm. But in *Much Ado About Nothing*, which presents that situation, Shakespeare conceived that cousin (Beatrice) as anything but such a woman. She is wittier and more caustic than anyone else in the play; everyone, though delighted to see others the victim of her coruscations, prefers to keep clear of them himself. Those who judge by appearances even think of her as heartless. Yet it is she who in a crisis proves alone to have loyalty, and to harbor more generous feelings than anyone else. She takes a

* suspicious.

simple position: her cousin could not be guilty of the immorality of which she is accused because Beatrice knows her to be incapable of it, no matter what the evidence to the contrary. It is infinitely more dramatic that the woman who, when occasion arises, shows herself to be loving and trusting should be one who does not wear her heart on her sleeve like a Pollyanna or a Rebecca of Sunnybrook Farm.

If one wished to write a play about a man who wades through slaughter to a throne, one's first thoughts would likely be of a cruel, hardhearted, conscienceless villain. And such, indeed, were Shakespeare's when he wrote his early melodrama *Richard III*. But in the fullness of his maturity, when he wrote the great tragedy of *Macbeth*, he conceived his hero as a sensitive, highly impressionable man of tremendous imagination, who commits his bloody deeds in a kind of defiance of his own nature.

If I wished to write a play about a young man who was forbidden to marry the girl of his dreams by her aristocratic mother, unless he could establish the fact that his own parents were of her class, my first thoughts would likely be of an honest, decent man of modest circumstances, simple, direct, forthright. Instead of such a stereotype, Wilde chose for his Jack a highly sophisticated, devious young man of wealth. The double life he leads (Jack in the country, Ernest in town) avoids the commonplaces attaching to the romantic lover and adds a fillip to his adoration of Gwendolen. His living in greater wealth, probably, than even Lady Bracknell possesses makes her snobbery all the more comic.

If I were writing a tragedy about a woman who conceives a passion for the son her husband has fathered in an earlier marriage, my first thoughts would probably be of a lecherous, over-sexed woman, a kind of Messalina. But Racine chose for his Phaedra a highly principled woman, whose conscience is tortured by the crime of her passion, who forgives herself nothing for her forbidden love.*

* These examples could be multiplied indefinitely. We were, in fact, going to give *Hamlet* as our first example. If one were going to write a tragedy about a young prince who, enjoined by his father's spirit to avenge his father's murder, finds it almost impossible to do so, one's first thoughts would probably be of a young man who "vacillates from sensibility and procrastinates from thought, and loses the power of action in the energy of resolve." This is Coleridge's Hamlet, this is (unfortu-

It would be absurd to pretend that we have here hit upon a principle. It would be too much to say that a playwright is *obliged* to have his main character endowed with traits which are in opposition to the environing situation. But it would certainly be safe to deduce from our examples that *a playwright is very wise to steer away from his first thoughts about the best characters for a plot, to the exact opposite direction*, since his first thoughts are likely to be the obvious, commonplace ones.

A one-act-play plot idea of which students, understandably, seem enamored goes like this: A college student is very much under the domination of his parent or parents. Over against objections at home he wishes very much to do something; for example, marry a girl (his mother doesn't want him ever to marry anybody; his parents want him to finish college first; or they object to this particular girl), or leave college to take a job or to study music (his parents have sacrificed everything for his college education; or they have a snobbery about a college degree), or go to a university now that he is being graduated (his parents think it necessary he go into the business world), etc., etc. The question of the play in any of these variations is: Will he forfeit his dream of happiness because of his parent (or parents)? Answer: He will. Now, for this plot the cliché would certainly be a young man who "vacillates from sensibility." He is too sensitive to oppose the forces obstructing him. This play promises to be dull before it is even written. But if the hero be not a slender, delicate, soft-spoken lad, but rather a kind of "Butch"—someone with the physique of a football player, sturdy, rugged, used to carving his own path in life—the capitulation of such a youth to parental demands has in it the stuff of drama.* [28]

---

nately) the Hamlet of most of the world, but it is not Shakespeare's. Because it is most of the world's, we decided not to obscure the point being made or puzzle the reader by using *Hamlet* as an instance. Nevertheless, popular impression notwithstanding, Shakespeare here again did avoid the cliché, did conceive of a hero whose temperament is in opposition to the situation in which he finds himself. His hero is at the opposite pole from Coleridge's. For proof and elaboration thereof, see the present author's *The Heart of Hamlet* (New York, 1960).

* Just as it is the stuff of drama that a diminutive, timid man (rather than a man of heroic cast) at the crucial moment should lead the troops over the hill in the face of enemy fire, and thus save the day.

"GETTING TO KNOW YOU"

We have said that it is necessary to know your characters intimately before you can write about them.

They will never come full-blown in your imagination. You must be thankful if they come at all with just a few key hints. You must, therefore, coax them into existence, like a conjurer. (It will not do to wait, pen in hand, for them to come full-rounded to you of their own volition.)

We hold that if a play is worth the writing, it merits having a notebook (or the equivalent) devoted to one's plans and tentative sketches for the play. There is no better use to which such a notebook can be put than assigning certain pages of it to the writing of a series of brief biographies of all the significant characters. Such a biography would carry an account of the parentage, financial circumstances, education, physical appearance, character traits, interests, dislikes, hobbies, of each of these persons of the drama. None of these biographical sketches, perhaps, can be composed in one day. One ought to read and reread what one has written of them, so they become more and more real to one, and add to them as new or better ideas appear.[29]

One thing is important to remember: *the dramatist must know a great deal more about his characters than he will ever be able to use in his play*.* Only when the author can sit comfortably in the center of his materials can he write with conviction. When he writes on the very edge of his knowledge, he is bound to find it a precipice from which sooner or later a false step will hurl him. Therefore, it is literally impossible to know too much about your characters.

IDENTIFYING YOURSELF WITH THE CHARACTERS

When you know your characters intimately and are ready to write your play, you must now contrive to identify yourself

---

* This dictum is, of course, true of every aspect of the materials employed in every kind of writing. For example, an author who really knows nothing about music or about the fine arts will do well to make no reference to either in his work. If, like many before him, he is foolish enough to do so, his ignorance will be obvious (through the superficiality, triteness, or faultiness of his reference). Even Keats' genius cannot excuse his "Hippocrene"!

with every one of your characters in turn. You conduct, as you write, a kind of breathless race from the interior of one character to the interior of another. As a character is speaking you must be inside of him, you must *be* he. When he has finished any given speech, you must not allow the next character to speak until you have rushed to take possession of the interior of *him*—even if he is to say no more than "Yes" or "No"—and when that next character speaks you must then be he.

Or, to put it another way, while writing you must not allow yourself the luxury of relaxing (as though you were a member of the audience) to enjoy the proceedings onstage. You must *be* onstage at the center of every detail of the proceedings.

To forget this is to run the risk which undoes many amateurs. They identify themselves with a particular character and use the others only to "feed" him lines (as a "straight" man does for a comic); they take possession of that one person and let the others shift for themselves. The resultant errors of such a method are manifold. The other characters become mere straw figures, mere supernumeraries. That one character, on the other hand—often because he becomes a vehicle for the author's self-portraiture or self-justification, a dangerous invitation to mock heroics—becomes a kind of stuffed man, overvirtuous more often than not, and given to harangues rather than to normal speech.

This identification with each character in turn is as necessary in the briefest moments of the play as in the longest. For example:

In *All's Well That Ends Well*, Helena has been nurturing an unrequited love for Bertram. The wise old Countess, his mother and Helena's protectress, suspects the girl's feelings and asks her outright whether it is not true that Helena loves her son.

COUNTESS

. . . Tell me truly.

HELENA

Good Madam, pardon me.

COUNTESS

Do you love my son?

HELENA

Your pardon, noble mistress!

COUNTESS

Love you my son?

HELENA

Do you not love him, Madame?

(I, iii)

(Note how these brief words bring vividly before us the older woman's amused insistence, the younger one's confused evasiveness, itself a confession.) Helena cures the King of a dangerous illness; her reward is to have the husband of her choosing. Before the assembled court, Helena chooses Bertram:

HELENA

This is the man.

KING

Why, then, young Bertram, take her; she's thy wife.

BERTRAM

My wife, my liege? I shall beseech your Highness
In such a business give me leave to use
The help of mine own eyes.

KING

Know'st thou not, Bertram,
What she has done for me?

BERTRAM

Yes, my good lord;
But never hope to know why I should marry her.

KING

Thou know'st she has rais'd me from my sickly bed.

BERTRAM

But follows it, my lord, to bring me down
Must answer for your raising? I know her well;
She had her breeding at my father's charge: *
A poor physician's daughter my wife!

                                                            (II, iii)

(Note how Bertram's few words reveal his indifference to Helena,
his snobbery, his cruelty, his impetuosity; note, too, how eloquent
Helena's silence is.) But Bertram is forced nonetheless to marry
her. In revenge he decides to leave the country at once. He takes
brùsque farewell of her with a hypocritical pretense that he will be
gone only a few days:

BERTRAM

'T will be two days ere I shall see you; so
I leave you to your wisdom.

HELENA

                                Sir, I can nothing say,
But that I am your most obedient servant.

BERTRAM

Come, come, no more of that.

HELENA

                                —and ever shall
With true observance seek to eke out that
Wherein toward me my homely stars have failed
To equal my great fortune.

* expense.

BERTRAM

Let that go:
My haste is very great. Farewell; hie home.

HELENA

Pray, sir, your pardon.

BERTRAM

Well, what would you say?

HELENA

I am not worthy of the wealth I owe; *
Nor dare I say 't is mine; and yet it is:
But like a timorous thief, most fain would steal
What law does vouch mine own.

BERTRAM

What would you have?

HELENA

Something; and scarce so much:—nothing, indeed.—
I would not tell you what I would: my lord—'faith, yes;—
Strangers and foes do sunder,† and not kiss.

BERTRAM

I pray you stay not, but in haste to horse.
(II, v)

Only by succeeding in being each of these characters in turn
could Shakespeare have been so marvelously true to both.

* own.   † part.

In Chekhov's *The Cherry Orchard*, soon after Madame Ranevsky's return to her old home and estate, Lopakhin informs her that he has good news for her: she knows that the cherry orchard on the estate is to be sold to pay her debts, but he has a way to save everything. If she will have the better part of her land cut up into building lots, and then lease them for summer cottages, she can make a fortune and have a regular income:

LOPAKHIN

Only, of course, the land must be cleared—the old buildings must be taken down—even this house, which isn't worth anything—and the old cherry orchard will have to be chopped down.

MADAME RANEVSKY

Chopped down? My dear man, you must forgive me, but you really don't know what you're talking about. If there is a single interesting thing, a single remarkable thing in our entire province, it is this cherry orchard.

LOPAKHIN

The only thing that's remarkable about your orchard is that it's big. The trees bear cherries every other year, and they're of no use because nobody wants to buy them.

(1)

Here again a dramatist, by identifying himself with each of the characters, portrays salient aspects of their make-up in just a few lines: Lopakhin, man of the new order, enterprising, unhampered by any considerations of beauty or tradition; Madame Ranevsky, a woman still living in a world that is swiftly passing away, and clinging to what it held of charm and memories.

CHARACTERIZATION BY DIALOGUE

The speeches we have quoted from *All's Well That Ends Well* and *The Cherry Orchard* will illustrate how powerfully characterization may be achieved in the dialogue of a play. Galsworthy said of good dialogue that it "is character."

No two people have the same habits of expression. In a way, all of us give out autobiographical hints every day of our lives by the very vocabulary we use. If a man readily speaks of another as a "highbrow," the speaker himself is probably a "lowbrow," for no one else would normally think of using the expression. If a man, describing his experiences in life, is moved to say figuratively, "And that was a home run!" or "There was I, sitting in the bleachers," he makes it plain that he spends much of his time in a ball park.

That Macbeth should cry at a moment of great emotion:

> I have no spur
> To prick the sides of my intent; but only
> Vaulting ambition, which o'erleaps itself
> And falls on th' other.*
>
> (I, vii)

is a result of his being used to being on horseback.

When Polonius instructs his man Reynaldo on the inquiries to be made of Laertes' conduct in Paris, the old man reveals only too well his training in matters legal (italics ours):

> *Your party in converse,* him you would sound,
> Having ever seen in the *prenominate crimes*
> The youth you breathe of guilty, be assur'd
> He *closes with you* in *this consequence.* . . .
> "I saw him enter a house of sale,†
> *Videlicet,* a brothel, or so forth."
>
> (II, i)

Everyone who knows the play thinks of Hamlet as a man of vast horizons: that is directly attributable to the enormous range of his interests: he refers often to books, matters connected with warfare, sports, fencing, law, gardening—to list only a few.

* the other side.   † a brothel.

Pastor Manders carries everywhere with him (in *Ghosts*)
the marks of his profession:

> That is very nice and dutiful of him. . . .
> There are many occasions in life when one must rely on other
> people; things are so ordered in this world. . . .
> The Orphanage is to be consecrated, so to speak, to a higher
> purpose. . . .
> People would be only too eager to interpret our behavior as a
> sign that neither of us had the correct faith in Higher Provi-
> dence. . . .
> We have no right at all to offend the weaker brethren. . . .
> Thank God, he is now trying to lead a decent life, I'm told. . . .
>
> (1)

And he makes clear that he is indifferent to the arts when he says
to Mrs. Alving of her son:

> It would be unfortunate, indeed, if his absence and absorption
> in art and that sort of thing were to blunt his natural feelings.
>
> (1)

Manders' phraseology not only bespeaks the clergyman but also
indicates a narrow habit of mind, and more than a little of his
social background.

Perhaps the most obvious way to indicate social background
is through the use of dialect and idiomatic expressions common
to a particular group. We need not be told that Mrs. Gogan (in
O'Casey's *The Plough and the Stars*) is an uneducated Irish-
woman, as she replies to the accusation that she talks too much
about death, that such thoughts are "a creepy thing" to indulge in:

> It is, an' it isn't; it's both bad an' good. It always gives meself
> a kind o' thresspassin' * joy to feel meself movin' along in a
> mournin' couch,† an' me thinkin' that, maybe, th' next funeral
> 'll be me own, an' glad, in a quiet way, that this is somebody's
> else's.
>
> (1)

* She means "surpassing."   † She means "coach."

This speech from O'Neill's *The Hairy Ape* plainly reveals the speaker to be a member of the lower orders:

> Aw, yuh crazy Mick! Aw, take it easy. Yuh're aw right, at dat. Yuh're bugs, dat's all—nutty as a cuckoo. All dat tripe yuh been pullin'— Aw, dat's all right. On'y it's dead, get me?
>
> (1)

But dialect and idiomatic expression must be used with a great deal of discretion. Too much of it in a play can be dull. And one must be careful never to use an idiom which may convey an impression never intended. It is likely that Arthur Miller meant in *The Death of a Salesman* to picture a typical American family, but as Mary McCarthy justly points out, he often sounds as though he were rather depicting a certain kind of Jewish family, even though he uses no Jewish dialect. Lines like these:

> He's not to be allowed to fall into his grave like an old dog. Attention, attention must be finally paid to such a person.
>
> (1)

do seem to have the accents strictly of the Bronx.

Another warning seems apropos here. Certain of our novelists, in pursuit of complete naturalism, have developed in their works a style of conversation in which everyone speaks in words of one syllable in sentences always simple and short. If naturalism is indeed their objective, that kind of speech can be as far from the realities of life as the involved false elegancies of the most third-rate of nineteenth-century novelists.

> What are you talking about? I don't know what you're talking about, honest I don't. You don't make sense. I don't follow you at all.

That sort of discourse will be readily accepted as mirroring the mind of a semi-literate man; but it is too much to ask us to think that an educated one would talk that way. People of any education, though they ought to avoid pomposity, on the whole do not speak exclusively in short simple sentences (listen to yourself next time you are talking to a friend); nor do they have a vocabulary limited to one hundred words. Listen to a truly convincing conversation between two civilized people who have just met, a magazine editor and a portrait painter, a charming woman, both unaffected and straightforward in their talk, from S. N. Behrman's brilliant play *Biography:*

KURT

You're one of these tolerant people, aren't you—see the best in people?

MARION

You say that as if tolerance were a crime.

KURT

Your kind is. It's criminal because it encourages dishonesty, incompetence, weakness and all kinds of knavery. What you call tolerance I call sloppy laziness. You're like those book-reviewers who find something to praise in every mediocre book.

MARION

You are a fanatical young man.

KURT

Having said that you think you dispose of me. Well, so be it. I'm disposed of. Now let's get down to business.

MARION

You are also a little patronizing.

KURT

(Pleased.)

Am I?

MARION

However, I don't mind being patronized. That's where my tolerance comes in. It even amuses me a little bit.

(Crossing to piano seat.)

But as I have to change for dinner perhaps you'd better—

KURT

Exactly.

MARION

Please sit down.

(A moment. She sits on piano bench facing him.)

KURT

(Goes to piano and talks to her across it.)

I am editor of a magazine called Every Week. Do you know it?

MARION

It seems to me I've seen it on newsstands.

KURT

You've never read it?

MARION

I'm afraid I haven't.

KURT

That is a tribute to your discrimination. We have an immense circulation. Three millions I believe. With a circulation of that size you may imagine that the average of our readers' intelligence cannot be very high. Yet occasionally we flatter them by printing the highbrows *—in discreet doses we give them, at intervals, Shaw and Wells and Chesterton. So you'll be in good company anyway.

MARION

I will?

KURT

Yes. I want you to write your biography to run serially in Every Week. Later of course you can bring it out as a book.

MARION

My biography!

KURT

Yes. The story of your life.

MARION

I know the meaning of the word.

KURT

The money is pretty good. I am prepared to give you an advance of two thousand dollars.†

MARION

Good Heavens, am I as old as that—that people want my biography?

* Kurt's use of the word "highbrows" is of course ironic; he is thinking of the low taste of his average reader, and the word is perfect here.
† This was in 1932!

KURT

We proceed on the theory that nothing exciting happens to people after they are forty.

MARION

What a cruel idea!

KURT

Why wait till you're eighty? Your impressions will be dimmed by time. Most autobiographies are written by corpses. Why not do yours while you are still young, vital, in the thick of life?

MARION

But I'm not a writer. I shouldn't know how to begin.

KURT

You were born, weren't you? Begin with that.

MARION

I write pleasant letters, my friends tell me.—But look here, why should you want this story from me—why should anybody be interested?—I'm not a first-rate artist, you know—not by far—I'm just clever—

KURT

(Bluntly.)

It's not you—it's the celebrity of your subjects.

MARION

(Amused.)

You're a brutal young man—I rather like you.

Notice how effectively both persons are revealed in this charming, natural dialogue. Notice, too, how much more literary the vocabulary of the young man is, though in not any ostentatious way; it is easy to understand that he is preoccupied with writings. The woman, on the other hand, although her discourse is literate, is far less literary; before she says so, it is clear that she is not interested in writing or the art of writing—and that is to the point of the play. The passage may stand, as is usual with Mr. Behrman, as an admirable example of characterization through dialogue.

In the passage just quoted it will be remarked that not a line is static. As the dialogue proceeds, it does more than depict the characters: it advances the plot too. Kurt and Marion are destined to fall in love; this piece of dialogue begins with their being total strangers to each other; before the close of the brief passage we feel the glimmerings of greater intimacy. Moreover, the chief business of the play, Marion's writing of her autobiography, has been firmly introduced as a basis for the workings of the plot.[30]

CHARACTERIZATION THROUGH ACTION

In *Biography*, Leander Nolan, a politician who expects to be a U.S. senator shortly, reappears in Marion's life. When they were very young, living in the same town, they had an affair, which has left an indelible impression upon him. He is rather put out to discover that Marion has difficulty at first in even remembering him. He has come to see her in a mood of sanctimonious repentance for their early sin, and is appalled to find that she does not think of it as a sin at all. He hints that he has heard of the free life she has been leading. Amused, she teases him by assuming the role he has picked for her. He blurts out his suspicions grimly:

NOLAN

Well, I suppose it's impossible to live one's life in art without being sexually promiscuous.

(He looks at her accusingly.)

MARION

Oh, dear me, Bunny! What shall I do? Shall I blush? Shall I hang my head in shame? What shall I do? How does one react in the face of an appalling accusation of this sort? I didn't know the news had got around so widely.

NOLAN

Well, so many of your lovers have been famous men—

MARION

Well, you were obscure. But you're famous now, aren't you? I seem to be stimulating, if nothing else—

NOLAN

If I had then some of the fame I have now you probably wouldn't have walked out on me at the last minute the way you did. . . .

She irritates him by calling him by his old nickname, Bunny. He comes back to his point:

NOLAN

Do you think it hasn't been on my conscience ever since, do you think it hasn't tortured me!

MARION

What, dear?

NOLAN

That thought!

MARION

Which thought?

NOLAN

Every time I heard about you—all that notoriety that's attended you in the American papers—painting pictures of Communist statesmen, running around California with movie comedians!

MARION

I have to practice my profession, Bunny. One must live, you know. Besides, I've done Capitalist statesmen too. And at Geneva—

NOLAN

(Darkly.)

You know what I mean!

MARION

You mean—

(She whispers through her cupped hand.)

you mean promiscuous? Has that gotten around, Bunny? Is it whispered in the sewing-circles of Nashville? Will I be burned for a witch if I go back home? Will they have a trial over me? Will you defend me?

NOLAN

(Quite literally, with sincere and disarm-
ing simplicity.)

I should be forced, as an honest man, to stand before the multi-tude and say: In condemning this woman you are condemning me who am asking your suffrages to represent you. For it was

I with whom this woman first sinned before God. As an honorable man that is what I should have to do.

MARION

And this has worried you—actually! . . .

NOLAN

(Gloomily contemplating her.)

I can't forget that it was I who—

MARION

Did you think you were the first, Bunny? Was I so unscrupulously coquettish as to lead you to believe that I—oh I couldn't have been. It's not like me. . . .

NOLAN

(Stands over her almost threateningly.)

You're lying to me to salve my conscience but I won't have it! I know my guilt and I'm going to bear it!

(1)

This passage, as we shall see in a minute, is quite vital to the plot. In the meantime, note how brilliantly and seemingly effortlessly the characters are being delineated.

Presently Nolan learns that Marion is doing her life story:

NOLAN

You must leave me out of that story!

MARION

But Bunny, how can I possibly leave you out?

NOLAN

You must, that's all!

MARION

But how can I? You were too important—think of the role you played in my life. By your own confession, Bunny darling, you —you started me. That's a good idea for a chapter heading, isn't it? "Bunny Starts Me." I must put that down.

NOLAN

This is no joke, Marion.

(With menace.)

I warn you—

MARION

Warn me! Let me understand you. Are you seriously asking me to give up an opportunity like this just because—

NOLAN

(Rises and gets down from the model stand. Speaks with brutal command.)

Opportunity! Cheap exhibitionism! A chance to flaunt your affairs in a rag like this.

(Indicating magazine on piano.)

I won't be drawn into it. I can tell you that!

(He is in a towering rage.)

MARION

(After a pause.)

I know that by your standards, Bunny, I'm a loose character. But there are other standards, there just are.

NOLAN

Not in Tennessee!

(II)

She refuses to make any promises, and he is too poor a judge of character to understand that she would never do anything to jeopardize him. Kurt comes in, and she leaves the two men alone.

> (NOLAN goes to KURT and reaches out his hand to him.)

NOLAN

How do you do, young man?

KURT

> (Very much surprised.)

How do *you* do?

> (He looks at him narrowly, his head a little on one side, a terrier appraising a mastiff.)

NOLAN

I am very glad to see you.

KURT

Isn't that nice?

NOLAN

You may be surprised to learn that on the one occasion when we met you made quite an impression on me.

KURT

Did I?

NOLAN

You did. Sit down. In fact—I hope you don't mind—if you will allow me as a prerogative of seniority—to ask you a few questions. I have a purpose in mind and not—I trust—an idle purpose.

KURT

Shoot!

> (Sits.)

Anything to enlighten the professor!

> (He knows he is going to be pumped and has decided to be casual, naive, and even respectful.)

NOLAN

> (Clearing his throat.)

Now then—your present position on the magazine you represent—have you been on it long?

KURT

About two years.

NOLAN

And before that?

KURT

Newspaper work.

NOLAN

And before that?

KURT

Tramping around the world. Odd jobs. Quite a variety.

NOLAN

College?

KURT

Believe it or not—Yale—two years—worked my way through
—washed dishes.

NOLAN

Very interesting preparation—very interesting— Tell me now
—your present work—do you find it interesting? Is the re-
muneration satisfactory?

KURT

Two hundred smackers a week. That's twice what I've ever
earned in my life before.

NOLAN

Now then—to come to the point—no doubt you've heard of
my prospective father-in-law, Mr. Orrin Kinnicott?

KURT

Heard of him? We pay him the compliment of imitation. He
is our model, our criterion, our guiding star!

NOLAN

As you know, Mr. Kinnicott's interests are varied. He owns some powerful newspapers in my state. The other day I heard him say that he wanted a new man in Washington.

KURT

(Playing naively excited.)

Now that's something to give one's eye-teeth for!

NOLAN

(Pleased at the result.)

I think it might be possible to swing it—very possible.

KURT

God, what a break!

NOLAN

As it happens, Mr. Kinnicott is at present in town. I shall arrange an appointment for you in the next few days. Naturally, I expect you to keep the matter entirely confidential.

KURT

Naturally! You needn't worry on that score, Senator, I assure you.

NOLAN

Thank you, Mr. Kurt. That is all I ask.

(A pause.)

KURT

Mr. Nolan—do you mind if I ask *you* something?

NOLAN

Certainly not.

KURT

You won't consider me impertinent?

NOLAN

(With a smile.)

I don't object to impertinence, Mr. Kurt. I was often considered impertinent myself when I was your age.

KURT

Why are you making me this offer?

NOLAN

I am not making you an offer. I shall merely attempt to expedite—

KURT

Why? The first time we met we didn't exactly hit it off, now, did we? Why then are you going to all this trouble?

NOLAN

I have discussed you with Miss Froude, who is an old friend of mine and whose opinion I greatly respect. She thinks very highly of you, Mr. Kurt. My own impression—

KURT

(Inexorably.)

Why? What, as they say, is the pay-off?

NOLAN

I'll tell you. I'll tell you quite frankly. I don't want Miss Froude's autobiography, which you have persuaded her to write, to appear in your magazine. I want it killed!

KURT

Oh! You want it killed?

NOLAN

Exactly.

KURT

Why?

NOLAN

Marion knows why. We needn't go into that.

KURT

(Wounded by a sudden and devastating jealousy.)

Good God! You! You too!

(II)

This is action in the best sense of the word. And in furthering the action of his play the dramatist has been strongly painting his characters. Nolan is shown as the self-confident politician, naively committed to the conviction that everything in life can be managed through a "deal." Kurt is shown as clever, superior, and sardonic, as he pretends to play Nolan's game; then, at the conclusion of the passage, his sudden outcry of jealousy gives us a view of what is working inside him.

Because of the very nature of drama, the most important

method of revealing character is through the action itself. We must, in plays, know people chiefly by what they *do*.

Shortly after the opening of *Hedda Gabler*, Tesman, after admiring the new bonnet of his aunt, Miss Tesman, places it on a chair. Presently Hedda comes in. After a little conversation:

HEDDA

(Interrupting.)

Tesman, this servant will never do.

MISS TESMAN

Berta will never do?

TESMAN

Whatever put that into your head, dear?

HEDDA

(Pointing.)

Look at that! She has left her old hat lying around on a chair.

TESMAN

(Upset.)

Why, Hedda—

HEDDA

Suppose anyone had come in and had seen it!

TESMAN

But Hedda! That bonnet's Aunt Julia's.

HEDDA

Is it?

MISS TESMAN

(Picking up the hat.)

Yes, indeed. And what's more, it's not old.

(1)

Hedda, of course, knew perfectly well that the new hat could not have been an "old" one of the servant's; the insult was calculated. This, one of Hedda's first actions in the play, though it is a small one, is a strong stroke in the etching of her character.

In the world's great plays, the characters are forever revealing themselves by their actions. In *Oedipus Tyrannus*, Oedipus, from the moment he begins to quarrel with Tiresias, shows that fatal recklessness which will bring him to disaster. The same is true of Lear when he disinherits his most loving and beloved daughter because she cannot make a pretty speech declaring her love for him. When Beatrice (in *Much Ado About Nothing*) comes forward as her cousin's only defender (see page 192) we know more about her than at any other moment of the play. Phaedra (see pages 69–74) makes us know, in the very way she discloses her fatal passion for Hippolytus, against what personal inner terrors that passion is struggling. Algernon, in withholding Jack's cigarette case until he is ready to give it back (see pages 35–41), demonstrates his delightful cheekiness. A measure of the importance of action in delineating character is the fact that if all the soliloquies in *Hamlet* were omitted, despite one's reluctance to part with them, the essential qualities of Hamlet would still be there to be grasped by the deeds he performs in the play.

There never was a wiser dictum than "By their fruits ye shall know them." Nowhere is this truer than in drama.[31]

TWO ONSTAGE, AND THREE

Aeschylus, earliest of Athenian dramatists to write for a theater, began with plays in which, in addition to the Chorus, there were only two characters present in any given scene. (*The Seven Against Thebes* is a magnificent example of what he was able to achieve in tragedy with the use of this technique.) The limitation of this practice is that *when only two persons are on-*

stage, it is possible to portray only one of them at a time.* The
other character inevitably acts as a foil to that portraiture. An
interesting proof of this will be found in Edward Albee's dramatic one-act play, *The Zoo Story.* Here the author has cast
only two characters, Jerry and Peter. Although, as we have
said (see pages 123–38), a park bench and a knife are used as two
distinct dramatic personalities in lieu of people, the bench and
the knife cannot, of course, speak. In consequence, it is really
only one of the two men, Jerry, who is characterized in the
round. Peter can do little more than act as his foil for the purposes of characterization, though he serves nobly the purposes
of plot.

When Sophocles introduced a third actor, and the dramatist could now have three characters onstage at once, a major
revolution in stage technique was thereby effected. (Aeschylus'
Agamemnon, The Libation Pourers, and *Eumenides,* a late triolgy,
employ the third character after Sophocles' innovation—but in
Aeschylus' own way.) *When three characters are onstage together, two of them can be delineated at the same time,* the third
acting as a foil; moreover, the emphasis can shift from minute to
minute, so that first one, then another, is being used as the foil.
The shift can be more rapid and frequent than when only two
characters are onstage.

If the reader will go over the passages we have thus far
quoted, he will see how this is the case. In the dialogue between
Algernon and Jack on pages 35–41, it is Algernon who is being
portrayed; in that between Algernon and Lane, pages 51–54, it
is Lane who is characterized. In the passage from *Othello,* pages
56–63, it is Othello who is depicted; toward its close, only two
lines of Desdemona are part of her characterization:

> O! my fear interprets. What is he dead?

and

> Alas! he is betrayed. . . .

—these showing, even with death at hand, her courage and
honorableness. In the passage from *Phèdre,* pages 69–74, it is
Phaedra whose character is revealed. In our third selection from

* Of course, in the exchange of dialogue between two characters,
for a certain space one of the characters is being delineated, and then
the emphasis may shift, so that that character now becomes the foil
while the other is being delineated.

All's Well That Ends Well, pages 196–99, it is Helena who is being portrayed. In our first passage from *Biography,* pages 204–7, it is largely Kurt, until Marion's last two speeches, where the emphasis veers to her; in our second, pages 208–11, it is Nolan; in our third, pages 211–13, it is more Marion than Nolan; in our fourth, pages 213–18, it is Nolan up to Kurt's

> Mr. Nolan—do you mind if I ask *you* something?

—when Nolan becomes a foil for Kurt's portraiture.

Now, notice what happens when three people are onstage at the same time. This is the scene, referred to by Kurt in our fourth selection from *Biography,* when Nolan and Kurt meet for the first time. Nolan and Marion are present; Kurt is ushered in:

MARION

This is Senator Nolan—Mr. Kurt.

NOLAN

(Glowering.)

I am not Senator Nolan.

MARION

But you will be.

(She offers him a cup of tea, he takes it.)

Can't I just call you that—between ourselves? It gives me such a sense of quiet power. And maybe it'll impress my visitor. Do have a cup of tea, Mr. Kurt.

(She gives him one.)

KURT

(Puts his hat on sofa left.)

I am not impressed by politicians. And I didn't come to drink tea. I am here on business.

(Nevertheless he takes a hearty sip.)

MARION

Well, you can do both. They do in England. American businessmen are so tense.

KURT

I'm not a businessman.

NOLAN

Well, whatever you are, you are very ill-mannered.

KURT

(Pleased.)

That's true!

MARION

(Delighted.)

Isn't it nice you agree? For a moment I thought you weren't going to hit it off.

NOLAN

In my day if a boy came in and behaved like this before a lady he'd be horsewhipped.

KURT

Well, when you get into the Senate you can introduce a horsewhipping bill. Probably bring you great kudos.

NOLAN

You talk like a Bolshevik.

KURT

Thank you! You talk like a Senator!

> (MARION wants to laugh but thinks better
> of it. She looks at KURT with a new eye.)

MARION

> (Quickly offering him more tea.)

Another cup, Mr. Kurt.

KURT

> (Taking it.)

Thank you.

MARION

And one of these cakes. . . .

KURT

> (Taking it.)

Thank you.

> (Eats cake.)

Having said, from our respective points of view, the worst thing
we could say about each other, having uttered the ultimate
insult, there's no reason we can't be friends, Senator. Damn
good cake. No lunch as a matter of fact.

MARION

That's what's the matter with him—he was hungry—hungry
boy—

NOLAN

(Puts teacup on piano.)

He probably wants to sell you some insurance.

KURT

Not at all. I'm not here to sell. I'm here to buy,

MARION

A picture!

KURT

Do I look like a picture-buyer?

MARION

As a matter of fact you don't.—But I haven't anything to sell except pictures.

KURT

(Confidently.)

I think you have.

MARION

(To NOLAN.)

This young man is very tantalizing.

NOLAN

Well, why don't you ask him to state his proposition and have done with it?

MARION

(Turns to KURT and repeats mechanically.)

State your proposition and have done with it.

KURT

(Puts his cup down on table rear of sofa left.)

What a nuisance women are!

NOLAN

(Starting toward him.)

Why, you insolent young whelp—I've half a mind to—

KURT

(Pleasantly.)

That's an impulse you'd better control. I wrote this lady a business letter asking for an appointment. She granted it to me at four o'clock. It is now six. In that interval I've climbed these five flights of stairs three times. I've lost over an hour of my life going away and coming back. An hour in which I might have read a first-class book or made love to a girl or had an idea—an irreparable hour. That's rudeness if you like. It's unbusinesslike. It's sloppy.

(To MARION)

Now will you see me alone or will you keep me here fencing with this inadequate antagonist?

MARION

You are unquestionably the most impossible young man I've ever met. Go away!

(1)

Because three people are here onstage together, all three can be depicted, two at a time while the third acts as a foil for them—and the emphasis can shift to a different pair from speech to speech.

Perhaps the most amazingly dexterous scene in drama is the play scene in *Hamlet*. Here (III, ii, 95–280) the variety is dazzling. At its opening, in the brief colloquy between Claudius and Hamlet ("How fares our cousin Hamlet?"), it is Hamlet who is important; next, in his few words with Polonius, it is the latter ("I did enact Julius Caesar . . ."). Then, the Players being ready, Shakespeare is able to etch telling touches in the characters of four people: Hamlet, Ophelia, Claudius, and Gertrude, because the Players become the foil to set off the others.

It is not to be concluded that there is anything wrong with having only two characters onstage together. At certain moments of the majority of plays it is highly necessary to have two only, to shut out everyone else and focus attention on a pair of characters alone—now on one, now on the other.[32] A brilliant example of this is the passage quoted from *Othello* on pages 56–63.

CHAPTER TEN

Dialogue

His words, like so many nimble and airy servitors, trip about him at command. MILTON, *Apology for Smectymmuus*

It is easier not to speak a word at all than to speak more words than we should. THOMAS À KEMPIS, *Imitation of Christ*, I, 29

They never taste who always drink;
They always talk who never think.
PRIOR, *Upon a Passage in the Scaligerana*

'Tis a task indeed to learn to HEAR:
In that the skill of conversation lies. YOUNG, *Love of Fame*, V, 57

Sermo animi est imago; qualis vir, talis et oratio est.* SYRUS, *Maxims*

La parole a été donnée à l'homme pour déguiser sa pensée.†

TALLEYRAND

Four things come not back: the spoken word, the sped arrow, time past, the neglected opportunity. OMAR IBN AL-HALIF

Words are but the shadows of action. DEMOCRITUS

Le secret d'ennuyer est celui de tout dire.** VOLTAIRE

Conversation . . .
Should flow, like waters after summer showers,
Not as if raised by mere mechanic powers. COWPER, *Conversation*

Quand celui à qui l'on parle ne comprend pas et celui qui parle ne se comprend pas, c'est de la métaphysique.†† VOLTAIRE

* Talk is the image of the mind; as a man is so is his speech.
† Speech was given to man to disguise his thoughts.
** The secret of being a successful bore is in telling everything.
†† When the man being addressed does not understand, and the man speaking does not understand—this is Metaphysics.

The observation of Omar Ibn Al-Halif quoted above ought to be engraved in the mind of every dramatist. Onstage, the word once spoken cannot be withdrawn; it is an arrow already shot which has hit a mark, intended or not intended; it belongs to time that is past and cannot be canceled; and if it was written carelessly by the dramatist, it becomes forever a neglected opportunity.

LEVELS OF CONVERSATION

From the outset we have stressed the fact that in the theater comprehension must be achieved, moment by moment, instantaneously, at the moment action and dialogue are being presented. No time is allowed the audience for reflection on the meaning intended.

The question is thus raised as to whether or not there are any limitations thereby imposed upon the dialogue. Obviously, *if there are any criteria* for what may be said onstage, *they are comprehensibility and interest.*

Does the need of comprehensibility mean that the dramatist, to insure it, is reduced to using monosyllabic words and/or only very short sentences and fragments? That is nonsense, of course; people who go to the theater are generally on a higher level than to require being addressed as illiterates. Nor is it true that an endless string of elementary words fitted into short sentences and fragments is inevitably immediately comprehensible. Suppose you came upon this bit of dialogue:

SHE

I would have done anything for you.

HE

Anything except let me alone. Or letting me get away. Letting me be free of you. Even in those days you were full of tricks. Woman's tricks. You women don't have to learn them. They come by instinct. You know how to make a man dependent on you. You do it by pretense. You pretend to be helpless. You pretend to put yourself entirely in a man's hands. As though

you were at his mercy. Before he knows it he's a slave. He has
to ask permission for everything. He can't take a step without
asking first. He can't do anything on his own.

(There are, unhappily, dramatists convinced that it is necessary
to write in this style.) In what the man says, each sentence or
fragment—taken one at a time—is easy enough to follow. But
the speech taken as a whole is confusing because a succession of
such short sentences and fragments is not only monotonous, it
is bedeviling as well. A considerable aggregation of individualized
ideas makes for chaos; the mind cannot take it all in. (This is
certainly true of an extended passage written in that style. We
have, after all, invented only one fairly brief speech.) Nothing
here is subordinated to anything else. Everything is apparently
of equal importance, and therefore nothing is of any importance.

Now let us see how the dramatist George Bernard Shaw
actually wrote the man's speech in *Man and Superman:*

ANN

I would have done anything for you.

TANNER

Anything except let me get loose from you. Even then you
had acquired by instinct that damnable woman's trick of heap-
ing obligations on a man, of placing yourself so entirely at his
mercy that at last he dare not take a step without running to
you for leave.

Everything intended in our wretched sixteen sentences and
fragments has been said neatly and forcefully in Shaw's two.
Despite the length of Tanner's second sentence, it would be immediately understood by a theater audience.

Comprehensibility, then, is not really a matter of the length
of sentences. Is it a matter of simplicity of vocabulary?

That depends upon what one means by simplicity. Look
again at the most "artificial" passages we have quoted, those from
The Importance of Being Earnest on pages 35–41 and 51–54
where a maximum of elegance has been achieved in the dialogue.

The conversation is certainly not monosyllabic; on the other hand, there is not a word in either passage which would not be part of the most modest of vocabularies.

> Some aunts are tall, some aunts are not tall. That is a matter that surely an aunt may be allowed to decide for herself.

The elegance obviously is not the product of a Johnsonian vocabulary; it comes rather from the structure of the sentences. It would be easy to ruin the effect by changing that:

> Some aunts are tall, some aunts are not tall. Every aunt ought to be allowed to decide about her height herself.

Naturally, since dialogue at its best *is* character, a peasant must be given the speech of peasants and an uneducated man uneducated speech; for them the language must be uncomplicated. In the speech of his cultivated people a dramatist has particular limitations. He must not only manage that they do not sound illiterate; he must also debar from their vocabularies words which would be puzzling even for a minute to a well-bred audience, for that could only mean a halt in attention to the play itself. Such are words

1. which, though not particularly difficult and quite possibly part of a cultivated person's vocabulary, are not frequently enough in use to be immediately familiar (*animadvert, butte, eschew, frore, gloze, xenophobe*);

2. which are idiomatic to a small segment of the population (*baukie, bushwhacker, chee-chee, dunt, usquebaugh*);

3. which are too technical, such as bloom in the sciences (*corneous, formulary, medullary, pediform*), the social sciences (*dichotomy, epistemological, phalansterism*), the arts (*enharmonic, hypostyle*), sports (*cantle, fair ball, gone to ground, luff, martingale*), religion (*ciborium, dulia, precentor*), law (*amicus curiae, corpus juris*), the trades (*cam, cant hook, enface, peen*).

Of course, since this is a rule, it is capable of exceptions—as in the case of a stuffy or pedantic or narrow personality, or a person who uses words without reference to their meaning.

Dialogue, then, can be written on any level, from the most illiterate to the most cultivated, as long as the criteria of comprehensibility and interest are observed.

In this matter, as in all matters pertaining to the stage, the only reality that can be achieved is the illusion of reality. Far more important than giving a character the words he would use in life, is giving him and every other person of the drama the *rhythms* of speech used in life. If Kurt (page 205) had spoken in this fashion to Marion when she admitted not having read his magazine:

> It doesn't matter. It only proves you've got a brain. Our magazine is a best seller. Millions buy it, three millions, I believe. We have to satisfy them, of course. You can't expect three million readers all to be intelligent—you can figure that out. But we can't afford to let them know that we know. They've got to be flattered. So every once in a while we print Shaw, Wells, and Chesterton, but not too much of them and not too often.

—the language would have been less unsuitable to a man like him than the rhythms in which he is made to speak above. Behrman, however, with a perfect ear, wrote his speech thus:

> That is a tribute to your discrimination. We have an immense circulation. Three millions I believe. With a circulation of that size you may imagine that the average of our readers' intelligence cannot be very high. Yet occasionally we flatter them by printing the highbrows—in discreet doses we give them, at intervals, Shaw and Wells and Chesterton.[33]

The only school for learning the various rhythms of speech is for the dramatist to train his ear to listen to the talk going on about him—to memorize the rhythms, to jot them down, to make them part of his knowledge. This is a significant aspect of Browning's power as a poet; his dramatic monologues talk straight to you with immediacy, leaping over rhyme and traditional poetical constructions:

She had

A heart—how shall I say?—too soon made glad,

> Too easily impressed; she liked whate'er
> She looked on, and her looks went everywhere.

Browning was a master at creating the illusion of real speech, not so much by the use of everyday language (which few poets prefer), but by reproducing the rhythms in which men and women speak.

RHYTHMS OF SPEECH AND THEIR EMOTIONAL VALUES

If it is true that each individual has his characteristic rhythms of speech, it is also true that everyone's rhythms of speech vary with his emotional state. Nothing can be more effective in a dramatist's work than well-calculated rhythms mirroring the emotional values that are to be projected.

Othello's mind having been poisoned against Desdemona by Iago, he is asked by the villain to be patient:

IAGO

Patience, I say; your mind, perhaps, may change.

OTHELLO

> Never, Iago. Like to the Pontic sea,
> Whose icy current and compulsive course
> Ne'er feels retiring ebb, but keeps due on
> To the Propontic and the Hellespont,
> Even so my bloody thoughts with violent pace
> Shall ne'er look back, ne'er ebb to humble love
> Till that a capable and wide revenge
> Swallow them up.

(III, iii)

A good actor would probably not pause (except briefly at "Hellespont") while delivering Othello's lines, the irresistible sweep of which powerfully expresses the wave of violence which is engulfing him. The swelling tide of the rhythm is an expression of the huge surge of passion in Othello's breast.

Shakespeare's mastery of the manipulation of rhythms for dramatic purposes is not the most negligible facet of his genius.

In *King Lear*, after Lear has been found wandering in his madness by Cordelia's men, he is ministered to by her physician.
This is the scene in which he awakens from the effects of the
restorative medicine, to find himself dressed again in robes be-
fitting royalty, to his bewilderment, in the presence of his long-
lost daughter:

CORDELIA

He wakes. Speak to him.

DOCTOR

Madam, do you; 'tis fittest.

CORDELIA

How does my royal lord? How fares your Majesty?

LEAR

You do me wrong to take me out o' th' grave.
Thou art a soul in bliss; * but I am bound
Upon a wheel of fire, that mine own tears
Do scald like molten lead.

CORDELIA

Sir, do you know me?

LEAR

You are a spirit, I know. When did you die?

CORDELIA

Still, still, far wide!

* Heaven.

DOCTOR

He's scarce awake. Let him alone awhile.

LEAR

Where have I been? Where am I? Fair daylight?
I am mightily abus'd.* I should e'en die with pity,
To see another thus. I know not what to say.
I will not swear these are my hands. Let's see.
I feel this pin prick. Would I were assur'd
Of my condition!

CORDELIA

    O, look upon me, sir,
And hold your hands in benediction o'er me.
No, sir, you must not kneel.

LEAR

        Pray, do not mock me.
I am a very foolish fond old man,
Fourscore and upward, not an hour more or less;
And, to deal plainly,
I fear I am not in my perfect mind.
Methinks I should know you, and know this man,†
Yet I am doubtful; for I am mainly ** ignorant
What place this is; and all the skill I have
Remembers not these garments; nor I know not
Where I did lodge last night. Do not laugh at me;
For (as I am a man) I think this lady
To be my child Cordelia.

CORDELIA

And so I am! I am!

* deceived.   † (Kent).   ** entirely.

LEAR

Be your tears wet? Yes, faith. I pray weep not.
If you have poison for me, I will drink it.
I know you do not love me; for your sisters
Have, as I do remember, done me wrong.
You have some cause, they have not.

CORDELIA

No cause, no cause.
(IV, vii)

Lear's halting accents mirror perfectly his calm (after his raging violence), his bewilderment, his brokenheartedness; Cordelia's, the pity which chokes her and the tenderness which moves her to say as little as possible so that he will not be disturbed about his past injustices to her. It is one of the sublime moments in world drama.

It has been remarked how throughout *Antony and Cleopatra* the rhythms tend to be made of brief phrases, so that we feel the heat of the Nile—as though the climate and the passion which work upon the two lovers make longer speech too difficult:

CLEOPATRA

I know, by that same eye, there's some good news.
What says the married woman?—You may go:
Would she had never given you leave to come!
Let her not say, 'tis I that keep you here.
I have no power upon you; hers you are.
(I, iii)

But all skilled dramatists know the emotional importance of rhythm. In *Hedda Gabler* Brock makes clear his boredom with the fussy Tesman; they are talking of Lovborg:

TESMAN

And imagine it—I'm delighted to hear that he's become quite the reformed character.

BROCK

So I hear.

TESMAN

And he has also published a new book, hasn't he?

BROCK

Yes he has.

TESMAN

They say it's made quite a sensation!

BROCK

An extraordinary sensation.

TESMAN

Imagine! Isn't that good news, though! A man of his unusual talents—I was so upset that he had gone hopelessly to the dogs.

BROCK

Everyone thought that.

TESMAN

But I can't imagine what he's going to do now! How on earth is he going to make a living, huh?

(1)

In *The Cherry Orchard*, as Madame Ranevsky looks out the window onto her beloved orchard, all the sweetness of treasured memories echoes in the rhythm of her murmured:

Oh, my childhood, my days of innocence! This was the nursery in which I used to sleep; from here I looked out into the orchard;

every morning I used to wake with happiness. In those days
the orchard was just as it is now; nothing has changed.

(Laughs with pleasure.)

White, all, all white! Oh, my dear orchard! After the dark and
gloomy autumn and the chill winter, you are young again, and
full of happiness—the angels from heaven have never left you.

(1)

In *Cyrano de Bergerac* the raptures of a moonlit night and
the pain of the aching love in his breast pour out from Cyrano
as he stands beneath Roxane's balcony (Brian Hooker's translation):

CYRANO

Yes!—yes—
Night, making all things dimly beautiful,
One veil over us both— You only see
The darkness of a long cloak in the gloom,
And I the whiteness of a summer gown—
You are all light— I am all shadow!—How
Can you know what this moment means to me?
If I was ever eloquent—

ROXANE

You were
Eloquent—

CYRANO

You never heard till now
My own heart speaking!

(III)

The hauteur of Lady Bracknell breathes through every
phrase of her rounded periods:

Mr. Worthing, I confess I feel somewhat bewildered by what
you have just told me. To be born, or at any rate bred, in a

hand-bag, whether it had handles or not, seems to me to display a contempt for the ordinary decencies of family life that reminds one of the worst excesses of the French Revolution. And I presume you know what that unfortunate movement led to? As for the particular locality in which the hand-bag was found, a cloak-room at a railway station might serve to conceal a social indiscretion—has probably, indeed, been used for that purpose before now—but it could hardly be regarded as an assured basis for a recognized position in good society.

(I)

The agonized cry of Bessie alone with Nora in the besieged room, in O'Casey's *The Plough and the Stars*, after she has been shot by rifle fire through the window, in its rhythms conveys perfectly the gasping of a mortally wounded woman:

Merciful God, I'm shot, I'm shot, I'm shot!—Th' life's pourin' out o' me!

(To NORA.)

I've got this through—through you—through you, you bitch, you!—O God, have mercy on me!

(To NORA.)

You wouldn't stop quiet, no you wouldn't, you wouldn't, blast you! Look at what I'm afther gettin', look at what I'm afther gettin'—I'm bleedin' to death, an' no one's here to stop th' flowin' blood!

(Calling.)

Mrs. Gogan, Mrs. Gogan! Fluther, Fluther, for God's sake, somebody, a doctor, a doctor!

(IV)

The indignation of the self-righteous speaks through the phrases of Madame Arcati, the medium, in this speech from Noel Coward's *Blithe Spirit*. Madame Arcati, invited by the Condomines to give a séance for them so that Mr. Condomine might get material for a mystery story, has brought back from "over yonder" the ghost of his first wife, who has since caused much mischief. In a desire to get the medium to undo her accomplishment, Mrs. Condomine has told Madame Arcati her husband's original purpose; Madame Arcati draws herself up to demand whether she had been invited in a spirit of mockery; Mrs. Condomine replies that her husband had merely wished to become familiar with some of the "tricks of the trade" of a medium. Madame Arcati is furious:

> Your attitude from the outset has been most unpleasant, Mrs. Condomine. Some of your remarks have been discourteous in the extreme and I should like to say without umbrage that if you and your husband were foolish enough to tamper with the unseen for paltry motives and in a spirit of ribaldry, whatever has happened to you is your own fault, and, to coin a phrase, as far as I'm concerned you can stew in your own juice!

(II, ii)

In Tennessee Williams' *The Glass Menagerie*, Amanda speaks throughout in the rhythms common to those whose talk rattles on without control:

> The only way to find out about those things is to make discreet inquiries at the proper moment. When I was a girl in Blue Mountain and it was suspected that a young man drank, the girl whose attentions he had been receiving, if any girl *was*, would sometimes speak to the minister of his church, or rather her father would if her father was living, and sort of feel him out on the young man's character. That is the way such things are discreetly handled to keep a young woman from making a tragic mistake! [34]

(v)

THE LANGUAGE OF DRAMA

Consider this passage from William Dean Howells' *Criticism and Fiction*:

> Matthew Arnold complained that he found no "distinction" in our life, and I would gladly persuade all artists intending greatness in any kind among us that the recognition of the fact pointed out by Mr. Arnold ought to be a source of inspiration

to them, and not discouragement. We have been now some hundred years building up a state on the affirmation of the essential equality of men in their rights and duties, and whether we have been right or been wrong the gods have taken us at our word, and have responded to us with a civilization in which there is no "distinction" perceptible to the eye that loves and values it. Such beauty and grandeur as we have is common beauty, common grandeur, or the beauty and grandeur in which the quality of solidarity so prevails that neither distinguishes itself to the disadvantage of anything else.

Now, there are two kinds of words or phrases from which a writer may select his vocabulary. One class may be represented by such words as *beauty, grandeur, truth;* the other by such words as *Matthew Arnold, table, violet.* The first class consists of words which express a concept apart from any particular or material instance: such words are called *abstract.* The second class consists of words which designate a thing or happening or class of things or happenings which can be perceived by our senses; such words are called *concrete.* The abstract word *beauty* presents nothing to our senses; the concrete word *table* does.

The passage cited from Howells contains many abstract words: *distinction, life, greatness, kind, recognition, fact, source, inspiration, discouragement, state, affirmation, equality, rights, duties, right, wrong, civilization, beauty, grandeur, solidarity, distinguishes, disadvantage.* The author is discussing abstract ideas, and has chosen abstract words. We commonly meet with this kind of abstract language in books of philosophy and economics; in literature, as in the present instance, we sometimes find it dominant in critical discussions. The effect of such abstract language is to keep us in a region of pure, non-experiential thought.

But in creative literature abstract language is to be tolerated, when necessary, only as a necessary evil. The language of the novel, the short story, poetry, and the drama—because they are concerned above all with the realities of human experience—must be largely the language of experience, the record of the world as presented to our senses or our imagination. This is the language made up of concrete expression, as in this speech of Christy's from *The Playboy of the Western World:*

And I the son of a strong farmer, God rest his soul, could have bought up the whole of your old house awhile since, from the butt of his tail-pocket, and not have missed the weight of it gone.

I, son, strong, farmer, God, rest, his, soul, could have bought up, old, house, butt, tail-pocket, missed, weight, gone. Even *whole,* an abstract word, is here part of a concrete expression, *whole of your old house.* Or, as in this speech of Serafina from Tennessee Williams' *The Rose Tattoo:*

Four thousand—three hundred—and eighty. The number of nights I held him all night in my arms. Sometimes I didn't sleep, just held him all night in my arms. And I am satisfied with it. I grieve for him. Yes, my pillow at night's never dry—but I am satisfied to remember.

(I, v)

or Alvaro's from the same play:

My name is Mangiacavallo, which means "Eat-a-horse." It's a comical name, I know. Maybe two thousand and seventy years ago one of my grandfathers got so hungry that he ate up a horse.

(II)

Here everything is concrete again. In the drama concreteness is necessary even when ideas are being discussed; look again, for example, at Tanner's two sentences from *Man and Superman* (page 229). Nolan, in *Biography,* does not merely reflect on the promiscuous sexual life artists live (according to him); he adds concretely as part of his charge against Marion:

painting pictures of Communist statesmen, running around California with movie comedians!

The importance of concrete expressions to the man of letters is that they are the stuff out of which images are made. And images are the source of vividness, power, and immediacy of meaning. From abstract phrases no images emerge.

Imagery has been the lifeblood of poetry. It is the reason

that poetry is a more intense, more condensed, more compact, more vivid, more stirring means of communication than prose:

> Swing low, sweet chariot,
> Comin' for to carry me home.
> I looked over Jordan and what did I see,
> Comin' for to carry me home?
> A band of angels comin' after me,
> Comin' for to carry me home.

One could write a chapter on the ideas which come thronging from four lines of William Blake:

> To see the world in a grain of sand,
>   And a heaven in a wild flower;
> Hold infinity in the palm of your hand,
>   And eternity in an hour.

That is because imagery seizes upon the imagination with suddenness and compulsion. We understand at once, and what we understand brings with it, because of the associational values of imagery, a host of related notions.

Drama being a concentrated method of presenting life, it has always had a strong affinity for poetry. The great dramatists of the golden age of Athens were great poets as well: Aeschylus, Sophocles, Euripides, and Aristophanes. The same was true of the giants of the Elizabethan age in England: Shakespeare, Marlowe, Beaumont and Fletcher, Webster, Ford. Racine is held by some Frenchmen to be the greatest poet of their language. Ibsen's earliest plays were poetic dramas; so is *Peer Gynt*—and the poet's feeling for language is everywhere in Ibsen's later dramas. In our time Christopher Fry in England and Maxwell Anderson have preferred to write poetic dramas. And the qualities which make Tennessee Williams one of our foremost current dramatists are, above all, those associated with his dialogue, which constantly comes very close to being poetry. As a matter of fact, more and more of our contemporary dramatists are becoming aware of the need of poetry in the theater: that is one of the most encouraging signs in the theater of today.* (For example, *The*

* Alvin Sapinsley has made several experiments with TV plays in

Chalk Garden, The Rope Dancers, The Member of the Wedding, which are full of the stuff of poetry.)

Small wonder! Consider the energy and power of lines like these:

From Christopher Fry's *The Lady's Not for Burning*:

HUMPHREY

                He says the Day of Judgment
Is fixed for tonight.

MARGARET

          Oh no. I have always been sure
That when it comes it will come in autumn.
Heaven, I am quite sure, wouldn't disappoint
The bulbs.

and:

MARGARET

        I shall go and change my dress;
Then I shall both be ready for our guests
And whatever else may come upon the world.

and:

THOMAS

        Now you, for instance,
Still damp from your cocoon, you're desperate
To fly into any noose of the sun that should dangle
Down from the sky.

                                    (1)

---

verse—one of them a Western! See *Even the Weariest River*, in B. Grebanier and S. Reiter, *Introduction to Imaginative Literature* (New York, 1960), pp. 941–62.

From Maxwell Anderson's *Elizabeth the Queen:*

ELIZABETH

What malicious star
Danced in my sky when you were born, I wonder?

ESSEX

What malicious star danced in the sky
Of Ireland, you should ask.

ELIZABETH

Oh, my dear,
You are a child in council. I saw them start
To draw you into this, and tried to warn you—
But it was no use.

ESSEX

They drew me into nothing.
I saw their purpose and topped it with my own.
Let them believe they've sunk me.

(I, iii)

Poetry is almost the natural vehicle for speech in the theater, for the life of the theater is in the projection of a compelling illusion.

Now, in prose, ideas are presented more or less with some kind of logical sequence; and hence imagery is less generic to prose than to poetry. Nevertheless, in creative prose the image is a riveter of our attention or a welcome oasis in the desert. In the theater, where attention must be riveted at every moment, when prose is used it avoids abstract language and is studded, at its best, with imagery. From Ibsen's *Rosmersholm:*

REBECCA

Don't you think it may be a little late?

KROLL

No doubt it would have been wiser if we had checked the stream at an earlier point in its course.

and:

KROLL

You bury yourself here in your historical collections. I don't want to speak disrespectfully of family trees and all that; unhappily there's no time for that kind of hobby. You can't conceive how things are all over the country. Hardly one accepted idea hasn't been turned upside down. It will be a huge task to root out all the errors again.

(1)

From Shaw's *Saint Joan:*

JOAN

One thousand like me can stop them. Ten like me can stop them with God on our side. You do not understand, squire. Our soldiers are always beaten because they are fighting only to save their skins; and the shortest way to save your skin is to run away.

From Shaw's *In the Beginning* (the first part of *Back to Methuselah*):

ADAM

I like you; but I do not like myself. I want to be different; to be better; to begin again and again; to shed myself as a snake sheds its skin. I am tired of myself. And yet I must endure myself, not for a day or for many days, but for ever. That is a dreadful thought. That is what makes me sit brooding and silent and hateful.

(1)

From *The Importance of Being Earnest:*

GWENDOLEN

Are there many interesting walks in the vicinity, Miss Cardew?

CECILY

Oh, yes, a great many. From the top of one of the hills quite close one can see five counties.

GWENDOLEN

Five counties! I don't think I should like that. I hate crowds.

CECILY

I suppose that is why you live in town?

GWENDOLEN

Quite a well-kept garden this is, Miss Cardew.

CECILY

So glad you like it, Miss Fairfax.

GWENDOLEN

I had no idea there were any flowers in the country.

CECILY

Oh, flowers are as common here, Miss Fairfax, as people are in London.

GWENDOLEN

Personally I cannot understand how anybody manages to exist in the country, if anybody who is anybody does. The country always bores me.

CECILY

Ah! This is what the newspapers call agricultural depression, is it not? I believe the aristocracy are suffering very much from it just at present. It is almost an epidemic amongst them, I have been told. May I offer you some tea, Miss Fairfax?

GWENDOLEN

Thank you.

(Aside.)

Detestable girl! But I require tea.

(II)

From Synge's *Playboy of the Western World:*

CHRISTY

If I can wring a neck among you, I'll have a royal judgment looking on the trembling jury in the courts of law. And won't there be crying out in Mayo the day I'm stretched upon the rope with ladies in their silks and satins snivelling in their lacy kerchiefs, and they rhyming songs and ballads on the terror of my fate.

(III)

From Emlyn Williams' *The Corn Is Green:*

MORGAN

All of a sudden, with one big rush, against that moon, and against that High Street—I saw this room; you and me sitting here studying, and all those books—and everything I have ever learnt from those books, and from you, was lighted up—like a magic lantern.

(III)

From Thornton Wilder's *Our Town:*

STAGE MANAGER

Most everybody's asleep in Grover's Corners. There are a few lights on: Shorty Hawkins, down at the depot, has just watched the Albany train go by. And at the livery stable somebody's setting up late and talking.—Yes, it's clearing up. There are the stars—doing their old, old crisscross journeys in the sky. Scholars haven't settled the matter yet, but they seem to think there are no living beings up there. They're just chalk—or fire. Only this one is straining away, straining away all the time to make something of itself.

(III)

From S. N. Behrman's *Serena Blandish:*

SIR EVERARD (who is one hundred years old)

I can remember when I was a boy of ten or twelve picking currants with my chum Jocelyn— Yes, I can remember that day very well. I can remember the sun on the back of my neck and the smell of the swamps and the foliage. But those years between—between twelve and a hundred—they are vague— they are vague.

(I, iii)

Consider how much feebler these speeches if Kroll had said:

No doubt it would have been wiser if we had registered our objections earlier.

and:

You are out of communication with affairs. I don't want to underestimate traditions, but we can't occupy ourselves with trivialities. You can't conceive the present conditions. Every old concept has been discredited. It will require great effort to achieve our objectives.

or Joan:

Their superior numbers do not deter me. You do not understand, squire. Our soldiers are not successful because they are
not led by principle. They fail because they are interested only
in self-preservation.

or Adam:

I should like renewed opportunities for my endeavors. . . .
That is why I make for such difficult companionship.

or Gwendolen and Cecily:

Is the vicinity of interest, Miss Fairfax?
Yes, much can be seen from a nearby elevation.
Much? I detest congestion.
I suppose that is why you prefer habitation in town?
The garden is in excellent condition, Miss Cardew.
So glad of your approbation, Miss Fairfax.
I had no conception that there was any horticultural activity in
the country. . . .

or Christy:

If I become guilty of mayhem here, I'll cause considerable
interest when I am brought to judgment.

or Morgan:

I suddenly achieved an appreciation of your generosity to me
in cultivating my understanding.

or the Stage Manager:

All activity has ceased in Grover's Corners with a few exceptions. The celestial bodies, however, have not ended their labors.
It is said that there is no life in them. Our own planet continues
to attempt achieving self-improvement.

or Sir Everard:

I can remember my boyhood, I can remember the recent past, but not the experiences in between.

These rewritings are a species of assassination, we know. Between them and their originals, to borrow Dogberry's phrase, comparisons are indeed odorous.[35]

WORD ORDER

In classical Latin it would have been possible, because of grammatical endings, to arrange the sentence

The good boy loves the farmer's daughter

in any one of the following ways without altering the fundamental idea (*puer* = the boy, *bonus* = good, *filiam* = daughter, *agricolae* = farmer's, *amat* = loves):

1. Puer bonus filiam agricolae amat.
2. Bonus puer filiam agricolae amat.
3. Filiam agricolae puer bonus amat.
4. Agricolae filiam puer bonus amat.
5. Amat filiam agricolae bonus puer.
6. Amat puer bonus agricolae filiam.

But the actual meaning varies in each version. The first would have been the usual rendition of our English sentence: subject at the beginning, followed by its modifier; next, the object, followed by its modifier; and at the end of the sentence, the verb. For emphasis this normal order was broken, the principle being that the beginning and the end of a sentence are the strongest positions. In the second version, therefore, the stress is on "good," and the meaning is something like: "It's a *good* boy who loves the farmer's daughter" (not a bad boy). In the third version the emphasis is on "daughter," and the meaning is something like: "It's the *daughter* of the farmer whom the good boy loves" (not the farmer's wife or the farmer's money). In the fourth version "the farmer's" is important, and the meaning is something like: "It's the *farmer's* daughter whom the good boy loves" (not the senator's). In the fifth and sixth versions the stress is on "loves." In the fifth, there is a secondary stress on "boy," and the meaning is something like: "He *loves* the farmer's daughter, does the good boy" (he does more than like her, or, he doesn't dislike her). In the sixth version, the secondary stress is on "daughter," and the meaning is something like: "He *loves* her, does the good boy, that farmer's daughter." The Latin language had no need of italics.

In English, where there are no grammatical endings, word order is much less elastic.

> The good boy the farmer's daughter loves.
>
> or
>
> The farmer's daughter the good boy loves.
>
> or
>
> Loves the good boy the farmer's daughter.

are inscrutable. With us, meaning is heavily dependent on the order in which words appear. (Compare "The good boy loves the farmer's daughter" with "The farmer's daughter loves the good boy"—obviously not the same thing!)

Nevertheless, it is as true in English as it was in Latin that *the strongest positions in a sentence are the beginning and the end*. In this sentence:

> I hope you will be prepared, when you see him again, to forget your disappointment and behave like a human being, as we all expect you to do.

—there is a lack of force because the opening and closing of the sentence are allotted to the least forceful ideas. Such loosely constructed discourse is acceptable enough during the rounds of impromptu daily conversation; moreover, facial expression, gestures, and vocal inflection can italicize what is important. What distinguishes eloquent talkers, however, from most of us, is their ability to put their thoughts in more effective arrangement. In written prose and, above all, in drama—where everything is highly selective and no time can be expended on fumbling attempts to be precise—something better is called for than loose construction. Although our sentence is, perhaps, the more usual (and therefore, perhaps, the more "natural"), it would be far more effective on the stage if rearranged in this way:

> When you see him again, I hope you will be prepared to forget your disappointment and, as we all expect you to do, behave like a human being.

Now the most striking ideas, "when you see him again" and "behave like a human being," are in the most forceful positions.

In *Biography*, Nolan does not say:

> If a boy came in, in my day, he'd be horsewhipped if he behaved like this before a lady.

—though that is perhaps the way the sentence would come out in life during the heat of discourse. What Nolan does say, far more effectively, is:

> In my day if a boy came in and behaved like this before a lady he'd be horsewhipped.

The dramatist here has accentuated the difference in age between Nolan and Kurt at the opening of the sentence, and concluded with the strongest idea, "horsewhipped."

Opening and conclusion are of cardinal importance in dramatic talk—though it is strange how many dramatists seem unaware of the principle—because of the very nature of dialogue. *The beginning of one speech is the link with the speech just ended; its conclusion is the link with the speech about to be heard.*

For this reason, the principle must be enlarged to apply to each speech as a whole, as a unit. *The opening of any given speech and its close must generally be allotted to the most important things being said.* When Kurt is trying to convince Marion that she ought to write her autobiography, he does not say:

> Your impressions will be dimmed by time. Most autobiographies are written by corpses. Why wait until you're eighty? While you are still young, vital, in the thick of life, why not do yours?

Here the force is dissipated in the middle of the speech, which ends weakly. Mr. Behrman wrote:

> Why wait until you're eighty? Your impressions will be dimmed by time. Most autobiographies are written by corpses. Why not do yours while you are still young, vital, in the thick of life?

Here the speech begins with force, and the ending is cumulative in power.

To work at revision of this kind in one's dialogue can be to achieve astonishing improvements. Though it is common enough in life that we end our remarks with parenthetical phrases like "as you know," "of course," "by the way," "so I hear," it is, for example, wise to make them truly parenthetical by tucking them in somewhere before the conclusion of a speech. As an ending for a given speech:

> You're bound to hear from him, I'm sure.

can be improved to:

> You're bound, I'm sure, to hear from him.

or—better:

> You'll hear from him, I'm sure—you're bound to.[36]

HOW LONG SHOULD A SPEECH BE?

It is likely today that any producer looking over the manuscript of a new play, if he saw page after page of long speeches, would toss the work aside and read no further. To overcome this prejudice against many long speeches, one has to have an already established reputation; any newcomer submitting a play with speeches as long as those in O'Neill's *The Iceman Cometh* would probably never get a hearing. (Of course, if one has the reputation of an O'Neill, there is no problem, for the producers will come running to him.)

A frequent question is: How long can a speech be? Obviously, it is, on the one hand, impossible to measure the correct length of a speech by inches or the number of words or syllables it contains. On the other hand, the action of a play can hardly be carried on through dialogue made up exclusively of brief one-sentence speeches in this style:

> Where were you last night?
> I was out.
> I phoned you but nobody answered.
> I'm sorry.
> I told you I was going to call.
> I forgot.

You must have had something important to do.
No, I went to a movie.
Were you trying to avoid talking to me?
No, why should I?
It looked like it.
Well, you're wrong.
Barbara thought it looked like it.
Well, she's wrong too.
We could be, I suppose.
You are, I assure you.

While very brief stretches of such dialogue can be very effective at moments of tension, even they must be broken by speeches a little longer, as in this passage from R. C. Sherriff's *Journey's End:*

STANHOPE

What are you looking at?

RALEIGH

Nothing.

STANHOPE

Anything—*funny* about me?

RALEIGH

No.—I'm awfully sorry, Dennis, if—if I annoyed you by coming to your company.

STANHOPE

What on *earth* are you talking about? What do you mean?

RALEIGH

You resent my being here.

STANHOPE

Resent you *being* here?

RALEIGH

Ever since I came—

STANHOPE

I don't know what you mean. I resent you being a damn fool,
that's all— Better eat your dinner before it's cold.

RALEIGH

I'm not hungry, thanks.

(III, ii)

A long procession of brief one-sentence speeches would not only
soon become wearisome; it would take forever to carry on the
business of the action.

The passage from the final scene in *Othello* (see pages
56–63 shows a wonderful alternation between brief and longer
speeches for dramatic effect.

As for the longer speeches, it is, as we have implied, impossible to limit them by number of words or lines. Since it is
manifestly the case that speeches can be too long, what is the
limitation which must be imposed upon them?

The salient fact about any given speech is that it must constitute a unity. It is safe to say, therefore, that *any given speech
must convey only one important dramatic idea and/or only one
ruling emotion*. Thus, in this exchange of dialogue:

TOM

(Coming into the room.) Why, hello, Henry!

HENRY

Hello, Tom! I just arrived. I'm sorry, but I'm leaving this afternoon.

—Henry's speech, though brief, is too long, for it contains two different ideas, Henry's arrival and imminent departure. The dialogue ought to go something like this, so as to separate the two ideas:

TOM

(Coming into the room.) Why, hello, Henry!

HENRY

Hello, Tom!

TOM

When did you get in?

HENRY

I just arrived.

TOM

Staying a while?

HENRY

Sorry. I'm leaving this afternoon.

Earlier epochs had not our prejudice against lengthy speeches, but the principle of unity in each speech was always respected by the great dramatists. If the reader will turn back to pages 69–74, he will note that in the passage quoted from Racine's *Phèdre*, Hippolytus' first speech is devoted to reassuring Phaedra that Theseus may be still alive. Phaedra's first speech shows her losing her battle with her passion. Hippolytus' second speech shows his misconstruing her words as referring to her husband. Her second speech, though long, has perfect unity: by identifying Hippolytus with Theseus she at last expresses her fatal passion. His third speech shows him suddenly understand-

ing her drift. Her third speech is an attempt to recover her forfeited dignity by a pretense that he has misinterpreted her words.
His last speech is an effort to quit her presence before the approaching storm he feels imminent can break. Her last speech,
again long, is a dramatic declaration of love in undisguised language. His trying to interrupt and, later, his turning away from
her are both breaks in her outpouring, and give unity to each
of the three parts of her speech, making it three distinct speeches
in effect.*

From this example it is clear that *any significant action unaccompanied by words on the part of one character may serve
as a paragraph ending to the talk of another character*. One character's suddenly smiling or shaking his head or throwing something into a trash basket, without an accompanying speech, has
the same effect as a piece of interrupting dialogue.†

As long as some of Hamlet's soliloquies are, none of them
is a word too long. This is one of the longest speeches in existence:

> O, what a rogue and peasant slave am I!
> Is it not monstrous that this player here,
> But in a fiction, in a dream of passion,
> Could force his soul so to his own conceit **
> That from her working all his visage wann'd,
> Tears in his eyes, distraction in 's aspect,
> A broken voice, and his whole function suiting
> With forms to his conceit? And all for nothing!

---

* French scholars will here protest that the stage directions were
added by our translator (which is true) and that in the original, where
there is a total absence of them, this last speech is printed, like all the
others, in a solid, uninterrupted block. Our translation is an English
acting version of the play. But the translator has added no stage directions
not implicit in the lines which Racine wrote. It is obvious that when
Phaedra cries, "I—I love you," the rapid rush of words which follows
can be explained only on the grounds of her not wishing him to speak
yet. And at the end of the passage we have quoted, she herself says, "If
but your eyes one moment deigned to look at me"—a clear indication
that he has turned away from her. The stage directions only make ex-
plicit what a scrutiny of the lines would demand of a director.

† Note Austin's first lifting the hamper of champagne and then
picking up Monica's wraps in the passage quoted from *The Second Man*,
pages 75–78. These actions break his speeches into two parts.

** imagination.

For Hecuba!
What's Hecuba to him, or he to Hecuba,
That he should weep for her? What would he do,
Had he the motive and the cue for passion
That I have? He would drown the stage with tears
And cleave the general ear with horrid speech,
Make mad the guilty and appall the free,
Confound the ignorant, and amaze indeed
The very faculty of eyes and ears.
Yet I,
A dull and muddy-mettled rascal, peak
Like John-a-dreams, unpregnant of my cause,
And can say nothing; no, not for a king,
Upon whose property * and most dear life
A damn'd defeat was made. Am I a coward?
Who calls me villain, breaks my pate across,
Plucks off my beard and blows it in my face,
Tweaks me by the nose, gives me the lie i' the throat
As deep as to the lungs, who does me this?
Ha!
'Swounds, I should take it; for it cannot be
But I am pigeon-livered, or ere this
I should have fatted all the region kites †
With this slave's offal. Bloody, bawdy villain!
Remorseless,** treacherous, lecherous, kindless †† villain!
O vengeance!
Why, what an ass am I! Sure, this is most brave,
That I, the son of a dear father murdered,
Prompted to my revenge by heaven and hell,
Must like a whore, unpack my heart with words,
And fall a-cursing, like a very drab,
A scullion!
Fie upon't! Foh! About, my brain! I have heard
That guilty creatures sitting at a play
Have by the very cunning of the scene
Been struck so to the soul that presently ***
They have proclaim'd their malefactions;

* self.   †† inhuman.
† birds of prey of the sky.   *** immediately.
** pitiless.

For murder, though it have no tongue, will speak
With most miraculous organ. I'll have these players
Play something like the murder of my father
Before mine uncle. I'll observe his looks;
I'll tent * him to the quick. If he but blench,†
I know my course. The spirit that I have seen
May be the devil, and the devil hath power
To assume a pleasing shape; yea, and perhaps
Out of my weakness and my melancholy,
As he is very potent with such spirits,
Abuses ** me to damn me. I'll have grounds
More relative †† than this. The play's the thing
Wherein I'll catch the conscience of the King.

(ii, ii)

(Just before this soliloquy, Hamlet has conceived the idea of presenting a play at court to test the guilt of Claudius; it came to him through a hint in the lines recited by the First Player from an old tragedy on *Dido and Aeneas*.) This soliloquy is designed, above all else, to apprise the audience of Hamlet's intentions in presenting the play before the King. Despite its length this speech has unity, for it contains only one ruling emotion—Hamlet's exasperation at the differences between the Player's freedom to express his feelings over a fiction and his own inability to act or say a word in a cause that is not fiction—and only one significant dramatic fact—his announcement of his purposes in giving the play. The speech, in consequence, is certainly not too long, for it respects the fundamental principle of unity. We are made to feel, moreover, that the dramatic fact (the intention of giving the play) is the cause of the pouring out of his exasperated impatience in the first part of the speech. It is his excitement over the prospect of giving the play which fathers the impatience which opens the soliloquy.

We could multiply the instances where a long speech is quite short enough. Such a speech is Jack's concerning Algernon:

JACK

It pains me very much to have to speak frankly to you, Lady Bracknell, about your nephew, but the fact is that I do not

* probe.   ** deceives.
† flinch.   †† convincing.

approve at all of his moral character. I suspect him of being untruthful.

LADY BRACKNELL

Untruthful! My nephew Algernon? Impossible! He is an Oxonian.

JACK

I fear there can be no possible doubt about the matter. This afternoon during my temporary absence in London on an important question of romance, he obtained admission to my house by means of the false pretense of being my brother. Under an assumed name he drank, I've just been informed by my butler, an entire pint bottle of my Perrier-Jouet, Brut, '89: a wine I was specially reserving for myself. Continuing his disgraceful deception, he succeeded in the course of the afternoon in alienating the affections of my only ward. He subsequently stayed to tea, and devoured every single muffin. And what makes his conduct all the more heartless is that he was perfectly well aware from the first that I have no brother, that I never had a brother, and that I don't intend to have a brother, not even of any kind. I distinctly told him so myself yesterday afternoon.

(III)

This speech is unified by one emotion and one idea: the indictment of Algernon, and the facts that make the indictment. Such a speech is Mrs. Alving's in *Ghosts:*

MANDERS

How did you manage to keep such a state of things secret?

MRS. ALVING

That's been my unending fight, day by day. After Oswald was born, it seemed to me that Alving improved a little. But not for long. Then I had to begin fighting twice as hard, a life and death struggle, so that the world might not know the kind of man my son had for a father. And you know how clever Alving was at winning over people. No one seemed able to believe anything but the best of him. He was one of those people whose life does not damage their reputation. But finally, Mr. Manders—you must know the whole story—the most disgusting thing of all happened.

(1)

This speech achieves unity by being an account of matters leading up to "the most disgusting thing of all."

Or these two speeches of the Captain from Strindberg's *The Father:*

DOCTOR

But there are many kinds of women.

CAPTAIN

Modern science has proved there is only one. I've recalled, recently, two experiences in my life which confirm it. I was strong and, not to boast, handsome when I was young. One time I was aboard a steamer, sitting with a couple of friends in the bar. The young stewardess came in, flung herself down next to me, burst into tears, and sobbed out that her sweetheart had been drowned. We gave her our sympathy; I ordered champagne. After the second glass I brushed her foot. After the fourth, her knee. Before morning I had consoled her.

DOCTOR

That was just one of those winter flies.

CAPTAIN

Well, here's the second experience: a real summer fly. I was at Lysekil. A young married woman was staying there with her children while her husband was in the city. She was religious, severely principled, preached sermons to me. I think she was entirely respectable. I loaned her first one book, then another, and when she left, strange to say, she gave them back to me. It was three months later that I found her card with a "declaration" in those same books. Oh, it was innocent, of course—as innocent as a declaration of love can be from a married woman to a stranger who never made any advances. And the moral of this is: don't trust too much.

(II)

Or these two of Ellida from Ibsen's *The Lady from the Sea:*

WANGEL

You cannot be allowed to choose—*I* will not allow you.

ELLIDA

You couldn't prevent my making a choice—you can't and nobody else could. You could forbid me to go away with him—to throw in my lot with his—if I chose to do that. You could detain me here by force, against my will. All that you could do. But the choice which my soul would make, my choice of *him* and not of you—I mean, in case it turns out that that is the way I must choose—that you could never prevent.

WANGEL

Yes, you're right. I could never prevent that.

ELLIDA

So, there's nothing that will help me resist! Here at home there is not a thing that holds me, that binds me. I have no roots in your home, Wangel. The children—their hearts, I mean—aren't mine, have never been mine. When I go with him tonight or out to Skioldvik tomorrow—if I do go—there's not a key for me to surrender here, not an order to leave behind me for anything under the sun. You see I am rootless, how rootless, in your house! How, from the moment I came here, I've been an outsider! [37]

(v)

Before we leave the subject, a word of caution may be in order concerning long speeches. One thing a single speech should never do is to mirror a complete reversal in emotion before it comes to its conclusion; for example, a man expresses his misery over his past life, suddenly thinks of a reason to be happy, and then resolves to alter the whole cast of his life—all in one speech. This is the kind of offense that in our century a number of writers of propaganda drama have committed. The effect of this sort of thing is highly alien to that of the drama: it reeks of the oratorical, which is by nature anti-dramatic.

Suppose, as some scholars have blindly imagined, that Hamlet, *during* the soliloquy we have quoted, had hit upon the idea of presenting the play—that it had not occurred to him any earlier. If Shakespeare had attempted that, the unity of the soliloquy would have been annihilated. For, in that instance, we should have heard first Hamlet's exasperation, and then, out of the clear sky, and with no connection, the inspiration for giving the play—a violent alteration in mood and emotion. But, as Shakespeare has actually written it, we are given to understand that the exasperation is largely owing to Hamlet's burning impatience to give the play, as he has already conceived of doing. The design of the soliloquy is first the effect (the exasperation) and then the cause (the giving of the play).

CHAPTER ELEVEN

Tragedy and Comedy

The world is a comedy to those who think, a tragedy to those who feel.
HORACE WALPOLE, *Letter to H. Mann*

In tragic life, God wot,
No villain need be! Passions spin the plot.
MEREDITH, *Modern Love,* 43

In this world there are only two tragedies. One is not getting what one wants, and the other is getting it.   WILDE, *Lady Windermere's Fan,* III

Sunt lacrymae rerum.*   VIRGIL, *Aeneid,* I

The tears live in an onion that should water this sorrow.
Antony and Cleopatra, I, ii

Castigat ridendo mores.†   Motto of the Opéra Comique, Paris

As the crackling of thorns under a pot, so is the laughter of a fool.
Ecclesiastes, VII, 6

Laughter! O thou reviver of sick Earth!
MEREDITH, *The Appeasement of Demete*

The low mimic follies of a farce.
W. DILLON, *Horace's Art of Poetry*

If that is not Sensation,
I don't know what it is.   LEWIS CARROLL, *Poeta Fit Non Nascitu*

From the standpoint of many a theatergoer, a play, to paraphrase Gertrude Stein, is a play is a play. He may not pause to

* There are tears in things.
† He chastises manners with a laugh.

identify any given drama beyond saying that it is serious or funny. But the dramatist must certainly know at the outset whether the play he is about to write is to be a tragedy, a comedy, a melodrama, a farce, or something in between tragedy and comedy. He must know in advance because his treatment of his materials will depend mightily on which kind of play he purports to write. The result can be only a mess if a work that is following the paths of tragedy suddenly veers into those of comedy or vice versa. Each type of play has its own objectives and therefore its own methods of procedure. Our discussion in this chapter—once again we repeat that we speak from the point of view of the dramatist, not of the critic—must therefore not be taken as a sort of battle over critical labels, but rather as a consideration of criteria important to the writer.

The kind of play an author can create is sometimes unalterably determined by his materials. The story of Romeo and Juliet could never make anything but tragedy—despite various disgusting attempts to travesty it into farce. The materials which are basic to Wilder's *Matchmaker* are not only beyond the possibility of becoming tragedy; they are equally beyond the possibility of high comedy and could make only for farce. The original story of King Lear ended with the old king's being restored to his throne; because Shakespeare wished to write a tragedy, he was compelled to change that ending. If the story of Hamlet did not end as it does, but showed Hamlet triumphant and alive—the play could not be a tragedy. *The Importance of Being Earnest* could never have been a tragedy with the plot materials it contains.

But there are many instances where the story materials could be used for either tragedy or comedy. The Antonio-Shylock story of *The Merchant of Venice* and the Hero-Claudio story of *Much Ado About Nothing* could easily have been used for tragedy if their plots had been shaped toward a tragic end. If Brutus had been conceived as a villain and Julius Caesar as a hero, a play on that subject could have been written without venturing into tragedy as Shakespeare's play does. In some of the topics we have suggested for scripts in our early chapters, the story could be directed toward ends either tragic or comic. Obviously, the dramatist must know which way he is to go and.what are the effects he must manage, before he starts out.

TRAGEDY

The history of tragedy in the Western world is not unfamiliar to many, but it is worthwhile briefly recounting it for the sake of establishing clearly what the purpose of tragedy is. It apparently originated in ancient Greece as part of the ceremonies connected with the Festival of Dionysus. In one respect that holiday corresponds to the Christian Lent and the Hebrew Day of Atonement. It was the occasion on which each citizen of Athens could achieve *katharsis,* inner purification. When tragedies were first written for the theater in the golden age of Athens, dramatists participated in a public competition. Each contestant submitted a trilogy, three tragedies connected in subject matter.* A committee selected the authors of the best tragedies, and on a succession of days each dramatist was allotted his day for the presentation of his trilogy. At the conclusion of the festival, one of the playwrights was awarded a prize by public applause.† The audience was composed of the entire citizenry of Athens, who were present in the theater, as part of their religious and civic duties, to achieve through *katharsis* a greater inner well-being.

We know from Aristotle's *Poetics* how this inner purgation was to be attained. Every normal human being carries with him a certain weight of pity and awe. When these are channeled into the activities of daily life, they equip a man with compassion, on the one hand, and, on the other, with a sense of his place in the general scheme of things. But the ordinary transactions of living do not allow sufficient scope for the expression of this pity and this awe. And when they remain unchanneled in action and are kept unexpressed within him, they begin to fester, to damage his spiritual health. An excess of pity degenerates a man into a sentimentalist, ready to weep over matters unworthy

* There survives but one trilogy, Aeschylus' *Agamemnon, The Libation Pourers,* and *Eumenides.*

† It is an indication of the astonishing level of public taste in that era that the prize was most often given to their sublimest poet, Aeschylus, and next most often to their greatest dramatist, Sophocles.

of tears: he will, for example, sorrow for the hardened criminal awaiting execution but be indifferent to the murderer's victim. An excess of awe degenerates a man into a coward or a neurotic.

The Athenian attending the theater, by identifying himself with the hero of a tragedy, was able vicariously to undergo the hero's tragic experience, in this way channeling his own pity and awe. He was thus able to unburden himself of these emotions. When the tragedy was over he was chastened into a sober comprehension of human destiny and his own place in the order of things. He left the theater with better perspectives and in a state of better spiritual health.

Though drama has undergone many changes and expansions since the golden age of Athens, the function of tragedy has not changed. We are always in need of this spiritual cleansing and chastening. Our own lives (we thank the stars!) rarely partake of the truly tragic. We are not afforded the opportunity to expend ourselves on grand or noble issues. Our own griefs are important enough to us privately, but seen objectively they are likely to be more trivial than magnificent. Thus, day by day we accumulate a sickening store of vexations and frustrations. We go to see a tragedy and it achieves the purposes for which tragedy was first conceived: we identify ourselves with the hero, suffer vicariously with him in his experiences, and are cleansed. We dash out our eyes with Oedipus, yet retain our sight; with Electra we help direct her brother's sword against their mother, yet remain innocent of the heinous crime of matricide; we drink the poison with Romeo, we carelessly choose the envenomed rapier with Hamlet, we plunge with Othello the dagger into the breast —we go through their death throes, yet remain alive and physically sound. And we come away saddened but purged of triviality, chastened but seeing more into the heart of things.

Part of the awe which we feel at the catastrophe is an exaltation. The downfall of the tragic hero involves a sort of transfiguration—as though at the catastrophe his were the role and privilege to stand representative of the human race, and by his experience expiate our failings. His ruin may be the product only of youthful impetuosity (as with Romeo) or of something almost criminal (as with Electra and Macbeth), but his sufferings transform him—for he reaps a harvest he has sown—at his downfall into a sacrifice offered by all of us.

This, then, is the high function which tragedy is called upon to fulfill. No matter how labeled, no play is a tragedy that cannot fulfill it. Tragedy is, perhaps, higher in its purposes than the exercise of any other human activity. Its province is, by its very nature, austerely delimited. Within its purlieus we may smile a little, even laugh a little (for example, with the Fool in *King Lear*, at Polonius, Osric, and the Gravediggers in *Hamlet*), provided the mirth does not shatter the seriousness of the atmosphere.

At this point it would be well to suggest a cardinal reason for the artistic failure of many pseudo-tragedies. A tragedy must not leave us indignant, for if it does how shall we, being inflamed, be purged? It must not leave us depressed, or how shall we be cleansed? Indignation or depression over the events portrayed in a play prevents our identification with the tragic hero and thus robs us of the powerful and overwhelming emotion afforded by true tragedy. Indignation or depression is outside the province of tragedy. This is not to say that there is not room on the stage for plays which arouse the indignation of the audience. Ibsen's unremitting attack on human hypocrisy and deceit has resulted in some of the world's greatest dramas—*A Doll's House, The Wild Duck, An Enemy of the People*. It is simply to say that such plays are not tragedies (as Ibsen was perfectly aware), and that they are not composed as tragedies must be composed. As for plays which succeed in depressing the audience, it is not possible to argue with a public that is willing to pay its hard-earned cash for tickets for a play which is guaranteed to make life seem unbearable. The popularity of some such plays in our time places the matter beyond dispute. It is of no moment to the present discussion that we belong to the sector of the public which prefers to avoid such plays, no matter how conscientiously they represent life or how well they are executed. We can think of better things to do with our time and money. However, applauded or not applauded, plays which leave the audience depressed are not tragedies, and our point is that having not the purposes of tragedy, they have not its requirements either.

Now, a tragedy must evoke both pity and awe in the audience. Pity is compassion. *Awe is evoked by the revelation of man's littleness in the face of the complexities he must deal with (God, Nature, Society), and by man's greatness of soul in stand-*

ing up, despite his littleness, against those complexities. Pity
without awe is not enough for tragedy; it too readily degenerates
into bathos (for example, Dickens' *The Old Curiosity Shop*).
It is in the absence of awe that most would-be tragedies fail.

THE TRAGIC HERO

*The purgation which tragedy makes possible can be attained
only through the identification of the individual member of the
audience with the hero of the tragedy.* Unless the member of
the audience can *be* that tragic hero during the performance, he
cannot experience vicariously what happens to that hero—and
upon that the *katharsis* depends. This results in a requirement
peculiar only to tragedy: *in a tragedy the identification of the
audience must be with the central character,* who is the tragic
hero. In other kinds of plays identification may be with the
central character or with some other character. *In tragedy, the
interest must center about the central character.* In other kinds
of plays the focus of interest may be elsewhere.

And since the tragic hero must be the central character, *the
climax must be a deed of the tragic hero.* As in all good plays,
that climax must be an expression of the character traits of the
central character. It is youthful recklessness which brings Romeo
to ruin, and it is that same youthful recklessness which causes
him to kill Tybalt. It is Othello's failing that he too rashly loses
his judgment, and that same rash loss of judgment is responsible
for his concluding that the handkerchief in Cassio's possession
was given him by Desdemona. It is Hamlet's violent impulsive-
ness which brings about his downfall; it is that same violent im-
pulsiveness which causes Hamlet's unreasoning killing of Polonius.*

In order to make audience identification with the tragic
hero possible, certain qualifications are called for in the central
character. Aristotle has analyzed with precision what these
qualifications are. *The hero must be not too good a man,* for
though we should pity his fall it would make us indignant. *He
must not be too wicked,* for then we should not pity him at all,
but rejoice in it (as in the fall of a Hitler or a Stalin). If he is

---

* See the present writer's *The Heart of Hamlet* (New York, 1960),
pp. 183–91.

too good, we cannot identify with him, since we know ourselves to have failings; if he is too bad, he can only alienate us. Macbeth, among Shakespeare's tragic heroes, is a crucial instance. Though Macbeth is a murderer, Shakespeare through the magic of his art manages to retain our sympathies for his hero; we feel him to be, despite his crimes, essentially a good man foundering in evil; if we were made ever to feel otherwise, the play would deteriorate into melodrama, as does *Richard III*.

The hero of a tragedy must be a man or a woman essentially good whose character is marred by a fatal shortcoming, a weakness which causes his ruin—the *tragic flaw* of Aristotelian fame.

He must also be a man above average or the commonplace in his qualities. This criterion has nothing to do with social rank. Thomas Hardy's hero in *Jude the Obscure*, despite his lowly station in life, is a truly tragic figure because of his qualities of soul which raise him above the average; so is the same author's Eustacia in *The Return of the Native;* so are Joseph Conrad's Lord Jim and his heroes in the stories *The Secret Sharer* and *Karain*.

We cannot identify with an average or commonplace man. However large may be our talk about the average man and our boasted sympathies with him, we never include ourselves in the designation. The average man is always somebody else. Privately nobody thinks of himself as commonplace. We are all aware of noble possibilities; granted the opportunity to act out our role in an appropriately stately setting, the world should soon see! No, we may pity the average man, but we cannot help also somewhat looking down on him, for we ourselves are not, we know, average. Hence, we do not identify with him in a play, for in him there can be no awe. We can identify only with a hero who is above the general run of men. The hero of Theodore Dreiser's *An American Tragedy* (which, by the way, is not a tragedy), though coming from origins no lower than Jude's, is not a tragic figure because the author has intentionally and successfully portrayed him as commonplace. The same must be said of the hero of Arthur Miller's *The Death of a Salesman;* at the most we can but pity him. The "depressing" plays (and novels) of which we have spoken make it their business to have as heroes average men, mediocrities with whom no one will identify. These works are usually described as tragedies by their authors. No one need quarrel with the admirable social intentions of these writers. But a work does not become a tragedy because it is so labeled or because it is "sad." *

Conversely, a man in high social rank does not necessarily become a candidate for tragedy. A king with the soul of a mouse would make an even more inept tragic hero than a commonplace office clerk; his position might indeed make him all the more boring.

But a man of superiority of character who is also in a position of some social importance is likely to make a more impressive tragic hero than such a man in a humble position would. Such a man involves the destiny of more lives than his own. A tragic hero of rank carries more along with him to ruin than can a man of lowly station. The death of Abraham Lincoln was a greater tragic fact, for North and South, than the death of any Union or Confederate soldier. A hero of lofty place is more tragic, too, because he falls from a greater height. The hero of Alan Paton's deeply moving tragedy *Too Late the Phalarope*, an important member of his South African community, is an excellent example of such a hero. The fall of an eagle weighs more with us than the fall of a sparrow.

By definition a tragedy will show the hero's experiences ending in catastrophe. *The catastrophe will be brought about by the hero's own tragic flaw. It cannot be accident which brings about his downfall.* Accident is beyond logic or explanation—that is what one means by "accident"—and the audience could never identify itself with an all-determining action which is only an accident. An accident, when we witness it, is something which will not happen to us. It is an occurrence which we cannot and, if we are to keep our sanity, should not count upon.

---

* There is another pitfall in these works. When the hero is a mediocrity it is easily possible that some other character will rise above him in qualities. Such is Roberta in *An American Tragedy*. She is not only the hero's victim; she also possesses an ability to love far in excess of his wretched commonplaceness. As a result we sympathize, with or against our will, with her. If we sympathize with her, our feelings to that extent are against the hero, Clyde. A similar situation develops with regard to the son Biff in *The Death of a Salesman;* to the extent that he wins our sympathy we must disapprove of his father. Biff, indeed, had the possibilities of becoming the hero of a tragedy, but the author did not choose to write the play about him.

But since we are members of the human race, we can identify with a deed which is the product of human failings. We are made sorrowful by the ruin which the hero brings upon himself, but we are not depressed by it. For there is dignity in the catastrophe of which a man himself is somewhat the author.

Since we have spoken of Aristotle, the reader at this point may very well be asking how this last stricture applies to Aristotle's favorite play, *Oedipus Tyrannus*. Unfortunately there is no misconception more prevalent than the vulgar one which describes the classic Greek tragedies as exhibiting the remorseless operation of Fate. Careless authors of textbooks and glib book-reviewers have perpetuated the error by forever comparing a modern work showing the blind agency of Destiny with Greek tragedy, and Oedipus is always being summoned as the perfect analogy for a tragic hero crushed by Fate. Actually, no hero in the whole realm of drama is more completely the author of his own doom than Oedipus. He builds his own funeral pyre log by log, and *Oedipus Tyrannus* devotes itself almost exclusively to the showing of it. He is impelled toward self-destruction by his willfulness and heedlessness.

Consider his actions as they are revealed to us in the tragedy. Brought up by the King and Queen of Corinth as their son, he was disturbed at a feast by a drunkard's insinuations casting doubts on his origins. Oedipus begged the King and Queen for the facts, but they were so evasive that he journeyed to the Oracle to learn the truth. Characteristically, the Oracle answered a question he had not asked, and spoke of his murdering his father and committing incest with his mother. Horrified, Oedipus vowed to escape such crimes by never returning to Corinth. But he was not only a virtuous man; he was also a very reckless one. He had consulted the Oracle only because he was unsure of his parentage. Had he been wiser, in addition to avoiding Corinth, he could have taken measures to avoid the dreadful future forecast for him. To do that he need merely have also vowed never to kill any man older than himself and never to mate with any women older than himself. Yet, before long, refusing to clear the road for Laius' carriage, he slew his father in wrath; and soon after that recklessly permitted himself to be wedded to the widowed Jocasta, his mother. It is not to the point that he was unaware that these were his parents. He had been given sufficient warning to avoid both deeds. And this is the way Sophocles' audience unquestionably understood the play, as Aristotle's strictures make plain. Oedipus was his own destroyer. Oedipus a victim of Fate would be only pathetic, not tragic.

So, too, despite the unfortunate Prologue to Act I of *Romeo and Juliet*, where appears the inaccurate description of the pair as *star-crossed lovers*, Romeo brings himself to ruin because of his rashness. As we have already shown (page 109), he makes no attempt to deal with the family feud; yet, as we have seen, that need not have been too difficult. At the climax of the play, he deliberately embraces a policy of rashness as Tybalt re-enters after Mercutio's death:

> Alive in triumph, and Mercutio slain?
> Away to heaven respective lenity,*
> And fire-ey'd fury be my conduct † now!
> Now, Tybalt, take the "villain" back again
> That late thou gavest me. . . .
>
>   (III, i)

He rejects rational conduct, rushes into the arms of disaster, as though it, not Juliet, were his bride. After the climax this recklessness continues: he tries to kill himself in Friar Laurence's cell (III, iii). In exile, when his servant brings word that Juliet is dead (v, i), he at once decides to die too. He loses no time in buying poison of an apothecary. Soon, when he is back in Verona after a wild ride during which his "betossed soul" paid no attention to what his servant was telling him concerning Paris and Juliet, it never occurs to him first to see Friar Laurence to find out how matters stand; had he done so, he would have learned that Juliet was indeed not dead. But he is so eager for death that, rather than explain his presence at the tomb, he fights with Paris, whom he can see only as an impediment to self-destruction. His final act of recklessness is the drinking of the poison. He is clearly the author of his own doom, and that is why we can identify ourselves with him. We are all too prone to be rash when we should be patient.

Of course, accidents do occur in life, and since they do occur, they find a place, though not the cardinal place, in tragedy.

* mildness which is the result of reflection.   † conductor.

In a manner of speaking, everything that happens to an individual without his having first willed it is an accident—whether it be the unexpected appearance at one's house of a man or the tardiness of the morning train. And such an unheralded appearance of a man or the lateness of a train may in truth be but the first of a series of destructive events. But in a tragedy, such accidents, if they contribute to the catastrophe, must be shown as cooperating with the hero's tragic flaw, not themselves causing the catastrophe. For example, the lateness of a train may contribute to the catastrophe if we are made to feel that it is our hero's characteristic fault that, knowing the company's undependability, he made no provision for the contingency of the train's lateness. The sudden appearance of a man may contribute to the hero's fall if we are made to feel that their relationship makes stronger our hero's shortcomings.

In a tragedy, it is the hero's failings which start the rocks tumbling; accidents may convert the falling of a few rocks into an avalanche engulfing him. It *is* unlucky that Desdemona loses the handkerchief just when she does; her handkerchief lost another day might have caused no mischief. But were Othello other than he is and she other than she is, no catastrophe need have ensued from the loss. It *is* unlucky that Polonius should be hiding at that hour behind the Queen's arras; on another occasion Hamlet would perhaps have been in less of a ferment. But were Polonius other than he is or Hamlet other than he is, Polonius need not have lost his life and Hamlet need not have impetuously thrust the sword through the tapestry. It is unlucky that Friar Laurence's letter to Romeo in exile is never delivered; but Romeo's recklessness has involved him in disaster long before. His killing of Tybalt made his life forfeit at once. And even after the misfortune of the letter's delay, had Romeo had the wisdom to seek out Friar Laurence, his death and Juliet's might have been avoided. *The hero of a tragedy can never be merely the victim of circumstance.* This is an error that many dramatists anxious to indict society for the individual's misfortunes, have made. Accident can appear in a tragedy only as a force to make the hero's folly trebly catastrophic. All tragedy reminds us that once we give rein to our weaknesses, we may expect the chances of life to help bring us to grief.

The writing of tragedy becomes more and more unencouraged in our time,* largely because of the inroads of popular psychology and psychoanalysis. These tend to explain away evil as owing to forces outside individual responsibility. If a young man thrusts an arsenic cocktail down his doting parents' throats in his impatience to inherit their money, we say, "But of course! Poor boy! They ruined him by overindulgence. It isn't really his fault." Or if the parents in the case had been severe with their offspring, we say, "But of course! Poor boy! Didn't they realize how they were thwarting his childhood that time they refused to buy him a toy machine gun? How they were robbing him of 'togetherness' with boys of his own age? This act of his could have been foretold then." The hero robbed of his personal responsibility for his deeds can never figure as a tragic hero. Hamlet, if conceived as the victim of an Oedipus complex or some neurosis, becomes no longer responsible for his acts, and therefore no longer a tragic hero.

It is also true that tragedy cannot blossom in an atmosphere of skepticism or cynicism. The eighteenth century was such an age, and it produced no tragedies worthy of the name. Skepticism and cynicism look upon the sublime with a derisive smile, the product of jaded tastes. For tragedy to thrive there must exist a public which is not disdainful of the sublime.

Besides all this, the concepts of right and wrong are basic to tragedy. And in our time these concepts have been subject to attack from the social sciences. We are taught now that there is no such thing as an absolute right or an absolute wrong, that good and evil are relative to time, place, and environment. Human beings, however, continue to make their choices in life as though right and wrong, good and evil, were realities; human beings continue to select friends and avoid some people on the presumption that some people are good and others evil. And experience has not taught that human beings are wrong to do so, psychology and anthropology notwithstanding. If human beings continue to behave this way, the basis for tragedy seems firm enough—if the public be willing to listen to it. Every once in a while—though rarely—the writer of a good tragedy proves that.[38]

* Among the few notable modern tragedies: Miller's *A View from the Bridge*.

COMEDY

In Plato's *Symposium* Socrates observes "that the genius of comedy was the same with that of tragedy, and that the true artist in tragedy was an artist in comedy also."

It is true enough that comedy and tragedy are not totally dissimilar in the impulses which bring them into being. Tragedy makes us understand how necessary it is to live with a sense of perspective of our personal limitations and failings and of our place in the scheme of things. So does comedy. Comedy and tragedy both deal with human beings who have either lost this perspective or else have never owned it.

Comedy, too, goes back to the celebration of Dionysus, god of procreation and fertility. In very ancient times it was customary for the celebrants to disguise themselves as various animals, while they sang songs of fertility with many a ribald sexual allusion. Instead of the purification of tragedy these embryonic comedies offered the euphoria of laughter.

Later, during the Festival of Dionysus comedy was granted an honorable place at Athens, too. The great writer of comedies, Aristophanes, flourished during the Golden Age but, unlike his contemporary tragedians, did not establish the traditions in which comedy was later to be written. His plays are grotesque and fantastic, rather than realistic, and were intended exclusively for his own times. Occasionally there is matter, as in *Lysistrata,* universal enough to make the play endure. Loose in structure, brimming with ribald allusion and comment on contemporary affairs, they contained a great deal of horseplay and buffoonery. Their purpose was to evoke the release of laughter and to castigate certain citizens. The libretti which Sir William S. Gilbert wrote for the music of Sir Arthur Sullivan are among the few modern examples of comedy conceived (without the ribaldry) somewhat in the Aristophanic spirit.

The traditions for comedy begin, rather, with the days of the New Comedy, whose leading practitioner was Menander (c. 342–292 B.C.). His plays were imitated by the two chief Roman dramatists, Plautus and Terence. The characters in these plays are more or less ordinary people, and the plot interest and mirth come chiefly from the complications of the story. These traits comedy has always since maintained.*

The difference between comedy and tragedy is that tragedy deals with failings that are deeply moving, awe-inspiring, and worthy of pity; comedy deals with failings that are amusing, absurd, or contemptible. Tragedy is largely intuitive and emotional in its understanding of life; comedy is critical and intellectual. And since we all think and feel, comedy and tragedy each satisfy different and important human needs. The characters in a comedy are as busy compounding mischief as is the hero of a tragedy, but we look on their deeds not with awe and compassion, but with derision or amusement.

Tragedy concerns itself with individuals; comedy has always been more preoccupied with the social group, the foibles of the time, the absurdities of social relationships. Its focus is less on what is universal in man's soul than on what is typical of his conduct. Unlike the characters of tragedy, those of comedy are not idealizations of the quintessences of human nature, but people whose behavior is more like that of ordinary human beings— or even of people below the level of ordinary human conduct. Not that comedy excludes superior persons; but when superior people are represented in a comedy, either the comic emphasis is on their all too human frailties (Beatrice and Benedick in *Much Ado About Nothing*, Jack in *The Importance of Being Earnest*, Marion and Kurt in *Biography*) or else we look elsewhere than at them (Isabella in *Measure for Measure*) for the comic display of failings. Taken as a whole, a comedy is not concerned with what is divine in man. It prefers to fix a questioning eye upon the vagaries, follies, and pretenses of contemporary life. Comedy shows man in his rather silly or thoroughly absurd side.

When we say that comedy concerns itself with the contemporary, we do not imply that the setting for a comedy cannot be in any remote time or place. S. N. Behrman's infectious adaptation of Jean Giraudoux's *Amphitryon* is laid in legendary Greek

* During the Middle Ages, when the theater was almost entirely extinct, the word "comedy" was loosely applied to any writing, including the most serious, when the ending was happy. (This is the reason Dante called his great poem *The Divine Comedy*.) The medieval connotation of the word persists in many plays, such as *Twelfth Night*, where the plot is essentially serious and the resolution a happy one.

times, and introduces Zeus himself as one of the comic characters. But in such a setting—in any setting—*the characters of a comedy speak as members of a modern world.* No matter what the period in which his play is set, the writer of comedies causes his characters to talk and behave like moderns. (There would be no point in ridiculing customs and values already obsolete.)

The province of comedy, unlike that of tragedy, is a wide one. Because comedy undertakes to amuse, it does not necessarily stipulate that we laugh outright. Some of the world's best comedies are more likely to make us smile (Molière's *The Misanthrope*, Behrman's *Biography*). Some contain too much bitter truth to allow us more than a faint, or even a sardonic, smile (*Measure for Measure*). Some contain truth so grim that we cannot smile at all (*The Wild Duck*). Some are frankly boisterous in their fun (*The Comedy of Errors*). Some are irrepressibly gay and lighthearted (*The Importance of Being Earnest*). Some are kindly in their exhibition of human folly (Goldsmith's *She Stoops to Conquer*, Chekhov's *The Cherry Orchard*). Some are vitriolic in their onslaught on human depravity (Jonson's *Volpone*). Some comic dramatists merely shake their heads whimsically at the spectacle of human frailty; others apply a lash to it.*

The mirth we procure from comedy comes in varying de-

* It is clear from our examples that we consider satirical drama to be within the precincts of comedy. Some critics would not agree, and would point to *The Wild Duck* as a play whose tone is devoid of any but the grimmest mirth. They would also observe that in some serious plays which are not clearly either tragedy or comedy, as in O'Casey's moving *Juno and the Paycock*, there may exist strong satirical elements. We take cognizance in this chapter of five basic types of drama; these critics would speak of satirical drama as a sixth. Our interest is not in nomenclature, but in dramatic principles, and therefore we have no desire to quarrel over the classification. We do agree that, while it is possible to be quite specific in defining tragedy, melodrama, and farce, the task is not so simple with comedy or with that kind of drama which is intermediate between tragedy and comedy. But conceiving comedy to be as spacious in its realm as we do, we think that, laughter aside, a play whose prevailing tone is satirical must be classed as a comedy. For satire is, after all, a matter of tone. And when satire is strongly present in a play like *Juno and the Paycock* but does not capture the tone of the whole play, we prefer to think of the satirical as only an element in a play which is certainly not tragedy or comedy or melodrama or farce, but a kind of play, a distinct type, which is between tragedy and comedy. With this kind of play we deal later.

grees from humor and wit. *Humor is a matter of the situations* in a play; *wit is a matter of the manipulation of language.* Both humor and wit emanate from the presentation of the incongruous and the shock of the unexpected.

Since humor is a matter of situation, it is therefore to be looked for in the action of a play, and is consequently more basic to comedy than wit. It would be possible to have a comedy without wit; comedy without humor must be made of sad stuff indeed.

In the passage we have quoted from *Biography*, where Nolan first comes in to see Marion (see page 63), we have a characteristic representation of humor: the incongruity comes from Nolan's complacent expectation of being recognized and Marion's inability to place him.

In the second act of *The Importance of Being Earnest*, Algernon has intruded into Jack's retreat in the country under the pretense of being Jack's depraved brother Ernest, has been accepted as such by Cecily to her immense delight, and has just gone off with her into the house. A few minutes later:

> (Enter JACK slowly from the back of the garden. He is dressed in the deepest mourning, with crape hat-band and black gloves.)

MISS PRISM

Mr. Worthing!

CHASUBLE

Mr. Worthing?

JACK

> (Shakes MISS PRISM's hand in a tragic manner.)

I have returned sooner than I expected. Dr. Chasuble, I hope you are well?

CHASUBLE

Dear Mr. Worthing, I trust this garb of woe does not betoken some terrible calamity?

JACK

My brother.

MISS PRISM

More shameful debts and extravagance?

CHASUBLE

Still leading his life of pleasure?

JACK

(Shaking his head.)

Dead!

CHASUBLE

Your brother Ernest dead?

JACK

Quite dead.

MISS PRISM

What a lesson for him! I trust he will profit by it.

CHASUBLE

Mr. Worthing, I offer you my sincere condolence. You have at least the consolation of knowing you were always the most generous and forgiving of brothers.

JACK

Poor Ernest! He.had many faults, but it is a sad, sad blow.

CHASUBLE

Very sad indeed. Were you with him at the end?

JACK

No. He died abroad; in Paris, in fact. I had a telegram last night from the manager of the Grand Hotel.

CHASUBLE

Was the cause of death mentioned?

JACK

A severe chill, it seems.

MISS PRISM

As a man sows, so shall he reap.

CHASUBLE

Charity, dear Miss Prism, charity! None of us are perfect. I myself am peculiarly susceptible to draughts. Will the interment take place here?

JACK

No. He seems to have expressed a desire to be buried in Paris.

CHASUBLE

In Paris!

(Shakes his head.)

I fear that hardly points to any very serious state of mind at the last. . . . And now, dear Mr. Worthing, I will not intrude any longer into a house of sorrow. I would merely beg you not to be too much bowed down by grief. What seem to us bitter trials are often blessings in disguise.

MISS PRISM

This seems to me a blessing of an extremely obvious kind.

(Enter CECILY from the house.)

CECILY

Uncle Jack! Oh, I am pleased to see you back. But what horrid clothes you have on! Do go and change them.

MISS PRISM

Cecily!

CHASUBLE

My child! my child!

(CECILY goes toward JACK; he kisses her brow in a melancholy manner.)

CECILY

What is the matter, Uncle Jack? Do look happy! You look as if you had a toothache, and I have such a surprise for you. Who do you think is in the dining-room? Your brother!

JACK

Who?

CECILY

Your brother Ernest. He arrived about half an hour ago.

JACK

What nonsense! I haven't got a brother.

(II)

This is a fine example of the incongruity of situation which is involved in humor.

In *As You Like It* Rosalind and Orlando meet once at Court and immediately fall in love. When they meet for a second time it is in the Forest of Arden, and Rosalind is disguised as Ganymede, a boy. Orlando does not recognize her. Because he is disconsolate over his frustrated love for Rosalind, she promises to cure him of his love if he will practice the art of wooing Rosalind on her. When Orlando courts Ganymede half in jest, calling the youth "Rosalind," and not recognizing Ganymede to be indeed Rosalind, that is a scene of humor:

ROSALIND

Come, woo me, woo me; for now I am in a holiday humour, and like enough to consent:—What would you say to me now, an * I were your very very Rosalind?

ORLANDO

I would kiss before I spoke.

ROSALIND

Nay, you were better speak first; and when you were gravell'd for lack of matter, you might take occasion to kiss. Very good orators, when they are out, they will spit; and for lovers, lacking (God warn us!) matter, the cleanliest shift is to kiss.

ORLANDO

How if the kiss be denied?

* if.

ROSALIND

Then she puts you to entreaty, and there begins new matter.

ORLANDO

Who could be out, being before his beloved mistress?

ROSALIND

Marry, that should you, if I were your mistress: or I should think my honesty ranker than my wit.

ORLANDO

What, of my suit?

ROSALIND

Not out of your apparel, and yet out of your suit. Am not I your Rosalind?

ORLANDO

I take some joy to say you are because I would be talking of her.

ROSALIND

Well, in her person, I say—I will not have you.

ORLANDO

Then, in mine own person, I die.

ROSALIND

No, faith, die by attorney. The poor world is almost six thousand years old; and in all this time there was not any man died

in his own person, *videlicet*, in a love-cause. . . . Men have
died from time to time, and worms have eaten them, but not
for love. . . . But come. Now I will be your Rosalind in a
more coming-on disposition; and ask me what you will, I will
grant it.

ORLANDO

Then love me, Rosalind.

ROSALIND

Yes, faith will I, Fridays, and Saturdays, and all.

ORLANDO

And wilt thou have me?

ROSALIND

Ay, and twenty such!

(IV, i)

These passages all contain wit too. For example, Marion's
"Well, you sat somewhere. Where did you sit?" and "You look
like a—like a—Senator or something monumental like that";
Chasuble's "Charity, dear Miss Prism, charity! None of us are
perfect. I myself am peculiarly subject to draughts," and "In
Paris! I fear that hardly points to any very serious state of mind
at the last"; Rosalind's many *doubles ententes* on her being
Rosalind, her "Men have died from time to time, and worms have
eaten them, but not for love," and "Ay, and twenty such!"

Wit is a graceful and usually fetching adornment to comedy. (The exception is when wit is employed without charity to
human failings.) Indeed, it can find a place in any other kind of
play; *Hamlet* abounds in it. But the most ingenious wit cannot
exempt a comedy from being based upon situations which are
humorous. That is the trouble with a great many Restoration
comedies, which, because their plots are devoid of any interest
to a modern audience, seem to crackle like dry twigs after one

has read a half dozen of them, instead of flashing their merriment. *The Importance of Being Earnest* impresses one with its endless play of wit; but behind the scintillating lines lies a firm plot and a procession of very humorous situations.

We have stressed the fact that in tragedy the focus of all interest is the tragic hero; he is by necessity the central character of the plot, and his, also, is the climax. This is a requirement of no other kind of play. In comedy, plays between comedy and tragedy, melodrama, and farce, the focus of interest may or may not be the character central to the plot. Chekhov's masterpiece, *The Three Sisters*, has been the subject of a great deal of nonsensical comment because of the attempts of critics to decide which of the three sisters is the heroine. The truth is that all three sisters are equally the focus of interest, but not one of them is the central character. The plot in that play revolves about the machinations of their vulgar sister-in-law to dispossess them of everything they have in life, while they stand helplessly by, yearning for Moscow. The sister-in-law is the central character of the plot, though not the center of interest in the play; and the three sisters, so far as the plot is concerned, are (taken together) the second character.

In Behrman's high comedy *The Second Man*, Storey is the focus of interest, but he is not the central character (see pages 75–78). He is much more acted upon than acting (that is part of his character), and the central character in any play is always the doer of the action. The Proposition for this play is something like this:

> Condition of the action: Monica, infatuated with Storey and loved by Austin, tells the apparently unreceptive Storey that she is going to campaign him into marrying her. (Act I)
> Cause of the action: After she has allowed herself to become engaged to Austin, she tricks Storey into confessing that he does love her and succeeds in causing him to make advances to her. (Act II, scene i)
> Resulting action: Will Monica marry Storey? (Act II, scene ii, to end of play)
> Climax: Monica announces to Austin and Kendall that she is going to bear a child to Storey. (Act II, scene ii)

We have referred to the scarcity of tragedies in our time.

As much might be said recently for the scarcity of comedies as well.* Is the scarcity of comedy due to the fact that the history of the last few decades has been such a tale of nightmare and horror that we have forgotten how to laugh freely? [39]

BETWEEN TRAGEDY AND COMEDY

Since the late 1930's people old enough to remember and to think have been living in an atmosphere of unremitting tension. There has always been either a major war or the threat of one in the air. We have been forced to digest as realities the incredible atrocities of genocide; ovens into which thousands of human beings were thrust; concentration camps whose function has been to degrade and dehumanize men, women, and children; countries overrun without warning by foreign powers who machine-gun liberty out of existence. We have been threatened by the extermination of everything which gives meaning to life. We are threatened now with the annihilation of humanity itself. It becomes understandable that playwrights might feel either ashamed to indulge the comic spirit or else unequal to embrace it.

Nevertheless, viewed in perspective, our times might be said to need more than ever a blossoming of that same comic spirit.

> *O Laughter! beauty plumped and love had birth.*
> *Laughter! O thou reviver of sick Earth!*
> *Good for the spirit, good*
> *For body, thou! to both art wine and bread!*

* Earlier in the century this was not the case. Shaw gave us *Pygmalion* and *The Doctor's Dilemma;* Barrie, *The Admirable Crichton, Alice-Sit-by-the-Fire, The Twelve Pound Look,* and *Dear Brutus;* Houghton, *Hindle Wakes;* Maugham, *The Circle, Our Betters,* and *The Constant Wife;* Munro, *At Mrs. Beam's;* Milne, *The Truth about Blayds;* Coward, *Private Lives, Hayfever,* and *Design for Living;* Priestley, *Laburnum Grove;* Kelly, *The Show-Off;* Howard, *They Knew What They Wanted;* Kaufman and Connelly, *Beggar on Horseback;* Kaufman and Lardner, *June Moon;* Kaufman and Hart, *Once in a Lifetime, You Can't Take It with You,* and *The Man Who Came to Dinner;* Behrman, *The Second Man, Biography, No Time for Comedy, End of Summer,* and *Amphitryon;* Barry, *Holiday* and *The Philadelphia Story;* Thurber and Nugent, *The Male Animal;* Van Druten, *Old Acquaintance* and *The Voice of the Turtle;* Chase, *Harvey;* Kanin, *Born Yesterday.* But it would be impossible to make such an impressive list for the English-speaking stage of the last two decades.

It may be a kind of integrity which forces some writers to compose plays which leave us depressed, in such times as ours. But it must also be conceded that it takes more courage to write comedy today—courage, and a belief that our tottering world does have a future. Does one not owe it to humanity to keep such a belief—in the teeth of whatever incentives to pessimism?

At any rate, few playwrights have been writing tragedies, few have been writing comedies, in the last decades. Rather than either, a kind of play between the two has been the most representative in our times (discounting a current frenzy for musical comedies).

Such a play maintains a tone of seriousness throughout—interspersed though it may be with moments of comedy. It does not, however, like tragedy, leave us with chastened emotions, though often during the course of its action the audience experiences feelings akin to those evoked by various episodes in a tragedy. The difference from tragedy lies in the total effect—the absence of any purgation for the audience. The majority of plays written in the last decades has been of this species, and many of them have been excellent.*

Not being tragedies, such plays do not have tragic heroes. Again, the focus of interest may or may not be the central character of the plot. In Ervine's *John Ferguson* the interest centers on the old man who gives the title to the play; as far as the plot is concerned, he stands almost outside of it, like a sensitive onlooker; the central character of the plot, a minor source of in-

* For example, Galsworthy's *Justice* and *Loyalties;* Maugham's *For Services Rendered;* Dane's *A Bill of Divorcement;* Sherriff's *Journey's End;* Rattigan's *The Winslow Boy;* Eliot's *The Cocktail Party;* Morley and Langley's *Edward My Son;* Ervine's *John Ferguson;* O'Casey's *Juno and the Paycock* and *The Plough and the Stars;* Carroll's *Shadow and Substance;* O'Neill's one-acters *The Long Voyage Home, Ile, In the Zone, The Moon of the Caribbees,* and *Anna Christie, The Hairy Ape, The Iceman Cometh;* Behrman's *Meteor;* Rice's *Street Scene;* Kelly's *Craig's Wife;* Anderson's *Saturday's Children;* Green's *The House of Connelly;* Kingsley's *Dead End* and *Detective Story;* Hellman's *The Children's Hour, The Little Foxes,* and *Toys in the Attic;* Odets' *Awake and Sing;* Williams' *The Glass Menagerie, A Streetcar Named Desire, Summer and Smoke,* and *Cat on a Hot Tin Roof;* Heggen and Logan's *Mister Roberts;* Patrick's *The Hasty Heart;* Inge's *Come Back Little Sheba, Picnic* and *The Dark at the Top of the Stairs;* Wishengrad's *The Rope Dancers;* Shaffer's *Five Finger Exercise.*

terest, is his son. In O'Casey's masterful *The Plough and the Stars* there is such a great number of interesting people and situations that it is almost impossible to choose among them; but the central character of the plot is Bessie. In O'Neill's *In the Zone* (see pages 173–77), it is with Smitty that we sympathize; but he is entirely acted upon, and although Driscoll is not any more interesting than the other men, it is Driscoll who is the central character of the plot. Of course, in this kind of play it is entirely possible for the focus of interest to be the central character of the plot, too—as in Behrman's exciting study of the Napoleon complex, *Meteor.*

This kind of play between tragedy and comedy has not yet been given a satisfactory name. Many such plays (for example, *A Doll's House* and *Craig's Wife*) have been thought of justly enough as "problem plays"; but the name will not do as a general classification, since many other of these plays do not really deal with social problems as such (for example, *The Plough and the Stars* and *Anna Christie*). In an earlier work * the present writer, forced by the nature of what he was writing to find a name for this species of play, used the term "play of grave experience" as a designation. But he is by no means pleased with the appellation, thought it at the moment of conception too clumsy, and has little expectation or desire that it find currency. He suggests it again now, simply as a convenient handle, as a stopgap, until someone think up something better.[40]

MELODRAMA AND FARCE

Melodrama and farce have this in common, that both aim, in some degree, to shock the audience, to provide some sort of thrill.

Melodrama sets out to play upon the nerves by using the sensational and the unexpected. The type is familiar in the numerous examples of the "play of suspense"—murder or detective plays, or what are loosely called "thrillers." Some modern examples of these have been Stoker's *Dracula*, Christie's *Witness for the Prosecution*. But, in a technical sense, the term "melodrama" must not be construed as in any way derogatory. One

* B. Grebanier and S. Reiter, *Introduction to Imaginative Literature* (New York, 1960), pp. 209–11.

of the most thoughtful plays of the century, Pirandello's *Six Characters in Search of an Author*, is technically a melodrama. Melodrama has sometimes been used as a good vehicle for psychological insight, as in Hamilton's *Angel Street* (called originally *Gaslight*) or Emlyn Williams' *Night Must Fall*—both of them thrillers, too.

Farce sets out to shock us by any device it can summon to provoke laughter, the chief one being, of course, the unexpected. Often farce has no further objective than to divert and amuse— for example, Wilder's *The Matchmaker*. In the movies the Marx Brothers made a career out of such works. Such plays certainly require no apology; they claim no more than to provide an evening's entertainment, and that surely asks for no extenuation. Joseph Kesserling's *Arsenic and Old Lace* is a hilarious cross of melodrama with farce, and is thoroughly diverting. The chief concern the writer of such farces need have is not to yield to the temptation of steeping the play in vulgarity—which is the characteristic sin of this type. On the other hand, the term "farce" in a technical sense is no more derogatory than "melodrama." *The Importance of Being Earnest* might well be the envy of any writer of high comedy for its elegance and bubbling good spirits; Anatole France's *The Man Who Married a Dumb Wife* is a timeless satire on the medical and legal professions; and Wilder's *The Skin of Our Teeth* is a play of the noblest conception and idealism—and all are technically farces.

Melodrama and farce alike trouble themselves little about dramatic construction. Nobody is expected to take the story seriously, and the plot is usually loosely put together. Their business is to keep things moving, as diverting or thrilling situation follows diverting or thrilling situation—no matter how inconsequentially strung on the thread of plot.[41]

IDENTIFICATION

The hero of a tragedy must be such, we have said, as enables the individual member of the audience to identify himself with him; he is, of course, also the central character of the plot. This is not necessarily the case, we have also said, with the central character of a comedy, play of grave experience, farce, or melodrama. The central character of any of these types of plays may very well be a person whom we dislike or detest or disapprove of—for example, Hedda in *Hedda Gabler*, Gregers in *The Wild Duck*, Raphael Lord in *Meteor*. Satirical plays often pillory the central character.

But it is also true that *in any satisfactory play there must be at least one character for whom the audience has sympathy*. It is part of the experience of witnessing a play that the audience should take sides with one character or one group of characters against another character or group of characters. In a tragedy it is usual to take sides with the hero against his enemies or the people working against him.* But in other kinds of plays we may or may not take sides with the central character. If we take sides against him, as in *The Wild Duck, Hedda Gabler, The Three Sisters*, and *Meteor*, there must always be someone for whom we are cheering: Thea and (to a certain degree) Lovborg in *Hedda Gabler;* Gina and Hedvig in *The Wild Duck;* the three sisters in *The Three Sisters;* Ann, Doug, and Dr. Avery in *Meteor*.

Many people have confessed to a distaste for Jonson's *Volpone*, as mordant as its satire is. Their reaction is understandable, for there is no one in *Volpone* whom one can like.† *A play in which there is no one for whom one would give a row of pins cannot sustain the interest of an audience.* Shakespeare never painted a darker picture of the world than the one he presented in *Measure for Measure;* the earth seems creeping with putrescence in that vitriolic work. Nevertheless, in the midst of the blackness of the scene, he planted one of his most radiant and magnificent women, Isabella—a kind of Joan of Arc of integrity. Her presence in the play redeems the world, and

* *Macbeth* is the grand exception. By the witchery of his art, Shakespeare manages to hold our sympathy for his murderer-hero until the end, even while we "disapprove" of what Macbeth is doing. And while we wish well to Macbeth's foes, we at the same time cannot rejoice at Macbeth's fall—because somehow the dramatist has made him a true tragic hero. This play is almost unique in this double feeling evoked in the audience.

† Brilliant actors have been known to improve on their material—just as they as frequently will deliberately assassinate it. We once witnessed a performance of *Volpone* in which the actor impersonating Volpone managed by some dexterity to convey the conviction that everything he was doing was being done only out of a sense of fun; that made it possible to like him, and for the first and only time in our experience we found we could take sides in that play.

makes it possible for the audience to identify with her against all the villainy going on about her.

Sophisticates and cynics, take note! No one but a misanthrope wishes to leave the theater utterly detesting the human race.

CHAPTER TWELVE

~~~~~~~~~~~~~~~~~~~~~~~~~~~~~~~~~~~~~

Other Techniques

Everybody's doing it. Doing what?   Popular Song

Wie machen wir's, dass alles frisch und neu
Und mit Bedeutung auch gefällig sei? *   GOETHE, *Faust: Vorspiel*

Ex Africa semper aliquid novi.†
                           PLINY THE ELDER, *Historia Naturalis*, VIII

What is valuable is not new, and what is new is not valuable.
                                                    D. WEBSTER

For every man the world is as fresh as it was at the first day, and as
full of untold novelties for him who has the eyes to see them.
                                    T. HUXLEY, *A Liberal Education*

Dramatic form has always been conditioned by the physical circumstances under which plays have been given.

PHYSICAL ASPECTS OF THE STAGE

It is true, of course, that Greek drama owed its origins to the choruses sung by Dionysiac celebrants. Inevitably, when the first theater was built at Athens, it was conceived as a place where the Chorus might sing and execute its stylized dances. But once the Greek theater took the physical form it did, with an amphitheatrical shape, an arena for the Chorus to dance in, a façade with columns to represent the setting of a palace or temple —the plays written by the Greek dramatists were in a form more

* How shall we plan that all be fresh and new—
  Important matter yet attractive too?
† Always something new out of Africa.

or less prescribed by the Greek theater itself. The succession of dramatic scenes was always separated by passages for the Chorus, and the play was presented in this way without any thought of intermissions between scenes. Such a theater has little in common with the indoor theater with which moderns are most familiar, with its boxed-in stage, its representational scenery, its footlights and lighting effects, its audience obscured from the actors' vision. It is not surprising that some of the most successful performances of the Greek classics have been those given outdoors during the daytime in a setting somewhat approximating the Greek theater's acting conditions.

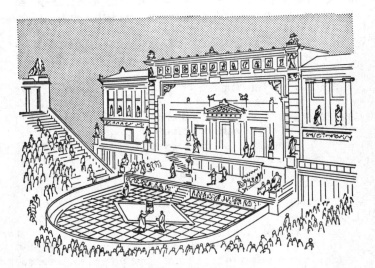

Conjectured reconstruction of the Theater of Dionysus at Athens, where the great Greek tragedies were produced.

In the Middle Ages drama began anew in the churches, then moved outside of the church building, and from there to market places. In its next development in England, plays were in the hands of the guilds, each of which, in certain towns, became responsible for presenting a different play on Corpus Christi Day. The audience would be stationed in various locales in the town, waiting for the succession of plays to arrive. These were mounted on large wagons, each wagon with its own little play, while the audience stood about the wagon watching the performance. That play finished, the wagon was drawn off to another square for another audience, while the next drama in the prearranged order of dramas was carted into the square left vacant. The conditions under which these miniature plays were offered invited a close relationship with the audience: on occasion the actor would descend from the wagon and continue his role among the audience—as when a Herod would come among the children, probably to make them squeal with delight at his hideous faces and threatening gestures. Such conditions also invited both realistic touches and down-to-earth comic effects; the medieval plays of England, despite the sacredness of their subject matter, sometimes contain both—for example, *The Second Shepherds' Play*.

In Elizabethan England drama became the most popular form of literary entertainment. Most of the thousands of plays which were written between the opening of the first theater (just outside London) in 1576 and the closing of the last of them, the Globe, in 1642, were performed in playhouses of similar design. The typical Elizabethan theater was a crude affair, not much more than an enclosed yard; its platform stage protruded into a space exposed to the mercy of the elements—the area where much of the audience stood about in no great comfort. Performances were given in the daytime. At the rear of the stage proper were exits on each side; the center back stage gave on to a slightly elevated "inner stage," which was normally concealed when not in requisition; above the stage proper was a balcony. There was no curtain to cut off the stage proper from the audience; there were, of course, no footlights, no scenery worth mentioning, no lighting effects. The inner stage was used for a number of purposes: it was the regular place for overhearing (for example, for Benedick, for Beatrice, for Othello, for Polonius, for Polonius and the King); when some basic furniture was required, such as thrones or beds—there is an almost total absence of deathbed scenes in Elizabethan drama—the pieces could be arranged in advance behind the curtain cutting off the inner stage, and at the appropriate moment the curtain could be opened to make the inner stage part of the scene; it served also for places

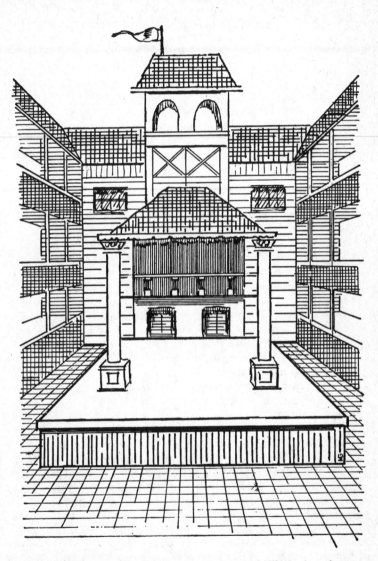

Reconstruction of the Fortune theater, a typical Elizabethan theater.
This theater seems to have had a curtained balcony, however, in lieu
of the characteristic curtained inner stage.

like caves (*The Tempest, King Lear*). The balcony was used to represent any kind of elevation: a balcony (*Romeo and Juliet*); an upper apartment (*The Comedy of Errors, Othello*); the walls of a town (*Henry V*).

Elizabethan playwrights conceived their dramas very much in terms of the peculiarities of the Elizabethan theater. Because of the apron and the fact that the audience stood about it in the same light as that of the stage, the soliloquy became a simple and natural enough device for communicating private information to the audience. An actor had only to move to the front of the apron and talk directly to the men standing just below him as if taking them into his confidence; at the end of the soliloquy he had but to take a few steps back to resume the action of the play. On our modern boxed-in stage, framed by footlights, the soliloquy is always an embarrassment, for the actor, instead of confiding in people standing about, is compelled to deliver his solo reflections into a black void.

Since there was no curtain that could cut off the stage from the audience, there was no way of separating scene from scene so that the audience might prepare itself for a change of locale or a lapse of time. To meet that expedient, Shakespeare employed the so-called "separation scene," a short scene between two longer ones and in which nothing much occurs, but which gives space between what has occurred and what is to follow, so that a lapse of time or change of place can be felt by the audience (*Romeo and Juliet*, IV, iv; *Othello*, III, ii). Had Shakespeare had available the modern curtain he would never have written most of those scenes.

The absence of a curtain also posed a problem in every tragedy, for Elizabethan tastes stipulated for a number of deaths in tragedy. What to do about characters killed onstage? For instance, at the end of *Hamlet* there are four corpses. With no curtain to bring down at the last line of the play, Shakespeare hit on the expedient of bringing in Fortinbras and his men to convey the bodies off.*

---

* This must unquestionably have been the necessity which mothered the invention. But Shakespeare, like all great artists, made much virtue out of the necessity: the last minutes of the tragedy are superb. Since the audience must be left not devastated by Hamlet's death, he employed Fortinbras' dialogue with Horatio at the conclusion for high poetic purposes, which were to make the *katharsis* complete.

Because there was no scenery, the Elizabethan dramatist seems often not to have asked himself whether any given scene was taking place in a particular room or street. There was no reason why he should have. All those bracketed descriptions like "a room of the castle," or "the garden," or "a street," which one finds in all editions of Shakespeare, are the additions of editors. Sometimes a close attention to what occurs in a given scene will reveal that the editorial designation is unacceptable—as in the case when the succession of people who appear in that scene could not all have made their way into "a room of the castle." The truth is that Shakespeare often was totally unconcerned about where the scene was taking place: he was simply bringing together on his stage a group of people, and it had nothing to do with the point of the scene whether they were meeting within four walls or out in the open. This tendency not to be tied down to a room, a street, or a field, operates toward giving these plays a certain spaciousness and timelessness.*

With the introduction of scenery, plays began to concern themselves more and more with the place in which scenes were laid. Many plays emphasize far too much the crossing from one chair to another, the going to fetch a cocktail, the rising and the sitting—as though this superficial and generally unmeaningful movement could atone for a lack of meaningful action in the dialogue. There have indeed been some twentieth-century dramatists who seem to feel that an audience's attention can be riveted by an endless series of entrances and exits for a glass of water, for a ringing doorbell, for attention to matters in the kitchen, and so on. A very little bit of such movement goes a long way in a drama.

Because in Shakespeare's time there was no curtain to separate scenes, scene followed scene without intermission. The Elizabethan stage had the advantage—which is lost in modern theaters, where intermissions are a sacred institution—of allowing the plays to proceed with great speed and accumulation of power. For the same reason, since there was no scenery to change, there was no reason why there should not be a multiplicity of

* On the rare occasions when it is important that the audience know precisely where a scene is set, Shakespeare makes that brilliantly clear (for example, *Romeo and Juliet*, ii, ii; the forest scenes in *As You Like It*; the storm scenes in *King Lear*).

scenes in any given act. (When the inner stage was needed, no time was wasted, for all that had to be done was to open the inner-stage curtain, and at the conclusion of that scene close it again.) A play like *Antony and Cleopatra* gains by the sense of its taking in the whole civilized world—made possible by the enormous number of individual scenes in that tragedy.

The presence of the audience in the same light as that on-stage, in full view (and sound!) of the actors, was, from our point of view, apparently a great inconvenience. Take the last scene in *The Merchant of Venice* as illustration. Jessica and Lorenzo enter upon what is supposed to be a moonlit garden. Think of what a Max Reinhardt kind of production could (and would) make of that! There could be a magnificent garden with the flowers laid out in parterres, with little walks, benches, and statuary; a huge willow tree might overshadow all, its branches gently swaying (through the operations of a wind machine off-stage); there could be a full radiant moon there to be seen, and, when the lovers come on, the moonlight could reflect on Jessica's hair and rebound with glints in Lorenzo's eyes. Someone could even be stationed offstage with a spray gun pumping Shalimar perfume into the air (courtesy of Guerlain & Cie.). How different from that was an Elizabethan production! There it was merely upon a bare wooden platform, without scenery, without moonlight, that the lovers entered in the unromantic light of a London afternoon. How was the dramatist to create the illusion he wished before an audience sharing the light of that London afternoon?

There was only one way to meet that challenge: to make the moonlight and the garden breathe in the lines:

LORENZO

The moon shines bright. In such a night as this,
When the sweet wind did gently kiss the trees
And they did make no noise. . . .

JESSICA

                    In such a night
Did Thisbe fearfully o'ertrip the dew,
And saw the lion' shadow ere himself. . . .

Already the stage is checkered with alternate moonlight and shadow! And presently Portia comes in, saying:

> That light we see is burning in my hall.
> How far that little candle throws his beams!
> So shines a good deed in a naughty world.

The Theatre Royal at Bristol, England—an exquisite eighteenth-century theater which is still thriving. Mrs. Siddons, Kean, and most of the great nineteenth-century actors performed on its boards. The theater is basically of the design which has been maintained in professional playhouses since then.

Even a London fog might be pierced by the radiance of such lines!

When the theater moved indoors in the late seventeenth century, lighting became necessary and scenery perhaps inevitable. By degrees the mechanical resources of the theater were developed. In our century electricity has made every kind of magic possible to the stage. As a result, the moonlight no longer

need be in the lines of a play; the dramatist can take care of it
in a stage direction. But such a stage direction is not really part
of the play; it is merely an order to the electrician. The temptation has been to succumb to the mechanical resources of the
theater, with a consequent impoverishment of the lines themselves.

It is familiar history that the Elizabethan age forms, with
the golden age of Athens, the great period of dramatic writing.
That bare wooden platform was an inconvenience, but it was
also a great challenge, and a dozen and a half great men rose to
meet that challenge with a dizzyingly large number of superb
plays. Is not the terrible decay of drama in the nineteenth century greatly due, among other things, to the development of the
mechanical resources of the theater? It is an equally familiar fact
that in our own time Hollywood, with the greatest mechanical
resources for making movies in the world, has been especially
remarkable for drowning the cinema plays in an excess of
stunning scenic effects; while France, Italy, England, and
Sweden, which have less to spend on productions, have preferred
to emphasize the cinema play instead of its settings. There is, of
course, no reason why drama cannot avail itself of the aid of
suitable scenery and lighting effects; but when the scenery and
the lighting effects take over at the expense of the play, drama
begins to die. The play must indeed be the thing.

In revulsion against some twentieth-century excesses, there
is a contemporary school of drama that would reduce scenery to
the minimum. It is probably true that for the presentation of a
really good play, all one truly requires is a large enough empty
space, good actors, and a good director.

Perhaps the most valuable development of the twentieth
century in the theater has been the wonderful resources now
available in lighting. Indeed, it has been proved that fine lighting
can stir an audience far more than can the most elaborate of
scenery. With superb lighting, scenery becomes nearly superfluous.

With the gradual elimination of sets and descending curtains,
lights and blackouts make it feasible to reintroduce the play with
a multiplicity of scenes, if the subject matter warrants it. Obviously, not all subject matters will. The drawing-room comedy,
for example, which most theater lovers will never willingly see

disappear, will always call for a form like the familiar three-acter, each act of a single scene or two scenes. But a play whose subject matter has considerable scope, written for a stage with only token scenery or none at all, might very well again be conceived in a multiplicity of scenes. The danger of this technique is that of making for a work which is too episodic, to the injury of the total effect. But the example of Elizabethan drama is enough proof that, under a controlling hand, this need not be the case. In our own time, expressionistic plays have often been written with a multiplicity of scenes.[42]

It should be superfluous to say that the three-act play, which we have throughout this work taken as the norm for the modern theater, is itself the product of the evolution of the boxed-in stage, and the physical conditions thereto appertaining.

NATURALISM

Realism, as we have implied, is a dramatic heritage that dates from the New Comedy of Menander; for no matter how artificial the plots of ancient comedy were, the characters were more or less ordinary people. This tradition of realism continues in the classical comedy of the great Molière and the dramatists following in his footsteps; moreover, the foibles of contemporary life are part of the content of classical comedy. With the development of a realistic approach in literature generally—especially in the field of the novel—during the nineteenth century, the situations presented in drama, as well as the characters, began to approach closer to the experiences of everyday life, without actually being "true to life." It must be admitted, however, that the realism of nineteenth-century drama was largely spurious.

The man who has been blamed for the tardiness of drama in going to everyday experience for its inspiration is Eugène Scribe (1791–1861), who provided a multitude of "well-made" plays for the delectation of middle-class Parisian society. The characters of his plays seemed to be everyday people, but the plots were highly artificial. As Mr. John Gassner has said of him, he "managed to create the illusion of reality on the stage with surface effects, and he taught a generation how to hold audiences with any kind of material. He did so by spinning out intrigues, by tangling up and then unwinding situations, and by producing discoveries and unexpected twists of circumstance. He turned playwriting into a virtuoso performance like tight-rope walking and sword-swallowing." * The plays of Scribe have nothing to say to us any longer. But one may pause to acknowledge the fact that he developed the "well-made" play to a form of high polish; Ibsen himself did not scorn to take over the mold from him, and for that alone Scribe deserves credit. Moreover, the concept that no play need be any the worse for perfection of form is one that has been taken very seriously by most of the major dramatists since Scribe.

But the very popularity of his superficial works was bound inevitably to cause a reaction. The strongest came from Émile Zola (1840–1902), the father of Naturalism in the novel.

Zola, deeply taken with Claude Bernard's *Introduction to the Study of Experimental Medicine* (1865), came to the unwarrantable conclusion that literature ought to enlist as a handmaid to science. This conviction was responsible for the long series of novels he wrote to document a deterministic theory of heredity and environment that science has by now discarded. Nor did he overlook the field of drama, in which he himself never achieved any success. In his *Naturalism in the Theater* (1881) he states his position:

> I am waiting for some writer to get rid of characters that are fictitious, of those symbols of good and evil which are worthless as human data. I am waiting to see environment determining the characters and the characters acting according to facts and the laws of their own disposition. . . . I am waiting for the hour when no more incredible stories will be told. . . . I am waiting, in short, until the Naturalism already victorious in the novel conquers the theater, and dramatists return to the source of science and the modern arts, to studying nature, to the anatomy of man, to painting life in exact reproduction. . . . The novel, because of its freedom of form, will continue to be the perfect tool of the century, perhaps; the stage must follow it. . . . The wonderful power of drama must not be overlooked. . . . No better vehicle for propaganda exists. . . . In Corneille's tragedies and Molière's comedies we find a pre-

* *From Ibsen to Eugene Ionesco* (New York, 1960), p. 4.

vailing analysis of character such as I deem necessary; plot is secondary and the work is a long treatise in dialogue on Man. But instead of an abstract man I wish to substitute a natural man, to place him in real surroundings, and to analyze all the physical and social causes which render him what he is. I believe, in brief, that the formula of the classics is a good one—provided that the scientific method is employed in studying society in the precise way that the science of chemistry is a study of compounds and their properties.

Before the nineteenth century had closed, Zola's own *Thérèse Raquin* was followed by a number of naturalistic plays: Henri Becque's *The Vultures* (1875) and *The Parisian Woman* (1885); De Porto-Riche's *A Loving Wife* (1891); De Curel's *The Fossils* (1893); Brieux's *The Three Daughters of Mr. Dupont* (1897); Strindberg's *The Father* (1887) and *Miss Julie* (1888); Hauptmann's *The Weavers* (1892) and *Drayman Henschel* (1898); Tolstoi's *The Power of Darkness* (1886).

Though the best naturalistic plays, such as *The Father*, show respect for form, the tendency of this school of playwriting has been toward formlessness. If, as the ideal is, the dramatist's eye is to be a camera, his ear a faithful dictaphone, the aesthetic principle of selection must be renounced—as the naturalistic novel, too, exhibits rather painfully. If the whole truth—that is, the truth in every one of its details—is to be recorded, the work must exhibit the shapelessness of life itself (as the novels of Theodore Dreiser). Yet, despite the boast of a scientific objectivity, Zola's novels and plays are not so objective after all. They are written from the premise that all human beings are no more or less than the product of heredity and environment—a premise that not even science would grant. Moreover, Zola was convinced that at bottom human nature is beastly, and that he undertook to prove; with that premise there must be many to take exception. It is sad to record that, however Zola's followers may have departed from some of his notions, the majority of naturalistic novels and plays emphasize the beastly in human nature—which can be only half the truth about the race—and are almost always overcast with an atmosphere of gloom—which can be only half the truth about the way life is lived. In them ideals and noble impulses are usually under suspicion, even though the dramatists themselves write usually out of compassion for the ills of humanity—a paradox, to say the least. In them no illusion or radiance is admitted either; the characters are usually drawn from the lower strata of society. Humor and wit usually do not live in the atmosphere of the naturalistic play.

The school has flourished in the twentieth century, and is with us still: for example, Strindberg's *The Dance of Death*, I and II; Hauptmann's *Rose Bernd* and *The Rats;* Brieux's *Damaged Goods;* Galsworthy's *Escape* and *Justice;* O'Neill's *Anna Christie;* Kingsley's *Detective Story;* Inge's *Come Back Little Sheba;* Gelber's *The Connection.* (There is some laughter in the O'Neill, Kingsley, and Inge plays.)

To the theory of Naturalism there are many valid objections. First of all, it is fairly ridiculous to attempt to enroll the arts as a subdivision of science along with chemistry, physics, geology, and the others. The methods of science must be those of analysis; the method of art can never be. The sciences must be based upon the facts, must proceed through an aggregation of the facts. The arts, being by their nature based upon certain agreed conventions (see Chapter One), cannot proceed that way at all. The arts and the sciences must be held as partners in the search for truth; each going its own road: the sciences by pursuit of analysis, the arts by pursuit of synthesis.

The objective of Naturalism of putting down all the factual details, however trivial, is not only a dull one; it is an impossible one. To record all that happens to an individual within but one day of his life would take a work of encyclopedic proportions. (Even Joyce's *Ulysses* had to be selective!) If, then, all the details can never be put down, why not omit all that is uninteresting? But to do that is to move away from Naturalism to Realism. The principle of selection is one that is imposed upon the arts by their very nature. That is why it would be fair to say that all the novels written by the Naturalists put together are less satisfying and less impressive than the single magnificent artistic achievement of Flaubert's realistic *Madame Bovary.*

If Naturalism is a contradiction in terms so far as the arts go, it is trebly so in the case of the theater. The very basis of success in the theater, powerful illusion, is a denial of all that Naturalism stands for. The very conditions under which plays must be given are equally a denial of the basis of Naturalism.

Mr. Walter Kerr examined all this very brilliantly in an essay on Gelber's *The Connection* (1960), a naturalistic play about dope addicts:

> Mr. Gelber . . . is aware that the promise of a shape that varies not at all from the actual shape of life is a fiction and perhaps a fraud. His solution is to admit to the fraud. . . . A presumed member of the management climbs onto the low platform to tell us, in garrulous fits and starts, that the actors are real [dope] addicts but that they are "improvising" a play for us. The "playwright" himself is drawn onto the stage, awkward and unhappy. Two photographers intrude. . . . Our attention is called, deliberately and repeatedly, to the presence of artifice, as though . . . it might now be killed by exposure to the light. Form is not concealed; it is mocked. Mr. Gelber would like, really, to laugh form out of existence, the better to get on with the real business of clocking, to the second, the shuffling, scratching, wearying "way it is." The naturalism itself would have satisfied the most resolute of Mr. Gelber's theatrical grandparents. Excellent actors suck their teeth, hide their trembling hands and eat pineapple with patient restraint. The language studiously avoids any attempt at literature. (On open ing a boil on the side of one man's neck, another faithfully asks, "What is all that green stuff, man?") Because these men listen to jazz while they wait, we listen to jazz while they wait—four or five times an act for four or five minutes at a time. . . . The naturalism comes off about as well as it always has in good hands: that is to say, it is impressive and unsatisfying. . . . I have a feeling that the distrust of art, because art may distort the truth, may in the end leave us with very little to hold in our hands.*

We feel that this is a perfect statement of the case against Naturalism in the theater.

* Walter Kerr on *"The Connection*—The Living End," New York *Herald Tribune*, June 5, 1960.

SYMBOLISM

The evil concomitant to the unflagging honesty of dramatists of the school of Naturalism has been a prosiness and dreariness antithetical to the theater and its world of magical illusion. The strongest influence operating against the flat-footedness of Naturalism in the theater has been Symbolism.

There is no word which has been more carelessly bandied about than the word "symbolism." Critical works, textbooks, lecturers use it frequently and glibly without defining it; young people follow suit. One suspects from the way it is used that very few have ever bothered to inquire what that impressive-sounding term actually signifies. Dictionary definitions are equally evasive. *The Century Dictionary*, a noble work, defines it as "the investing of things with a symbolic meaning or character; the use of symbols," and defines "symbol" as "an object, animate or inanimate, standing for or representing something moral or intellectual; anything which typifies an idea or quality; a representation; a figure; an emblem; a type." *Webster* is even looser in its definition of "symbol": "That which suggests something else by reason of relationship, association, convention." This would make every instance of figurative language a symbol, of course. When Shelley calls the clouds "Angels of rain and lightning!" he is using "that which suggests something else by reason of relationship, association." In the same way Keats may be said to be using a symbol when he calls the Grecian urn a "foster-child of silence and slow time," and "sylvan historian." But neither Shelley nor Keats was a Symbolist. Stendhal's novel *The Red and the Black* assuredly uses symbols for its title: red for the military, black for the clergy; but in the book itself there is no Symbolism.

We ask to be pardoned if we insist on clarifying this matter. A symbol is indeed something used to represent or stand for something else. The lion is a conventional symbol of courage; the scepter of power; the Cross of Christianity. In language a symbol suggests or portrays the thing signified by the associations of experience. The writer, however, has little use for such symbols as the three above, for, being public, they can too easily make for triteness. An author, wishing to intensify the meaning of his lines, will invent for a particular work the symbol or symbols which will be of significance to the meaning of that work. This is the case with Stendhal's title. By using "red" to symbolize the military, he evoked the color of the soldier's uniform, the blood that must be shed, and the courage required; by "black" he evoked the priestly garb, and the gravity and solemnity of the clergy.

In Enid Bagnold's admirable play *The Chalk Garden*, the title is again a literary symbol: in that drama Mrs. St. Maugham is a woman of general benevolence but arid heart; her good intentions are vain, for her inability to love anybody or anything makes her benevolence an unnourishing garden in which nothing can thrive. The symbol is further strengthened when Madrigal, the governess, exclaims impatiently: "You have not a green thumb, Mrs. St. Maugham."

The titles of *The Wild Duck* and *Ghosts* are both symbolic.

Now, the presence of a symbol does not constitute Symbolism in a work. Nor does the fact that a work is allegorical—this is perhaps the most usual confusion—make it a work of Symbolism. Symbolism is to be found in the tissue of the writing itself.

When a literary symbol recurs or persists in a work, the author is using symbolism as a device to deepen the imaginative meaning. Symbolism became a literary movement in France, home of artistic movements, in the late nineteenth century. But there was nothing essentially new in the method beyond the emphasis placed upon the importance of the symbolism, and the tendency to have the meaning of the work lie chiefly in the symbols.

Few works exhibit more brilliantly the use of symbolism than *Romeo and Juliet*. From their first encounter, the lovers speak of each other in images of light and radiance against a background of darkness, and they continue to do so throughout the play. When Romeo first sees Juliet he murmurs:

> Oh, she doth teach the torches to burn bright!
> It seems she hangs upon the cheek of night
> Like a rich jewel in an Ethiop's ear . . .
> So shows a snowy dove trooping with crows.

(I, v)

Shortly after, in the balcony scene, he cries, as he looks up from
the garden:

ROMEO

But soft! What light from yonder window breaks?
It is the east, and Juliet is the sun!
Arise, fair sun. . . .
Two of the fairest stars in all the heaven,
Having some business, do entreat her eyes
To twinkle in their spheres till they return.
What if her eyes were there, they in her head?
The brightness of her cheek would shame those stars
As daylight doth a lamp; her eyes in heaven
Would through the airy region stream so bright
That birds would sing and think it were not night. . . .

JULIET

What man art thou, thus bescreen'd in night,
So stumblest on my counsel? . . .
I would not for the world they saw thee here.

ROMEO

I have night's cloak to hide me from their sight. . . .

JULIET

Thou knowest the mask of night is on my face;
Else would a maiden blush bepaint my cheek . . .
                . . . therefore pardon me,
And not impute this yielding to light love,
Which the dark night hath so discovered.

ROMEO

Lady, by yonder blessed moon I swear,
That tips with silver all these fruit-tree tops—

JULIET

. . . Although I joy in thee,
I have no joy of this contract to-night.
It is too rash, too unadvis'd, too sudden;
Too like the lightning, which doth cease to be
Ere one can say it lightens.

(II, ii)

Again, Juliet says, while waiting impatiently for the Nurse's return from her embassy to Romeo:

Love's heralds should be thoughts,
Which ten times faster glide than the sun's beams,
Driving back shadows over lowering hills.

(II, v)

After the lovers have been secretly married, Juliet, anticipating Romeo's coming to consummate their union, murmurs:

Come, night, come, Romeo, come, thou day in night,
For thou wilt lie upon the wings of night
Whiter than new snow on a raven's back.
Come, gentle night, come, loving, black browed night,
Give me my Romeo; and when he shall die,
Take him and cut him out in little stars,
And he will make the face of heaven so fine
That all the world will be in love with night
And pay no worship to the garish sun.

(III, ii)

In Friar Laurence's cell, Romeo cries:

More honourable state, more courtship lives
In carrion-flies than Romeo: they may seize
On the white wonder of dear Juliet's hand. . . .

(III, iii)

When Juliet begs Friar Laurence for help, she tells him that rather than be unfaithful to Romeo by marrying Paris:

. . . Bid me go into a new-made grave.
And hide me with a dead man in his shroud.

(iv, i)

And in the last scene, Romeo cries as he enters Juliet's tomb:

A grave? Oh, no, a lantern. . . .
For here lies Juliet, and her beauty makes
This vault a feasting presence full of light. . . .
How oft when men are at the point of death
Have they been merry! Which their keepers call
A lightning before death. Oh, how may I
Call this a lightning!

(v, iii)

The persistence of these contrasting images of light and dark rules out the possibility of their being there by accident. They are deliberately employed, and with great sagacity. For they are perfect for making us understand how Romeo and Juliet are all love in the midst of a life about them that is all hate.

Shakespeare makes frequent use of symbolism. In *Macbeth* we find recurrent the image of new or borrowed clothes. When Macbeth, after being greeted as Thane of Cawdor, stands transfixed by his thoughts:

BANQUO

Look, how our partner's rapt.
. . . New honours come upon him,
Like our strange garments, cleave not to their mould,
But with the aid of use.

(i, iii)

After Duncan's arrival at their castle, Macbeth justifies to Lady Macbeth his unwillingness to commit the murder:

MACBETH

I have bought
Golden opinions from all sorts of people,

Which would be worn now in their newest gloss,
Not cast aside so soon.

LADY MACBETH

Was the hope drunk
Wherein you dress'd yourself?

(I, vii)

Once this image has been interwoven in the work, even Lady
Macbeth's injunction to her husband after the murder cooperates
with it; her words have a plain and a symbolic meaning at one
and the same time:

Get on your nightgown, lest occasion call us,
And shew us to be watchers.

(II, ii)

So too do Banquo's words after the murder is discovered:

And when we have our naked frailties hid,
That suffer in exposure, let us meet.

(II, iii)

Macduff says to Ross, who is on his way to Scone, that he has
decided himself to return to Fife:

Well, may you see things well done there:—adieu—
Lest our old robes sit easier than our new!

(II, iv)

Macbeth, giving the Two Murderers reasons for killing Banquo,
concludes:

And I will put that business in your bosoms,
Whose execution takes your enemy off,
Grapples you to the heart and love of us,
Who wear our health but sickly in his life.

(III, i)

The cutting down of the boughs from the wood of Birnam to
camouflage the troops marching against Macbeth is also a con-

tinuation of the image (v, iv), as is the throwing away of the boughs before Macbeth's castle:

MALCOLM

Now near enough: your leafy screens throw down,
And shew like those you are.

(v, vi)

The image is perfect for Macbeth's dissembling, and his ambition to wear the royalty that does not belong to him.

In *Hamlet* there are, among other recurrent images, persistent images of corruption, disease, and decay:

HAMLET

How weary, stale, flat and unprofitable,
Seems to me all the uses of this world!
Fie on 't! oh fie! 'Tis an unweeded garden,
That grows to seed; things rank and gross in nature
Possess it merely.

(I, ii)

Hamlet speaks to Horatio of "some vicious mole [blemish] of nature" in a man which will so infect his virtues that they

Shall in the general censure take corruption
From that particular fault. The dram of eale *
Doth all the noble substance often dout † . . .

(I, iv)

Marcellus almost gives voice to the significance of this recurrent image in his celebrated line:

Something is rotten in the state of Denmark.

(I, iv)

The image is fortified by the Ghost's description of the late king's death:

* evil.   † put out.

Upon my secure hour thy uncle stole,
With juice of cursed hebenon in a vial,
And in the porches of mine ears did pour
The leperous distilment; whose effect
Holds such an enmity with blood of man
That swift as quicksilver it courses through
The natural gates and alleys of the body,
And with a sudden vigour it doth posset *
And curd, like eager † droppings into milk,
The thin and wholesome blood. So did it mine,
And a most instant tetter bark'd ** about,
Most lazar-like, with vile and loathsome crust,
All my smooth body.

(I, v)

When Polonius accosts Hamlet to test his sanity, there is the Prince's brilliant quip:

HAMLET

For if the sun breed maggots in a dead dog, being a good kissing carrion— Have you a daughter?

POLONIUS

I have, my lord.

HAMLET

Let her not walk i' the sun. Conception is a blessing, but not as your daughter may conceive.

(II, ii)

And a few minutes later he is describing to Polonius the contents of the book he is reading:

Slanders, sir; for the satirical slave says here that old men have grey beards, that their faces are wrinkled, their eyes purging

* curdle.   † vinegar.   ** encrusted as if with a bark.

thick amber or plum-tree gum, and that they have a plentiful
lack of wit together with weak hams.

(II, ii)

Soon Hamlet is telling Guildenstern and Rosencrantz that

this goodly frame, the earth, seems to me a sterile promontory,
this most excellent canopy, the air, look you, this brave o'er-
hanging firmament, this majestical roof fretted with golden
fire, why, it appears no other thing to me than a foul and pesti-
lent congregation of vapours.

(II, ii)

In the "To be or not to be" soliloquy he speaks of "the native hue
of resolution" being

. . . sicklied o'er with the pale cast of thought.

(III, i)

In his subsequent interview with Ophelia he says to her:

Get thee to a nunnery; why wouldst thou be a breeder of
sinners? . . . I could accuse myself of such things that it were
better my mother had not borne me. . . . What should such
fellows as I do crawling between heaven and earth? We are
arrant knaves all; believe none of us.

(III, i)

In his mother's closet the images of decay take on a violence, in
his accusations against her:

Such an act
That blurs the grace and blush of modesty,
Calls virtue hypocrite, takes off the rose
From the fair forehead of an innocent love
And sets a blister there. . . .
Here is your husband, like a mildew'd ear,
Blasting his wholesome brother. Have you eyes?
Could you on this fair mountain leave to feed,
And batten on this moor? . . .
. . . Nay, but to live

In the rank sweat of an enseamed * bed,
Stewed in corruption, honeying and making love
Over the nasty sty. . . .
Lay not that flattering unction † to your soul,
That not your trespass, but my madness speaks.
It will but skin and film the ulcerous place,
Whilst rank corruption, mining ** all within,
Infects unseen. . . .
. . . Do not spread the compost on the weeds,
To make them rank.

(III, iv)

In the next scene, the King takes up the image:

We would not understand what was most fit,
But, like the owner of a foul disease,
To keep it from divulging, let it feed
Even on the pith of life.

(IV, i)

And again:

>   Diseases desperate grown
> By desperate appliances are relieved.

(IV, iii)

Hamlet's answer to the King's question "Where is Polonius?" is:

Not where he eats, but where he is eaten. A certain convocation
of politic worms are e'en at him. Your worm is your only
emperor for diet. We fat all creatures else to fat us, and we fat
ourselves for maggots.

(IV, iii)

As Hamlet is shipped off to England, Claudius cries:

>   Do it, England;
> For like the hectic †† in my blood he rages.

(IV, iii)

* greasy.   † ointment.   ** undermining.   †† fever.

Hamlet, hearing of the intended exploits of Fortinbras' army, says:

> This is the imposthume * of much wealth and peace,
> That inward breaks, and shows no cause without
> Why the man dies.
>
> (IV, iv)

Alone, in his next soliloquy he remembers that God

>   gave us not
> That capability and god-like reason
> To fust † in us unused.
>
> (IV, iv)

The entire scene of the Gravediggers, of course, cooperates with the image, particularly such passages as the one in which the First Gravedigger gives his professional opinion:

HAMLET

How long will a man lie i' the earth ere he rot?

FIRST CLOWN

I' faith, if he be not rotten before he die—as we have many pocky corses now-a-days, that will scarce hold the laying in— he will last you some eight year or nine year. A tanner will last you nine year.

HAMLET

Why he more than another?

FIRST CLOWN

Why, sir, his hide is so tann'd with his trade that he will keep out water a great while, and your water is a sore decayer of your whoreson dead body.

> (V, i)

---

* abscess.   † grow moldy.

And presently Hamlet is saying to Yorick's skull:

> Now get you to my lady's chamber, and tell her, let her paint
> an inch thick, to this favour * she must come.

The image of corruption and disease is perfect for the play; it makes us feel that Hamlet is operating in a Denmark that is indeed sick from the evil murder and incestuous marriage by means of which Claudius ascended the throne.

In the later nineteenth century, under the influence of Baudelaire, Symbolism flourished in the works of the great poets Mallarmé, Verlaine, and Rimbaud. What is of moment to the present discussion is that Symbolism began to make important inroads into drama. It is particularly interesting that some of the greatest successes with the method will be found in the plays of the two greatest Realists of the nineteenth-century and early-twentieth-century dramatists, Ibsen and Chekhov. Their impulse to avail themselves of Symbolism is explicable. They understood very well that something was required to alleviate the drabness and prosiness of the Realism for which they stipulated in their great plays. Ibsen had already proved himself an important poet before he turned to the ways of Realism, and Chekhov always had poetic vision. The result is that the outstanding examples of Symbolism may be sought in the dramas of these two outstanding Realists—which, in any other medium than the theater, might very well be a paradox.

Ibsen's *The Wild Duck, Ghosts,* and *The Lady from the Sea* and Chekhov's *The Three Sisters* make brilliant use of Symbolism.[43] The titles of the Ibsen plays afford a clue to the ruling symbol. But it has generally been overlooked that Ibsen was never more the Symbolist than in *A Doll's House.* Let us examine some passages from the opening pages of that play.

When the curtain rises, Nora comes in carrying some packages and is accompanied by a porter. One of her first actions is to open her purse and ask the porter how much she owes him. He tells her.

NORA

Here's a crown. Never mind, keep the change.

* face.

In a few moments Helmer opens the door of his study.

HELMER

Has my little extravagant one been letting money fly away again?

NORA

Oh, surely, Torvald, we can afford to extend ourselves a bit. It's the first Christmas when we haven't needed to pinch our pennies.

HELMER

Now, now! We can't afford to throw money away.

NORA

Yes, yes, let's throw away a little bit, just the least little bit! You'll be earning lots of money soon, you know.

HELMER

Yes, beginning New Year's. But it will be a whole quarter of a year before I get my salary.

NORA

It doesn't matter. We can borrow before then.

HELMER

Nora! Still my little featherbrain! If I did borrow a thousand crowns today, and you let them fly through your fingers during the Christmas holidays, and suppose a tile broke from the roof and bashed my brains in—.

It will be noted that from this very opening of the play there is recurrent talk about money. This concern with money is the pervasive image projected into the body of the lines throughout the drama. A few lines further on:

HELMER

(Taking out his wallet.)

What do you suppose I've got here, Nora?

NORA

Money!

HELMER

There you are.

(He gives her some banknotes.)

Naturally I realize that all sorts of things must be bought for Christmas.

NORA

(Counting them.)

Ten, twenty, thirty, forty . . .

Nora proceeds to show him her purchases; noticing that she has omitted buying anything for herself, he asks her what he can give her as a present:

NORA

You could give me some money, Torvald. Just as much as you feel you can spare. . . .

HELMER

But, Nora—

NORA

Oh, please, Torvald, please! I could hang the money in the loveliest gold paper on the tree. Wouldn't it be fun!

HELMER

What's the name they have for the little birds that are always making money fly away?

NORA

I know—spendthrifts. But please, Torvald! . . .

HELMER

If you really would keep the money I gave you and spent it on yourself. . . .

We do not desire to quote the entire play. This talk about money continues for pages between Nora and her husband. When Christina Linden comes in, she talks about her husband's dying:

NORA

And he left you nothing?

MRS. LINDEN

Nothing.

Then Nora tells her about Helmer's good fortune:

NORA

It's wonderful to have loads of money, and no need to worry, isn't it?

MRS. LINDEN

Yes. It certainly must be wonderful to have everything you need.

NORA

Not only everything you need, but loads of money, loads!

Nora now speaks of her having done embroidery work to supplement Helmer's income.

NORA

He didn't have much hope of promotion, and he naturally had to make more money.

She speaks of Helmer's illness, and how they had to go to Italy for his health.

NORA

It was a marvelous, exciting trip! And it saved his life. But it cost an awful lot of money, Christina.

MRS. LINDEN

I should imagine.

NORA

Twelve hundred dollars! Four thousand eight hundred crowns! That's a lot of money, isn't it?

MRS. LINDEN

How fortunate you had the money to spend.

NORA

Father gave it to us. . . . We had the money, and the doctors said no time must be wasted.

Soon Nora is confessing that her father did not give her the
money:

NORA

Papa didn't give us a cent. It was I who found the money.

MRS. LINDEN

You? That much money?

NORA

Twelve hundred dollars. . . .

MRS. LINDEN

And your husband never learned from your father that the
money did not come from him? . . . My poor Nora. So it had
to come out of your pin-money.

NORA

Of course. The whole thing was really my doing. When Torvald gave me money for clothes and things like that, I always
spent only half. I always bought the cheapest things. . . . And
besides that I made money other ways. I was very lucky last
winter. I got a great deal of copying to do. . . . It was wonderful to work in that way and earn some money.

The image of money persists in their talk. When Krogstad comes
to see Nora alone later in the first act, the talk again centers
around money.

NORA

If my husband learns of it, he will naturally pay you off at
once. . . .

KROGSTAD

When your husband was ill, you came to me to borrow twelve hundred dollars.

NORA

I didn't know of anyone else.

KROGSTAD

I promised you to find the money—

NORA

And you did.

KROGSTAD

I promised you to find the money on certain conditions.

There are few plays in the world in which an image persists so completely as here—and we have examined only the first act. The appropriateness of the money symbol must be clear. The theme of the play is not, of course, about money (nor is it, as is always being said, about the independence of women either). The matter at issue in *A Doll's House* is the fundamental dishonesty—and hence, dishonorableness—of most marriages, built as they are upon lies and pretenses. Nora is as much to blame, in Ibsen's eyes, as Helmer; only, it is she who comes to realize that their marriage has no foundation—that the only possible basis for a decent marriage is mutual respect. But this issue comes to the light, to its crisis, and to its resolution because of money. That is why the symbol is perfect.

Now, it cannot be too strongly emphasized that *the prevailing image which makes for Symbolism must be used with subtlety*. After our analyses, it might appear that in these plays the recurrent figure on each appearance strikingly announces itself to the audience's attention, as though a bell were rung each time.

Nothing is further from the truth. A highly intelligent playgoer might hear *Romeo and Juliet*, *Macbeth*, *Hamlet*, and *A Doll's House* without ever being conscious of the prevailing image—which is as it should be. Symbolism exercises itself to attack the audience on the emotional level, not on a conscious rational level. It is intended to deliver its meaning with the immediacy of music —as an emotion charging the atmosphere, rather than an idea. Indeed, the analogy with music is perfect. The French Symbolists were enthusiastic Wagnerians (in a day when Wagner had yet to find wide acceptance). They were deeply impressed with Wagner's skillful use of the leitmotif. The average music lover is not expected, during the performances of the Ring Cycle, to identify each motif consciously, saying to himself: "Ah, that is Siegmund's motif, that Fricka's, that Alberich's," as they appear in their marvelous interweavings in the score. Unquestionably the student will get an added intellectual pleasure from learning to identify each; but that is not asked of the average attentive listener, for music addresses us without any intellectual intervention or it does not address us at all. The prevailing image, which is the method of Symbolism, is a kind of leitmotif, which we imbibe almost subconsciously. That is its power. The minute the prevailing image becomes obvious—as it does in Ibsen's *The Master Builder*, a play not equal to his best—the very reason for Symbolism is defeated and the results become fairly distasteful. Symbolism, when obvious, tends to degenerate into the allegorical.

About allegory, it may be said that it is palatable to a modern audience only when the story and the characters are interesting in themselves—that is, only when, if one chose, the allegory could be ignored. When the story and the characters become only machinery to illustrate the allegory, we seem to be in a Sunday school, not the theater. Andreyev's *The Life of Man* suffers from this obviousness; Sherwood's *The Petrified Forest*, on the other hand, suffers nothing from its allegorical intentions, for it is excellent drama first and last.

Following Ibsen's example in his masterpieces, a number of dramatists have employed Symbolism to a greater or less degree: for example, Hauptmann in *The Sunken Bell*; von Hofmannsthal in *Death and the Fool*; Werfel in *The Goat Song*; K. and J. Capek in *The World We Live In*; Maeterlinck in *The Intruder*,

The Blind, and *Pélléas and Mélisande;* Yeats in *Kathleen ni Houlihan;* Bagnold in *The Chalk Garden;* Williams in *Orpheus Descending.*

As for the prevailing image in a work of Symbolism, though the audience ought not be made too conscious of it, the dramatist, of course, must have it constantly in mind: he must not only know what it is but he must decide on the places in the work in which it is to appear. His first problem here is to find the perfect image for the needs of his play. If his play has a theme which has to do with revenge, he might find advantageous, to give a random example, the image of blood or of a trap.[44]

Symbolism, naturally, is not a requirement in drama. But the fact that the world's leading Realists have found it expedient to employ it, might very well serve as an argument that it is a highly effective counterpoise to the always imminent dreariness of stark realism.

Actually, Symbolism has never been as much of a movement in drama as it has in poetry. A poet like Mallarmé in effect discarded the rational meanings of words in favor of the suggestive power of imagery and music over the intuitive apprehensions. The nearest that Symbolism in drama ever came to going anything like that distance is in the plays of Maeterlinck, who at the height of his success was thought by some to have world-shaking genius. But today most of his plays seem unbearably attenuated, and their heavy moodiness and sometimes laughable understatement too much contrived. For the rest, Symbolism has been valuable to dramatists most when used in conjunction with other techniques.

EXPRESSIONISM

Besides Symbolism, the most important new movement to bring alteration of techniques to the theater has been Expressionism. The school blossomed particularly in the 1920's, with an occasional more recent revival of its mannerisms. But the movement really originated in the experiments of Strindberg and Wedekind, much earlier.

The writers of this school have accused Realism in the theater of presenting only the external world, of ignoring the inner conflicts of the mind and the states of the soul; they have also felt that the return to poetic values, which came in with Symbolism, did nothing to penetrate the inner man. The trouble with drama, they decided, was that it had always been based upon the premise that the individual knows what he desires and where he is headed. To them the important thing was the confusion, and often the chaos, which reigns in the individual's soul. The term "expressionism" itself is intended to describe the fact that *in these plays the subjective feelings of the important characters are given full play to express themselves in the action of the play*. The form for these plays was more or less set by Strindberg's *The Dream Play* (1902) and *The Spook Sonata* (1907), with their nightmarish air; and on the English-speaking stage by O'Neill's *The Emperor Jones* (1920) and *The Hairy Ape* (1922). They were composed of a succession of short scenes presented as a "whirl of fragmentary events." The objective world in which we live, according to the theory, is simply the creation of the subjective perception of the characters involved. Life is therefore represented in these plays in deliberate distortion, sometimes as being totally amorphous—according to the soul-state of the beholder. Strindberg tells us in the preface to *The Dream Play*, the prototype of the school, that he was attempting to reproduce "the disconnected but apparently logical form of a dream. Anything can happen; everything is possible and probable. Time and space do not exist." The pattern keeps on changing and is woven from "memories, experiences, unfettered fancies, absurdities, and improvisations. The characters are split, double, and multiply; they evaporate, crystallize, scatter, and converge." Unity exists here only in the dreamer's consciousness. He "neither condemns nor acquits, but only relates." *

Obviously, in such a play the concept of logical plot, and hence of a guiding Proposition, has no place. Events follow one another without sequence of cause and effect; people come and go as though they were uninvited spirits which have materialized. In *The Dream Play* a character is found to change his age from youth to old age without notice. The past of the Emperor Jones's race comes thronging to him in the guise of suddenly objectified persons. The only logic of an expressionistic play is the logic of the subconscious. Expressionists talked a great deal about the importance of the psychological in their work, but the remarks

* Translation by Elizabeth Sprigge.

were misleading. For by that they meant not the delving into the motivations of character, which has always been true of important drama, but rather an unrestrained exhibition of the quirks and instabilities of which the mind is capable. Generally, these plays show a character's progress, or, more usually, deterioration, through a series of events at many times and many places. Georg Kaiser's *From Morn to Midnight* (1916), one of the most impressive of the school, shows the movement at its best. It tells the story of the revolt of a bank cashier against his dull existence and of his futile attempts to find another kind of life. Elmer Rice's *The Adding Machine* (1923), which in its day made a great stir on the American stage, tells an analogous story. An interesting recent example is Ionesco's *Rhinoceros*.

Thus, expressionistic drama rather easily turned typically into a statement of protest against contemporary society and its depersonalizing influence: for example, K. Capek's *R.U.R.*; Kaiser's *Gas*, I and II; Toller's *Man and the Masses;* Williams' *Camino Real*. The distortions and deliberate exaggerations and absurdities were employed with success for the purposes of comedy in Kaufman and Connelly's riotous *Beggar on Horseback* and, more recently, in Chase's *Mrs. McThing*. Odets' *Waiting for Lefty* and Miller's *The Death of a Salesman*, though belonging to this school and maintaining the dreamlike atmosphere found in Strindberg, are not given to the extreme distortions of their predecessors and are closer to Realism.

Because of the unreal atmosphere permeating expressionistic drama, it has always leaned heavily on scenery and lights, and a considerable amount of physical movement in the action, distorted to reflect emotional distortions. The use of symbols (not necessarily repeated as in Symbolism) has been standard in these plays. The school must be pronounced now as rather passé. It was interesting as experiment, but its faults were the very depersonalization it so studiously cultivated and something approaching hysteria in the tone of the play. Whatever value may attach to depersonalization of the characters, in the theater, as we have seen, it is imperative that the audience be able to identify with at least one character in a drama. It is asking the impossible for such identification to take place when the characters onstage have ceased being individuals. Expressionistic plays, too, are distracting in their alternation of moods, their proneness to noise and violence. Worst of all, there developed a sense of sameness about the various plays of the school. After a while they all seemed to be saying the same thing.

There is, of course, no reason why a dramatist should not try his hand at this kind of play. They do not seem very hard to write after one has mastered the more conventional three-acter, since they follow no law but that of free association. But it is worthy of note that before Strindberg invented the type, he had written *The Father* and a number of other well-knit plays; and that O'Neill, before *The Emperor Jones*, had behind him a number of powerfully constructed works: his group of admirable one-acters and the fine full-length play *Beyond the Horizon*. It is wiser to depart from tradition into such fields as Expressionism (where there is not much ground under one as he makes his way) only after he is sure of his control of what is traditional in form.* Then, if one chooses to break with tradition, one knows just where one is departing and why. Those who refuse to take this advice can never be free of the suspicion within themselves that all they have chosen is an easier way.

* Williams' *The Glass Menagere*, while not totally expressionistic, uses some expressionistic techniques with great success.

CHAPTER THIRTEEN

~~~~~~~~~~~~~~~~~~~~~~~~~~~~~~~

Subplots;
Secondary Characters

This is the poynt, to speken short and pleyn,
That ech of yow, to shorte with your weye,
In this viage, shall tellen tales tweye.

Prologue to *The Canterbury Tales*

In his narrative a due subordination is observed: some transactions are
prominent; others retire.   MACAULAY, *History*

A water was them by-twene,
And a brig all ouer it clene.   *The Holy Rood*

But ah! who can have too much of a good thing?

EBIRGENÄR, *Hamletje*

Enough is enough!   GRANRIEEB, *Punjabi Table-Talk*

The classic tradition in tragedy has always been averse to
the use of subplots. The intensity which is the great quality of
classical tragedy could only be dissipated by the intrusion of a
second story. The plays of the great Greek tragedians and those
of their greatest successor, Racine, are at one in this. The only
instance where Shakespeare comes close to the same practice is
in *Othello*, the most intense of his plays.

The tendency is the same in classical comedy, though less
stringently so. The comedies of Molière, for example, have sometimes embryonic subplots.

In England taste, from the beginnings of the theater, was less
for intensity than for scope. Part of that feeling of breadth which
one senses in Elizabethan drama comes from the playwrights'

addiction to multiple plots. Of this, Shakespeare is almost every-where representative. An extreme case is *The Merchant of Venice*, which has five distinct threads of story: the Antonio-Shylock-Portia story, the story of the wooing of Portia, the Jessica-Lorenzo story, the Gratiano-Nerissa story, and the story of the fortunes of Launcelot Gobbo. One of these is near the tragic, one of them is highly romantic, one of them is highly lyrical, one of them is comic, and the last belongs to low comedy; yet all five not only are so brilliantly interwoven that they are mutually interdependent, but they are also so wonderfully under control that they all interfuse into the tone of high comedy.

What Shakespeare has done in that play (though for most writers four subplots are three too many) might well stand as an exemplar for all dramatists. The plots run concurrently, but they also are intertwined. The story of the wooing of Portia is made to interweave with the main plot: it is because Bassanio wins Portia that she becomes Antonio's savior. The Jessica-Lorenzo story is interwoven with both the Shylock story and the Portia story. The Gratiano-Nerissa story is made dependent on the Bassanio-Portia story. And Launcelot Gobbo's fortunes involve him with every one of the other stories. This is unity (unity, indeed, through diversity, but unity just the same) in the highest sense of the term.

The main plot in *Much Ado About Nothing* is the Hero-Claudio story; the subplot is the Beatrice-Benedick story. In the case of this play, the audience is bound to be more interested in the characters connected with the subplot than with the central and second characters of the main plot. But, as we have seen, this is eminently possible in plays which are not tragedies—that is, that the focus of interest can be elsewhere than in the central character. Here again Shakespeare has intertwined the two stories. Beatrice and Benedick both figure in the unwinding of the main plot; and Hero and Claudio both figure in the Beatrice-Benedick story. As a matter of fact, it is the catastrophic ex-perience of Hero in church which brings about the crisis in the relationship of Beatrice and Benedick: they are able at last to voice their love for each other.

Perhaps the most magnificent use of a subplot in all world drama is in *King Lear*. Elsewhere not even Shakespeare manipulated one with equal power and range. From two different sources he chose the two stories of Lear and his daughters and Gloucester and his sons. What a master stroke to join them in one play! For at every turn of the tragedy these two stories cast light upon each other, sometimes by way of parallelism, sometimes by way of contrast. These are some of the parallels: Lear has two wicked daughters and one good daughter, Gloucester one wicked son and one good one. The wicked daughters are as evil as the wicked son. Lear and Gloucester each exiles the child who is loving. Lear and Gloucester are both stripped of everything by the wicked children. Lear loses his mind, Gloucester his sight. Cordelia forgives Lear all his injustice to her and comes tenderly to his aid when his plight is direst, Edgar forgives Gloucester all his injustice to him and stays by his side in his greatest hour of need. Cordelia restores Lear to peace, Edgar does the same for his father. Kent, in love and loyalty, gives up everything to serve Lear, Gloucester risks his very life to do the same. When Lear at length realizes his injustice to Cordelia, his concern is not for himself but for restitution to her and to all the homeless in his kingdom; Gloucester, when he at last learns the truth about Edmund, desires above everything to undo the wrongs done Edgar. These are some of the contrasts: Lear deserves only affection and loyalty from Goneril and Regan, Gloucester has done little to earn the love of Edmund; in Lear's wicked daughters there is no hint of goodness, Edmund has seeds of decency in his make-up though they were never encouraged to grow; Cordelia's stubbornness is somewhat responsible for her father's disastrous decision at the beginning of the play, Edgar is innocent of any wrong against his father; Cordelia knows very well the wicked nature of her sisters, Edgar is ignorant of his brother's real character; Goneril and Regan both become infatuated with Edmund, Cordelia is not especially interested in Edgar; the wickedness against Lear is perpetrated by women, that against Gloucester by his son (aided and abetted by Regan).

These are but some of the analogies existing between the two plots of the tragedy, analogies which fortify and throw into relief main plot and subplot. The two stories are united at a number of points: Goneril and Regan fall in love with Edmund and both wish to marry him; Regan is responsible for the blinding of Gloucester; Gloucester hazards everything to help

Lear; Edgar is present in the scene where Lear loses his reason; Edmund assumes power of death over Lear and Cordelia at the end.

No one, not even Shakespeare, could repeat this miraculous management of two plots so that they run concurrently and yet intertwine in all sorts of ways. Somewhat because of this intertwining, he was able to incorporate many themes into the tragedy:

1. Despite great love and kindness of a parent, some children will respond only with barbarous cruelty and inhumanity. (Lear-Goneril-Regan)
2. Despite unpardonable injustice of a parent, some children will respond only with loyalty and love. (Lear-Cordelia; Gloucester-Edgar)
3. True love will persist in the face of every deprivation and demand for self-sacrifice. (Kent-Lear; the Fool-Lear; Gloucester-Lear)
4. An ungovernable temper will cause a man to visit injustice on those whose love he has most cause to be sure of. (Lear-Cordelia; Gloucester-Edgar)
5. Wickedness and goodness are each not in monopoly by either sex. (Goneril-Regan-Cornwall-Edmund; Cordelia-Edgar-Kent-Albany)
6. Alliances among the greedy and self-seeking are sure to be short-lived. (Goneril-Regan; Goneril-Regan-Edmund)
7. To stand by silent while inhumanity is being meted out to a fellow human being is to invite villainy on one's own head. (Albany-Lear-Goneril)

If no one can be expected to repeat the miracle of *King Lear*, it is nonetheless true that a careful study of the play must prove infinitely rewarding to the student of dramaturgy, particularly on the subject of how subplots may be used to advantage.

Now, since a subplot must be sound too, *every good subplot should be capable of a sound Proposition and have an identifiable climax*. Such a Proposition and such a climax will follow the same laws as Proposition and climax for the main plot—with this exception: that the locating of the various steps of the Proposition and of the climax is much more fluid in a subplot; it is not possible to allocate them definitely to certain parts of the play, or even to discover a general tendency in their allocation. The reason for that is clear: since the subplot must depend upon the main plot, the proportioning of the subplot is subject to the requirements of the latter, and will be determined by the contribution it makes to it.

This is the Proposition and climax for Algernon's subplot in *The Importance of Being Earnest:*

1. Algernon learns of little Cecily's existence and decides to Bunbury with her, masquerading as Jack's wicked brother Ernest.
2. Because he is that wicked Ernest, he is accepted by her as soon as he proposes.
3. Will he be able to keep her to her promise of marriage when his true identity is known?

Climax: He declares that he will change his name. (It turns out that he is really a brother to Jack.) [45]

In Pirandello's *Six Characters in Search of an Author*, this is the Proposition and climax of the main plot:

1. A theatrical manager, attracted to the dramatic possibilities in a story that certain characters bring him, decides to make a play of their story.
2. In the process of fashioning the play, he meets with resistance from the characters, who do not want to submit to dramatic necessity.
3. Will he succeed in making the play?

Climax: He gets them to concede to playing the brothel scene in a way that satisfies him.

The subject of this main plot is the making of a play. The theme is that the author must control the characters, who always tend to act without regard to the necessities of the plot. (Here again the focus of interest is not in the central character, or even in the main plot, but rather in the characters of the subplot.) In this melodrama the main plot is concerned with a play; the subplot is concerned with living people. Thus, the old "play within a play" concept is reversed; the play being made becomes life, and the characters whose lives are the material for that play become part of a play within the play. The two plots meet in the climax. The subject of the subplot is: What is reality? Who or what is the real person? The theme is embodied in the person of the Father.[46]

SECONDARY CHARACTERS

The proposition of Sartre's fine one-acter *No Exit* is:
1. Garcin, stigmatized in his own mind by cowardice and wanting to think his way clear, fails to persuade Inez to leave him in peace.
2. When he tries to escape the stigma (this agony of mind being his torture) by getting Estelle to say he did not run away, he is prevented by Inez from believing in Estelle's opinion after all.
3. Will he have to exist forever with his agony of mind?
Climax: Out of cowardice he does not go through the open door. (This leaves him with Estelle, whose opinion means nothing, and with Inez, who hates him and whom he cannot persuade that he is not a coward.)

Now, the three characters who form the plot of *No Exit* have been painted with equal fullness; moreover, all three perform positive actions in the play. But unquestionably Garcin is the central character because the climax (which comes, as it should, near the very end of this one-act play) is his. However, it would be possible to make a Proposition and identify the climax of each of the other two in their relationship to the plot:
1. Inez, although she is aware that she and the other two are in this room in Hell to torture one another, cannot leave things alone and makes advances to Estelle.
2. Inez is put off by Estelle, who is interested only in a man.
3. Will she be able to prevent Estelle from getting Garcin?
Climax: She assures Garcin that Estelle is lying when Estelle assures him he is a real man.

And:
1. Estelle, whose reason for existence, in life and death, is to have a man and his admiration, invites Garcin to take her.
2. Estelle finds that he cannot make love to her because his mind is in anguish.
3. Will she be able to set his mind at rest so that he will love her?
Climax: She cannot get Garcin to help her push Inez through the door.

It should be possible to make a Proposition and identify a

*climax for each of the important characters in terms of his rela-
tion to the plot* in any play, if the plot is a sound one.

Thus, in *The Wild Duck*, looked at from the point of view
of Hialmar, who is actually the second character in the play,
his Proposition and climax go like this:

1. Hialmar reveals to Gregers the conditions of his marriage
   with Gina.
2. When Gregers reveals to Hialmar how the marriage took
   place (the setting up of the photography studio, Hialmar's living in the house of Gina's mother), Hialmar
   resolves to live henceforth without any illusions.
3. Will he cast off his self-delusions?

Climax: He disowns Hedvig. (As a consequence of her
   suicide, he will sink deeper than ever into his senti-
   mentality.)

It would be possible to make a Proposition and identify the
climax for Gina and Hedvig too.[47]

If *The Father* is looked at from the point of view of the
Captain, who is the second character in the play, his Proposition and climax go like this:

1. Asserting his domination, the Captain tells Laura that
   their child is to go to a boarding school, and thereby
   provokes her to insinuate that the child is not his.
2. Tortured by his suspicions, his will to dominate begins
   to buckle.
3. Will he go under in the struggle between them?

Climax: He throws the lamp.

In the same play, looked at from the point of view of the doctor,
the Proposition and climax are:

1. The doctor begins to think that the Captain may be in-
   sane.
2. Speaking with the Captain, he reverses his feelings and
   begins to believe that the Captain is sane.
3. To which decision will he come?

Climax: He sees the Captain behaving violently.[48]

In *The Importance of Being Earnest*, looked at from the
point of view of Gwendolen, the Proposition and climax would
be:

1. Gwendolen, when "Ernest" proposes to her, accepts
   him.
2. She discovers that he is not Ernest after all.

3. Will she marry him anyhow?

Climax: When he offers to undergo christening for her
    sake, she decides he is very brave and deserves her.

*A plot can also be looked at this way in terms of the central char-
acter and a character other than the second character.* For instance, a Proposition and climax can be stated for Jack in his
relation to Gwendolen:

1. Jack, on proposing to Gwendolen, learns that she would
   not marry him if his name were not Ernest.
2. He decides to insure marrying her by becoming Ernest
   in fact.
3. Will he succeed?

Climax: He announces that he intends to become chris-
    tened.[49,50]

This sort of analysis is of the utmost benefit if one wishes
to be sure of having a well-rounded plot of sufficient dimension.
The framing of a Proposition and statement of the climax for a
subplot (if there is one) is, of course, highly necessary. But to
do the same for *each* of the leading characters of the main plot
(and the subplot, if there is one) will not only reveal hidden
weaknesses; it will also present a challenge and opportunity for
enriching ideas.

CHAPTER FOURTEEN

Of Many Things

"The time has come," the Walrus said.
> LEWIS CARROLL, *Through the Looking-Glass*

All concord's born of contraries.   JONSON, *Cynthia's Revels*, v, ii

Amidst the soft variety I'm lost.   ADDISON, *Letter from Italy*

The thing to do is to supply light and not heat.
> WOODROW WILSON, Speech at Pittsburgh

When an authentic watch is shown,
Each man winds up and rectifies his own.   SUCKLING, *Aglaura*, Epil.

On est quelquefois un sot avec de l'esprit; mais on ne l'est jamais avec
du jugement.*   LA ROCHEFOUCAULD, *Maximes*

Yet Ah . . .
That Youth's sweet-scented manuscript should close!
> FITZGERALD, *Rubáiyát*

Sumite materiam vestris, qui scribitis, aequam
Viribus.†   HORACE, *Ars Poetica*, 38

Doubtless everyone has had this experience in the professional theater: at a highly dramatic moment someone comes in
or goes out shutting the door with such violence that the
walls of the set vibrate or ripple or threaten to come down. Or
at an amateur performance: after a highly satisfactory rendition of the play the final curtain declines to come down in a

* There exist sometimes fools with some talent, but there are none
who have judgment.
† You who write, choose a subject equal to your powers.

normal way, leaving the poor actors stupefied. In either case, whatever illusion had enthralled the audience was at that moment utterly obliterated.

Such little accidents remind us of a great truth that has always impressed us: the most enormous results are forever emanating from the most trifling changes, mistakes, carelessnesses, or improvements in all things connected with a play.

It is of comparatively small matters that we are now to speak, but they are matters which can bear considerable importance. This chapter is frankly a catchall for various odds and ends that have to do with playwriting. They might have been relegated to a series of appendices; but appendices frequently go unread.

LAST LINES

We have known many a good play to defeat itself only because the last lines in it were inept. *The final curtain must never be allowed to come down on speeches which are makeshift or casual. The tone predominant in a play must be sustained in the final speeches.*

The final speeches in a serious play must be serious. Here are some examples:

Hamlet

FORTINBRAS

                                        Let four captains
Bear Hamlet, like a soldier, to the stage,
For he was likely, had he been put on,
To have prov'd most royally; and for his passage,*
The soldiers' music and the rites of war
Speak loudly for him.
Take up the bodies. Such a sight as this
Becomes the field, but here shows much amiss.
Go, bid the soldiers shoot.

* death.

A Doll's House

NORA

No, I repeat. I can accept nothing from strangers.

HELMER

Nora—am I to be nothing more than a stranger to you?

NORA

(Taking her valise.)

Oh, Torvald, the miracle of miracles would have to happen!

HELMER

What is this miracle of miracles?

NORA

We would both have to change so—. Oh, I no longer can believe in miracles, Torvald.

HELMER

But I will believe. Tell me. We would both have to change so that—?

NORA

That our relationship will be a marriage. Goodbye.

(She goes out.)

HELMER

(With his face in his hands.)

Nora! Nora!

(He looks about him.)

Empty. She's gone.

(Hope springing in him.)

Ah! The miracle of miracles—?

(The reverberation of a heavy door closing is heard.)

Ghosts

MRS. ALVING

Oswald! look at me! Don't you know who I am?

OSWALD

(In a dead voice.)

The sun. The sun.

MRS. ALVING

(Rising in desperation, she clasps her
hands in her hair and cries.)

I can't stand it!

(Whispering, as though petrified.)

I can't stand it! Never!

(Suddenly.)

Where has he put them?

(She fumbles hastily in his breast-pocket.)

Here they are!

(She retreats a few steps and cries.)

No. No, no!—Yes!—No, no!

(She looks at him speechless with terror.)

OSWALD

(As before.)

The sun. The sun.

The Father

LAURA

Is that all you are able to say at this bed of death, Doctor?

DOCTOR

That is all! There's nothing more I know. He who knows more, let him speak.

BERTHA

(Running in, and coming to LAURA.)

Mother, mother!

LAURA

My child! My own child!

PASTOR

Amen.

The Cherry Orchard

Everyone has left the house but old Firs; the stage is empty, and one hears the stroke of the ax felling trees. Old Firs, quite ill, comes in; he goes to the doors and finds them locked:

FIRS

Locked! They've left.

(Sitting on sofa.)

They've forgotten me. It doesn't matter. I'll sit here a while.
I'll bet Leonid Andreyevich didn't wear his fur coat, and has
gone in his thin topcoat.

(Sighs.)

I didn't see to it. Ah, these young folk!

(Muttering.)

Life has passed me by as if I never lived.

(Lying down.)

I'll lie down a while. There's no strength in you. Nothing's
left you. It's all gone. Ach! I'm not good for anything.

>   (Lies motionless. A sound like that of a
>   snapped harp-string is heard, as if from
>   the heavens. All is quiet again, except for
>   the axe-strokes in the orchard.)

Cyrano de Bergerac

                              CYRANO

                                        One thing without stain,
Unspotted from the world, in spite of doom,
Mine own!—And that is—

>   (He falls into the arms of LE BRET and
>   RAGUENEAU.)

                              ROXANE

>   (Bends over him and kisses him on the
>   forehead.)

                                        —That is—

                              CYRANO

>   (Opens his eyes and smiles up at her.)

My white plume—

Elizabeth the Queen

PENELOPE

Dear Queen, would you let him go?
He goes to his death! Send, send after him!

(The queen lifts her head and shows a
face so stricken that Penelope, who has
gone to her, says no more.)

The Little Foxes

REGINA

Would you like to come and talk to me, Alexandra? Would
you—would you like to sleep in my room tonight?

ALEXANDRA

Are you afraid, Mama?

(REGINA does not answer, but moves
slowly out of sight.)

The final speeches in an amusing play must be amusing.

The Importance of Being Earnest

GWENDOLEN

Ernest! My own Ernest! I felt from the first that you could
have no other name!

JACK

Gwendolen, it is a terrible thing for a man to find out suddenly
that all his life he has been speaking nothing but the truth. Can
you forgive me?

GWENDOLEN

I can. For I feel that you are sure to change.

JACK

My own one!

CHASUBLE

(To miss prism.)

Laetitia!

(Embraces her.)

MISS PRISM

(Enthusiastically.)

Frederick! At last!

ALGERNON

Cecily!

(Embraces her.)

At last!

JACK

Gwendolen!

(Embraces her.)

At last!

LADY BRACKNELL

My nephew, you seem to be displaying sigus of triviality.

JACK

On the contrary, Aunt Augusta, I've now realized for the first time in my life the vital Importance of Being Earnest.

The Madwoman of Chaillot

COUNTESS

Well, let's go on to more important things. Four o'clock. My poor cats must be starved. What a bore for them if humanity had to be saved every afternoon. They don't think much of it, as it is.*

Biography

MARION

(Opens telegram and reads it.)

This is from heaven! Minnie, I want you to pack right away. We're leaving!

(She springs up.)

MINNIE

Leaving? Ven?

MARION

Right away. Tonight! This is from Feydie! Listen!

(Reads telegram aloud to MINNIE.)

"Can get you commission to paint prize winners Motion Picture Academy—wire answer at once. Feydie."

(Hysterically grateful for the mercy of

* Adaptation by Maurice Valency.

> having something to do at once, of being
> busy, of not having time to think.)

Something always turns up for me! Pack everything, Minnie.
I want to get out right away.

> (She rushes upstage right, picks up her
> hat and coat, and then runs to the stairs
> left.)

MINNIE

Don't you tink you better vait till tomorrow?

MARION

No, Minnie. Once the temptation to a journey comes into my
head I can't bear it till I'm on my way! This time, Minnie, we'll
have a real trip. From Hollywood we'll go to Honolulu and
from Honolulu to China. How would you like that, Minnie?

> (She starts up the stairs.)

MINNIE

> (For her, enthusiastic.)

Fine, Marion!

> (Calls after her as she runs upstairs.)

Dot crazy Kurt he goes vit us?

MARION

> (As she disappears into her bedroom.)

No, Minnie—no one—we travel alone!

These concluding speeches are particularly fine. Just before
them there has been serious business in the final break between
Marion and Kurt. But the play is a comedy—though with serious
matter in it—and these lines reaffirm the bright mood of comedy.

The last line, however, has just the right tinge of sadness in it to cause the play to end on the perfect tone.

STAGE DIRECTIONS

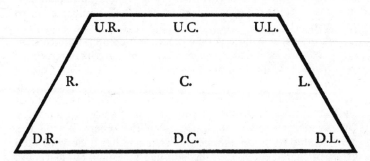

U.R. = upstage right. R. = right. D.R. = downstage right. U.C. = upstage center. C. = center. D.C. = downstage center. U.L. = upstage left. L. = left. D.L. = downstage left.

It is important for the dramatist to visualize the position and movements of the characters onstage at every minute. When these *directions* are indicated in the script, they *are always from the actors' right and left, not the audience's.* Downstage is that part of the stage nearest the audience. It is wise to keep stage directions to a minimum; good directors prefer not to be pinned down too much.

As for the emotional cues like: (Laughing.) or (Shouting.) or (Angrily.), the writer is wise to insert most of them after a scene is finished, if they are necessary. Otherwise, he runs the danger of having his emotional values in the directions instead of in the lines. Well-written lines need comparatively few such emotional cues. (Note their complete absence in Shakespeare's text, and how the lines make very plain what the emotion is.)

WRITING "BY SCENES"

Despite their preference for unity of time and place, the French classical dramatists, when their plays were published, would seem to have written on a superficial glance at their pages,

dozens of scenes for each act. This was actually, of course, not
the case. But it was a convention among them to consider any
given scene over when any character left the stage or when
another character entered. While their designation of each exit
and each entrance as constituting a new scene is an impediment
to the reader, the concept itself must have been a valuable one to
the writer.

A dramatist will be very wise, during composition, to *consider each exit and each entrance of a character as inaugurating a
new scene*. It will encourage him to make sure that each episode
of the play is complete in itself, as it should be. One might be
wise to begin, after the exit of a character or with the entrance of
another, writing on a separate sheet of paper—that is, each scene
(in the French sense) separated from the others. To do this
is to be able to examine honestly what one has done with each
group of characters. Everything slipshod will stand out glaringly.

SMALL REVISIONS

We have said several times that the smallest revisions can
make for the most important differences in effect. Never let even a
word stand if you feel that it does not say all it should. And be
particularly careful that your last line is the right one.

We have long been impressed, and have recently discovered
that many others have been equally affected, by the splendid line
with which Mr. S. N. Behrman brings down the curtain upon
the second act of *Rain from Heaven*. The line is so striking that
we have always suspected that it might very well have been the
product of felicitous revision. We applied to the dramatist for information on this head, and he has graciously certified that was
indeed the case.

To gauge the effect of the revision, we had better summarize
the story of *Rain from Heaven* up to the second-act curtain:

The action of the play takes places around 1933, when the
Nazi persecutions in Germany were beginning to indicate their
potential of horror, but when most people preferred to be
blind and deaf to what was going on under the direction of
Hitler. The scene is the living-room of Lady Lael Wyngate's
house, a short distance from London. It is a spring afternoon.

We meet Rand Eldridge and his older brother Hobart. Hobart, a wealthy American industrialist who cannot "visualize a cosmos in which he and his kind are not the central suns," is a man in his late forties, essentially coarse and hollow within. His brother Rand, about thirty, very attractive and rather shy, is currently an international hero because of his aviational exploits at the Pole; he does not particularly enjoy his fame.

Hobart, incensed that Lael is not at home to greet them when she expected Rand, expresses his ill-will against her. To him she is either "Bohemian" or "artistic"; "if you're artistic," he says, "you can be rude." Rand, devoted to his brother, who has financed all his expeditions, tells Hobart that he intends to ask Lael to marry him. Hobart, full of plans for Rand, tries to dissuade him: Lael "whose fortune has been built up by a lot of hard-working manufacturers," uses her money to support a Liberal weekly. Anything liberal is to Hobart "communistic." Rand's marriage to Lael would prove inconvenient to Hobart, who intends to settle in England and become a power there in leading the New Crusade, an English Fascist movement. Hobart intends to use Rand as a figure-head because of the young man's world popularity. For Rand to marry Lael would be, according to Hobart, "like Lindbergh marrying a young Emma Goldman." *

Lael comes in. She says that she has been to London "to pick up a German refugee. I found him so alone and charming that I've brought him back with me." The refugee, Hugo Willens, formerly a leading music-critic in Germany, turns out to have been an old skiing companion of Rand's, who met him originally through Hobart's wife, Phoebe. Lael is clearly an enchantress, sophisticated, generous, warm. Willens comes in. Recently emerged from a concentration-camp, he is a charming, urbane citizen of the world. Hobart baits him, anxious to prove that Hugo Willens, who is completely non-political, must have been a Communist; for Hobart, like many ill-informed people of his day, thoroughly approves of what Hitler is doing to "revitalize" Germany. The fact is that Willens got into trouble with the Nazis

* Emma Goldman was a notorious anarchist of the early decades of the twentieth century, the object of much talk because of her open practice of the doctrine of "free-love."

for writing a satire mocking them for their persecution of the
Jews, though Willens himself is "Aryan" enough, except for one
Jewish great-grandmother.

When Lael and Rand are alone, they are in each other's
arms at once. She confesses to having run away from her house
this morning, just as she has run away from Rand before, because, though she loves him deeply, there is nothing in the world
they agree about. Rand is astounded to hear this: they've never
discussed anything. Lael admits that she has always steered clear
of any discussions with him just because she knows they would
never agree, and she cannot bear quarreling with him. She knows
about Hobart's plan "to enlist Anglo-American youth for Fas-
cism." Rand, politically naive, asks, "Well, what's wrong with
that?" The very question shows that, though she does not wish
to give Rand up, they are worlds apart. She also admits, however, that she will probably end by succumbing to him because
of her love for him, though she owes it to her conscience "to put
up an awful fight." Rand, to whom their political differences
seem irrelevant, wants merely to know whether she has "affairs
with men." Half-angered and half-amused, she assures him that,
however sophisticated in thought, she is almost Puritanical in her
personal life. This is all Rand wished to know, and he can see no
possible obstacle to their marrying.

In the first scene of the second act, four days later, Lael
discovers that Hobart cannot be talked out of his Neo-fascist
plans. She hates all youth movements; "they all come to the same
thing. Boy Scouts with bayonets. Do you want a private army,
Hobart? Have you a little dictator hatching in your brain?"
Hobart admits that "democracy is passé." In business and private
life, dictatorship has proved itself successful to him, why not in
the political sphere too? Lael learns how Hobart plans to use
Rand for his movement, but delays having a show-down with
her lover about it. She is newly reminded of their incompatibility.

Phoebe, Hobart's wife, comes in. She has in the past had
an affair with Hugo Willens, and decides, quite wrongly, that it
was because of Lael that Willens left her. Willens honestly assures Phoebe that her "intuitions" concerning Lael and himself
are false. Phoebe does not believe him.

Alone with Lael, Willens confides in her, tells her of his boring affair with Phoebe, of how he left Phoebe only because he

couldn't endure her, how out of cowardice he had pretended he
was leaving her for another woman, and how now Phoebe has
decided this "other woman" is Lael. Seeing Willens' bitterness
over his life, Lael offers him the warmth of her friendship, and
confides to him her confusion about Rand. At her request he
agrees to stay on to help her "because an obsession may be destroyed." They are feeling very close to each other; at this moment Phoebe comes in, over-interprets their intimacy, and leaves
blind with jealousy.

In the second scene of the second act, Willens at last tells
Phoebe the truth about their affair: he has been unable to endure
her. "You bored me before anybody came. The only reason our
affair lasted as long as it did was because we were separated
months at a time, because I hardly saw you more than a few
weeks each year." In a fury, Phoebe tells Hobart that Lael is
having an affair with Willens. Skillfully, Hobart prods Phoebe
to reveal how she knows this to be a fact. Hearing the voices of
Rand and Lael, husband and wife go off to continue their mutual
torture. Rand comes in with Lael and insists on a "showdown."
He wants to rescue her from "this highbrow atmosphere and
these seedy people" she has surrounded herself with. She is still
evasive about marrying him. Willens enters, just as the conversation threatens to become a quarrel. Hobart comes in, having
learned of his wife's former relationship with Willens, and announces that Willens and Lael are lovers.

This brings us almost to the second act curtain. In a letter
to us, dated September 26, 1960, Mr. Behrman writes:

> My original curtain made Lael deny that she was Hugo
> [Willens'] lover, proved it in fact. And she had a speech in
> which she made a fool of the fascist [Hobart], then turned to
> Hugo and said something like: 'Well, Hobart is lying now.
> But maybe he has the gift of divination!' That was approx-
> imately the curtain line. We opened with that and it got a
> laugh all right and then I disliked the whole passage in which
> Lael denounces Hobart. . . .

Mr. Behrman canceled all that. Instead of it, he re-wrote the
passage following Hobart's "revelation" that Lael and Willens
are lovers, thus:

RAND

(Turns on HUGO.)

You dirty Jew!

LAEL

(Horrified.)

Rand!

HUGO

It's all right, Lael. This makes me feel quite at home.

HOBART

You swine! Maybe those people over there are right.

LAEL

Hobart, please remember—Herr Willens is not only my lover, he is also my guest.

(Smiles at HUGO.)

Hugo darling!

(Curtain)

Concerning this alteration, Mr. Behrman's letter continues: the old passage was cut out, the new brief speeches substituted, including

the present curtain line which is: 'Hobart, please remember—Herr Willens is not only my lover, he is also my guest.' This curtain line aroused considerable comment. I remember one critic said that it was the most significant curtain line he knew because it overthrew an entire code of morality.

This, we trust, has been a vivid demonstration of the re-markable improvements which may come from revisions. This alteration would be described as an act of sheer inspiration.

An examination of Ibsen's notebooks, published as *From Ibsen's Workshop*, will reveal the fact that some of his most powerful effects came to him during the process of revision. These few examples from *Hedda Gabler* are enough to show what that play gained from the dramatist's re-writing. In the first draft of the play:

1. There was no Mlle Diane.
2. There was no reference to Hedda's jealousy of Mrs. Elvsted's lovely hair.

Both of these, introduced in revision, figure importantly in pre-paring the climax. Also in the first draft,

3. The manuscript is destroyed not by Hedda but by Tes-man.

This makes Tesman the active character and Hedda the passive one, and assigns the climax to Tesman, who becomes, thereby, the more dynamic of the two. In the first draft too:

4. It is Tesman who lures Lovborg to Judge Brack's party.

The last two dramatic facts would have tended to make Tesman the central character, and ruin the balance of the plot. In ad-dition, the first version of the play reveals that Tesman and Mrs. Elvsted show knowledge of the relationship between Hedda and Lovborg in the past. In the scene between Hedda and Mrs. Elvsted in Act I, for example, Ibsen first wrote:

MRS. ELVSTED

But—but—oh, Hedda, there is *some one* that stands between us.

HEDDA

What do you mean by that?

MRS. ELVSTED

Some one who has hurt and injured him so profoundly—. But whom I don't believe he can ever forget in spite of that.

HEDDA

Who is it you mean?

MRS. ELVSTED

Yourself, Hedda.

HEDDA

Can this be—! Hush! Hush, he's coming! For God's sake, Thea
—let all this be between ourselves!

(Enter TESMAN with a letter in his hand.)

This passage now reads:

MRS. ELVSTED

(Gloomily)

A woman's shadow stands between Eilert Lovborg and me.

HEDDA

(Looking at her anxiously)

Who can *that* be?

MRS. ELVSTED

I don't know. Some one he knew in his—in his past. Some one
he has never been able wholly to forget.

HEDDA

What has he told you about this?

MRS. ELVSTED

He has only once—quite vaguely—alluded to it.

HEDDA

And what did he say?

MRS. ELVSTED

He said that when they parted, she threatened to shoot him with a pistol.

HEDDA

Oh nonsense! No one does that sort of thing here.

MRS. ELVSTED

No. And that is why I think it must have been that red-haired singing-woman whom he once—

HEDDA

Yes, very likely.

Aside from the great superiority in the writing, the revision makes one very important change. In the earlier version Hedda is put in a defensive position by the very fact that her old relationship with Lovborg is known; and it is beside the issue of the play—which is, in Ibsen's own words, Hedda's "want of an object in life"—that she should have to defend herself against other people's knowledge of her love-affair with Lovborg. In addition, of course, the revised scene, because of Hedda's apprehension that Thea *might* know, and its telling detail about the pistol, make for much more intensity. We have here obvious proof of the benefits of revision.

Here is another example which will show how important small revisions may prove to be. The first version of Michael Turque's one-act satire, *Shoptalk,** had considerable brilliance, but the deftness was almost ruined by the concluding speeches.

* This excellent comedy can be found in its entirety in *Introduction to Imaginative Literature* (1960), pp. 193–98.

In this comedy two men, Purvis and Bright, have been summoned to the office of the Director of a large corporation; the position of President is now open and these are the two men who are the candidates for the important post. It is up to each to prove that the other is unfit for the job: they can make any accusation against each other that they wish, but if any accusation that cannot be substantiated is made, it will count heavily against the accuser. After tentative attempts at injuring each other, Bright accuses Purvis of being ignorant of the fact that his own wife is an adultress. According to the rules of the game, Purvis may demand that Bright substantiate this grave charge: if he does not challenge Bright's proof, that would perhaps count against him; if he does challenge Bright's proof and Bright has no proof, Bright would be disqualified. Bright now taunts Purvis into demanding the proof. Mrs. Purvis, it turns out, has been ready to help Bright, and is waiting in the outer office. She comes in and certifies the truth of Bright's assertion. It looks as though Bright has proved his superior qualifications for the presidency, in having successfully deceived Purvis. But now Purvis takes a gun out of his pocket, and with it covers both Bright and his wife. Purvis calls upon the Director to agree that he has been provoked to the limits of self-restraint; he then cites a recent case in which a husband shot his wife and her lover for flaunting their love affair, and was exonerated for justifiable homicide. Purvis adds that he will have to call upon the Director to testify in his behalf as a witness to the flaunting of this love affair.

This is the first draft of the last passage of *Shoptalk:*

PURVIS

And so the situation is this, director. If you are willing to testify in my behalf before a grand jury, and the results of such a hearing are assured, then my path is clear.

DIRECTOR

Diabolical! This is extraordinary! Now understand, Mr. Purvis, what you propose is unprecedented.

(To himself.)

Frightening to think how it will affect future elections. Who would have thought it would come to this? Hmm.

(To PURVIS.)

On the other hand, as you pointed out, you would be perfectly justified in exercising righteous indignation.

BRIGHT

For God's sake, Director, don't let him do it!

(The telephone rings.)

DIRECTOR

(Answering the phone.)

Hello. Oh, yes, dear.

(Pause.)

How are the children? Good. Yes, I'll meet you at the restaurant in ten minutes. Right. Goodbye, dear.

(Hangs up the phone.)

Mr. Purvis—

(Pointing to the gun.)

I'm in no position to argue with you. You'll have to do as your conscience dictates.

MRS. PURVIS

(Crying.)

No!

DIRECTOR

If you don't mind, I'll go to lunch now. My wife is waiting for me. You know how they fuss if you're late. I'll be back in an hour. I assume that, by then, all the evidence * will have been presented.

> (DIRECTOR looks at PURVIS. Nods. Then he looks at BRIGHT, who has his head in his hands.)

Good. I'll give you my verdict after lunch. Good morning, gentlemen. Nice to have seen you, Mrs. Purvis. You must come again. Perhaps we can all get together some evening for a drink. And I promise you. No shoptalk.

MRS. PURVIS

Horrible, horrible!

> (As the DIRECTOR leaves the office the curtain descends.)

It was pointed out to the author that the last line made for a weak curtain, and also that the Director's last remarks imply that he does not expect the murder to come off. After reconsidering the entire passage, Mr. Turque rewrote it this way:

PURVIS

Here is the situation, Director. Although I hesitated to put you to any inconvenience, I'm afraid I shall have to call upon you to testify in my behalf before a grand jury. Of course, the results of this hearing are assured.

DIRECTOR

Diabolical! This is extraordinary. Now understand, Mr. Purvis, what you suggest is unprecedented.

> (To himself.)

Frightening to think how it will affect future elections. Who could have thought it would come to this? Hmm.

* The "evidence" in this case is the material offered by both men for their succession to the office of President. The "verdict" next referred to by the Director is on who shall get the position.

(To PURVIS.)

On the other hand, as you pointed out, you would be perfectly justified in exercising your righteous indignation.

BRIGHT

For God's sake, Director, don't let him do it!

(The telephone rings.)

DIRECTOR

(Answering the phone.)

Hello . . . oh yes, dear . . . How are the children? Good . . . yes, I'll meet you at the restaurant in ten minutes. Right. Good-bye, dear.

(He hangs up.)

Mr. Purvis—

(Pointing to the gun.)

I'm in no position to argue with you. You'll have to do as your conscience and your judgment dictate.

MRS. PURVIS

(Crying.)

No!

DIRECTOR

(Looking at his watch.)

I'll have to hurry. My wife is meeting me for lunch. You know how they fuss when you're late. I'll be back in an hour. I assume that by then all the evidence will have been presented.

(DIRECTOR looks at PURVIS, nods.)

Good! I'll give you my verdict after lunch. The final deliberation in serious matters should always be made over a glass of port.

MRS. PURVIS

(Her hands over her eyes.)

Horrible . . . horrible!

DIRECTOR

(Affably.)

Nice seeing you again, Mrs. Purvis. Your visits are much too rare. I know . . . perhaps we can all get together some evening for a drink. And, I promise you, Mrs. Purvis, no shoptalk. Well goodbye for now.

(As the DIRECTOR leaves, PURVIS still aiming the gun, the curtain descends.)

The revisions were trifling, but the results not. Note what is accomplished by transposing Mrs. Purvis' "Horrible . . . horrible!" Note, too, how much is changed by the omission of "You must come again" from the Director's last speech.

TYPING THE MANUSCRIPT

When printed, plays are arranged in various typographical ways. Very often the criterion is saving space, particularly in anthologies. But producers and directors prefer to have manuscripts typed in a certain form; not to follow it is to advertise the fact that you are an amateur. Throughout this book, therefore, we have sacrificed considerations of space (and money) in order to accustom the reader to the accepted form for play manuscripts:

1. The name of the character speaking in capitals centered above the speech.
2. The speeches single-spaced.
3. A double space between the end of a given speech and the name of the next speaker.

4. A single space between the name of the speaker and his speech.*

5. Stage directions and emotional cues on a separate line, when they break up a speech. The speech continues on the next line at the margin.* The exception is a stage direction' or emotional cue preceding a speech, in which case the speech can follow on the same line.*

6. The names of characters appearing within a direction always in capitals (for example, To HELEN.).

We have shown how the directions of the opening of a scene are typed (see p. 41.) These are to be kept on the right-hand half of the page, and single-spaced, as thus:

> Morning-room in ALGERNON's flat in Half-Moon Street. The room is luxuriously and artistically furnished. The sound of a piano is heard in the adjoining room.
>
> LANE is arranging afternoon tea on the table, and after the music has ceased, ALGERNON enters.

Preceding the first page of the play there should be a page listing the characters and giving a synopsis of scenes, in this fashion:

BIOGRAPHY

Cast of Characters
(in order of their appearance)

Richard Kurt, a young man in his mid-twenties
Minnie, Marion Froude's maid
Melchior Feydak, a Viennese composer
Marion Froude, a beautiful woman in her mid-thirties
Leander Nolan, about forty
Warwick Nolan, matinee idol and Hollywood star
Orrin Kinnicott, an elderly man of powerful physique
Slade Kinnicott, a smart young woman, his daughter

* To make for greater readability throughout this book we have allowed a double space instead of the usual single space of a typed manuscript. See our specimen of a typed manuscript page on page 364.

CHATTY PAYEVSKY (Cont.)

So explain already!

ELYOT QUOATER

(Fixes PAYEVSKY with an icy stare and then loftily addresses the others.)
I went to the ticket-office and got them to exchange it.
I don't know why you're all so astonished.
You know I'm quite experienced in traveling.

PROVINCETOWN MCNEAL

(Pleading with ELYOT.) Go, for the love of Christ, you mad tortured bastard !
Go, for your own sake!
    (Touched, ELYOT gives him a penetrating look.)
What the hell are you staring at?
    (He recites sardonically with soaring power.)
"Look in my face. My name is Might-Have-Been;
I am also called No More, Too Late, Farewell."
That's from Rossetti. Ever hear of him? I've been reading Swinburne too.
If they were here they'd have understood my side of it, Jesus but they would!

ELYOT QUOATER

(Still moved, but recovering his poise.) I know very well why you think so.
You think so because you think they drank.
You think I drink because I am a poet.
And I am a poet because I speak in lines.
And you pretend to think I think because
You drink you are a poet too—

PROVINCETOWN MCNEAL

(With a cry of anguish, like that of a hurt little boy.) Shut up!
    (He takes a drink from the bottle.)
Beloved God, let me clasp greedily to my white heart this lovely treasure,
this pearl of rarest price, this filthy, stinking bit of putrid flesh, which
is my own beautiful life.
    (He laughs a laugh of self-loathing.)
Well, so long mates! "Thus Thisbe ends!"
    (He dashes out, head sunk on chest. There is
    a long silence.)

CHATTY PAYEVSKY

(Speaking at last.) Listen, Elyot. I been a good friend to you. I ever
asked you to lend me a dollar or something?
    (ELYOT ignores him.)
Anything you wanted was always O.K. with me. You know that. Only one thing
I'm asking of you. Please, Elyot, please go away like Provincetown says. Please!

HENRY WEAVER

(Sternly to ELYOT, with a nod toward PAYEVSKY.) Nobody dast blame this man. A
playwright has got to dream. Tomorrow he'll make the last payment on the
house, and then everything will be different. Attention must be paid to
such a man!

KENTUCKY JONES

(Softly.) There's a beautiful purple bird that lives up there in the sky,
and it never comes down to earth to alight. You know why? It doesn't have
a head.

REUBEN FLOUR

(Irritably.) What's that got to do with it. He don't fly with his head, does he?

KENTUCKY JONES

(Gently.) No. But since he has no head, he has no mouth, and so it wouldn't

Manuscript page of an unpublished play, showing preferred arrangement.

Time: 1932.
The entire action takes place in Marion Froude's studio in
    New York.
Act I. About five o'clock of an afternoon in November.
Act II. Afternoon, two weeks later.
Act III. Late afternoon, two weeks later.

In the case of a play with more than one scene to an act
and/or different sets, it would read like this:
Time: The present, in a Midwestern college town.
Act I. Scene 1. The room shared by Charles, Richard, and
    Herbert in the college dormitory. An October after-
    noon.
        Scene 2. The porch of the Dexter family. The same
    evening.
Act II. Scene 1. Same as Act I, scene 2. Two weeks later,
    a Sunday afternoon.
        Scene 2. The same. An hour later.
Act III. The office of Dean Humphreys, the next morning.

It is customary to paginate the manuscript in the upper
right-hand corner, in this way: a roman numeral for the act, an
arabic numeral for the scene, and an arabic numeral for the page
of that act. Each act is paged right through the act; each new act
begins with page 1 again. Thus:

I—6. This is the sixth page of Act I. This act has not more
    than one scene.
I–1–6. This is the sixth page of Act I. This act will have more
    than one scene.
II–2–24. This is the twenty-fourth page of Act II, of which
    this is the second scene. This might be, for example, the
    third page of the second scene.
III–1–1. This is the first page of Act III, which will have
    (alas!) more than one scene.

*The average full-length play is not less than 90 pages and
not more than 120 pages, when typed according to the correct
form.* A three-act play averages between 30 and 40 pages per
act. The last act is usually shorter than the others.

There are many excellent typing services in New York that
specialize in typing play scripts. They will make the usual six
copies at a time, and also bind each copy in appropriate covers.

SELLING THE PLAY

The chief obstacles to the flourishing of drama on Broadway are the scarcity of theaters and the throttling demands of the various unions (of the stagehands, the electricians, the musicians) not concerned with the acting of the play.

Thirty years ago there were three times as many theaters available for the production of professional performances in New York as there are at the present. All along Forty-second Street and neighboring Broadway there are a large number of magnificent theaters (the best of their kind in their heyday) which are now devoted to the cinema. Other theaters, once devoted to legitimate plays, have been swallowed up by the hungry maw of television, for the purposes of broadcasting—sometimes a single half-hour show a week! This situation tragically limits the number of plays which can be given on Broadway during a season, and it also makes for an outrageous competitiveness for theaters based upon anything but the quality of what is being offered. The scarcity of theaters has made it possible for tickets to be sold out a year in advance of the first performance; all that is needed for that is to have a star in the cast—preferably, these days, a movie star. In the meantime, superior plays without that dubious artistic advantage may go begging for a theater. If some millionaire lover of the arts wished to indulge in a much needed philanthropy, he could not do better at this juncture than to build a string of theaters to be devoted exclusively to legitimate drama.

Yet the recent mushrooming of "Off-Broadway" performances all over the city proves that the theater public is larger than ever. These performances, though they are a blessing in the present drought of Broadway theaters, are no substitute for them. They are severely limited in the numbers they can accommodate, either by the size of the improvised playhouse or, if they are large enough, by union regulations. The producers cannot afford to hire top performers, and the shows are sometimes quite amateurish—though not always so. They nevertheless deserve the thanks of the drama lover for the very real services they are performing for the public, the dramatist, and the actor.

Another deterrent to the flourishing of drama in the professional theaters is the deadly strangle hold which unions have on them. Every theater must employ a certain minimum number of stagehands, whether they are needed or not, at a very high wage; each one of these men has a specific job to do; if he is to remove a lamp between scenes, it is quite possible that his union will not allow him also to remove a chair—another man may be required for that. Nearly every theater must pay the salary of four musicians whether they are needed in the playhouse or not. There was a time when a producer preferred single-set plays with a small cast and steered clear of plays that called for a number of sets and/or a large cast. But the cost of scenery and actors' salaries is now considered a trifle as compared with the constant drain on the budget of agreements forced by the unions.

Under such conditions, it becomes increasingly hard for the beginner to get a hearing. Yet producers are always complaining that they cannot find good plays. And some new dramatists do get their plays produced.

If you are going to undertake being a playwright, you must have the heart of a lion and the patience of a saint. *The important thing is to get your play read by a producer.*

To achieve that objective there is only one ideal way. When you are sure that your play is as perfect as you can make it—and to do less is to make certain the futility of your efforts to place it—you must find a play agent who will handle it. There are many good agents, and they are all listed in the directory. There are some spurious ones, too. It is easy to find out who the spurious ones are: they ask you for a fee for reading your script (and sometimes will offer criticisms for the same fee—criticisms which are likely to be of little value to you). No reputable agent is going to ask you for a fee for reading your play. He is as anxious to find salable plays as you are to sell your script, for his livelihood depends upon his doing so. The commission that he gets, when he sells a play, he will well have earned. Naturally, he will not be willing to handle a play that he feels has no chance, for his time and money are involved. But if he does accept your script, you have overcome the first obstacle. For he will see to it that your play is read by the right people.

Above everything, while your play is taking its chances in the world—even while you are trying to place it with an agent —do not wait with your tongue hanging out for the opening night. *Get busy on the next play*, make it a better one, and try to forget for at least weeks at a time the play that is out. The definition of a playwright is one who writes plays, not *a* play.

For the rest, it is well to remember that success depends upon many factors, some of which are purely those of circumstance. Since such is the case, all you can do is your best and your wisest.

We have done *our* best for you. Good luck!

An Appendix of
Suggested Exercises

We recommend that these exercises be kept in some sort of notebook, or at least filed together. It may very well be that some of the earlier exercises may turn out to be useful as material for the later ones; and all of them may prove their worth as reference. We further recommend that *all* the exercises be done, and that none be disdained because they *seem* simple. They have all been tested for their value in progressively developing thinking in terms of writing for the theater. It is this habit of mind which we hope the student will apply himself to cultivate.

CHAPTER ONE

1. Write a dialogue such as might be heard on a bus, trolley, or train. After your first draft, revise and compress what you have written to make the speeches more interesting and to imply some sort of characterization. Put in the stage directions and emotional cues only after you are satisfied with the script. Don't expect to write a masterpiece yet.

CHAPTER TWO

2. a. List a series of themes on the following subjects:
    (1) Love
    (2) Jealousy
    (3) Ambition
    (4) Idleness
    (5) Social rank
    (6) The values of big business

   b. Make a list of other subjects.
   c. For each subject in (b) list several possible themes.
   d. Choose two or three themes from (c) and invent for each a situation and the principal characters.
3. Read several of the plays whose situations have been listed—they are all worth the reading—and:
   a. State the leading theme of each play.
   b. Write a description of the leading characters in each play.
   c. Invent a different set of characters that might exhibit the same theme in a different plot.
4. Jot down a series of situations each of which might give rise to a play. Make a tentative statement of possible characters and theme for each.
5. a. Invent a different second character and a new situation for:
      (1) The woman of great compassion and generosity
      (2) The man of incorruptible honesty
      (3) The lightheaded, beautiful chorus girl
   b. Invent a series of three leading characters that you might wish to represent in a play.
   c. Invent a secondary character and a situation for each of the three in (b).
6. Start a collection of newspaper clippings which seem to offer possibilities for dramatic use. Don't overlook the news magazines. (The "Miscellany" column of *Time* sometimes contains choice items.)

CHAPTER THREE

7. Write an incident which might take place on a train, trolley, or bus. Be sure that the situation is sufficiently developed and that one person emerges as the important character.
8. Develop this situation: In a neighborhood store (a grocery, a candy store, a pharmacy, or a tailor's, for example) there has been a sign in the window: "Baby Carriage for Sale." Someone comes in to buy the carriage. Write the incident.
9. Write this scene. Materials for it will be found chiefly in Chapters IX through XIII of *Henry Esmond;* feel free to use any of Thackeray's dialogue in these chapters. Follow the suggestions we have made for the progress of the scene.
10. Jonathan has been paying court, without much success, to Maisie, a very pretty but lightheaded young woman whose

only passion in life is dancing. On innumerable occasions she has broken her engagements with him; it is no unusual occurrence for him to arrive to take her out and find her gone off with some other young man. On some of these disappointed evenings, he was greeted by her older sister, Ruth, who is genuinely sorry for the way Maisie has been treating him. By degrees Jonathan has come to appreciate Ruth's more solid qualities, and he has become more and more attached to her. Tonight on his way to their house, he found himself hoping that Maisie would be out and Ruth there. And so it turns out. As he talks to Ruth, he begins to understand that it is she he loves. She is totally unprepared for his revelations. Write this scene.

or

Conceive the two sisters in a different light. Ruth, desperate to get a husband, has no suitors. Since Maisie does not particularly care for Jonathan, she has deliberately disappointed him so that her sister could have some time alone with him. Jonathan is not interested in Ruth: the more unattainable Maisie is, the more he desires her. Tonight Ruth has decided to ensnare Jonathan. She succeeds. Write this scene.

CHAPTER FOUR

11. Read the following plays and make a tentative Proposition for each of them:

Othello

Hedda Gabler, by Ibsen

The Wild Duck, by Ibsen

Ghosts, by Ibsen

The Cherry Orchard, by Chekhov

Cyrano de Bergerac, by Rostand

The Father, by Strindberg

The Playboy of the Western World, by Synge

The Second Man, by Behrman

Biography, by Behrman

The Petrified Forest, by Sherwood

The Silver Cord, by Howard

The Circle, by Maugham

Elizabeth the Queen, by Anderson

Winterset, by Anderson

Six Characters in Search of an Author, by Pirandello

As You Desire Me, by Pirandello

The Glass Menagerie, by Williams

The Madwoman of Chaillot, by Giraudoux

The Chalk Garden, by Bagnold

Each of these plays has a firm, sound plot and should yield a clear Proposition. Begin by asking: what is the play about? Juggle with your answer to that question until you are able to frame the third step (*the resulting action*) in terms of a central character and a second character. Next, find the second step (*the cause of the action*) by finding the event, involving central and second character, which raises the question framed in the third step, and so forth. Be sure to state all three steps of the Proposition so that the central character is the subject of the sentence.

12. Now restate the Proposition in a final form for each of the plays dealt with in Exercise 11.

13. A high-school teacher of twenty-six has fallen in love with a young man of eighteen who is her pupil at school. Write a Proposition in which she is the central character. Write another Proposition in which he is the central character. You may introduce any other characters you wish. Begin by asking yourself what the play is to be about, and so forth.

CHAPTER FIVE

14. Carson McCullers wrote a brilliant novel called *A Member of the Wedding*. Later she dramatized it. The play, by the same name, was a great popular success, as it deserved to be because of its overtones of authentic poetry. But as a play it was very weak because of its poor plot structure; instead of a charming play, it could have been, with a firm plot, perhaps a great one. The materials for two different plays, both connected with the heroine's desire to be a part of the wedding, were in the novel. Read the novel (it is a short one) and then make two different Propositions for it; in one the soldier will figure as a character; in the other he will not. Then read the play as it was written, analyze the plot, and decide what is the matter with it.

15. Identify the climax of the other plays listed in Exercise 11:

Ghosts	*Six Characters in Search of*
The Cherry Orchard	*an Author*
The Second Man	*As You Desire Me*
The Petrified Forest	*The Glass Menagerie*
The Circle	*The Madwoman of Chaillot*

Elizabeth the Queen   *The Chalk Garden*
Winterset

16. Revise the story from the point where John and Susan are settled in New York. Manage a climax in which John does something to determine the answer to the question of the play. You are free to make the story end so that the answer is either in the affirmative or the negative. You will need, of course, a third character. Use, if you like, those already mentioned: Susan's sister, Susan's old beau, or the art critic; or, if you prefer, invent one of your own.

CHAPTER SIX

17. Look again at the Propositions you made for *The Member of the Wedding* in Exercise 14. If you are satisfied with them do the following; if not, make new Propositions that you can use:
    a. Decide upon the climax for each of these Propositions.
    b. Planning at first a three-act play for each, place the climax at the end of a projected Act II, and then work out the material to appear in each of the three acts.
    c. Are the resulting plans well proportioned? If not, why not? If not, try a four-act plan, with the climax at the end of Act III.
18. Read Sophocles' *Oedipus Tyrannus*, and as you read it jot down the facts of the story which were antecedent to the opening of the play, also noting the page on which each of these facts is brought in. Then rearrange these facts in their chronological order. Finally, consult the play again, with the chronological list in hand, to note the dramatic fitness of the moment where each is introduced.

CHAPTER SEVEN

19. Why would neither be a climax?
20. Analyze the plays you have read for the central character, the second character, and the third character needed in the climax. Decide which of the other characters came into being because of their connection with the Proposition or the climax.

21. a. Decide how the characters other than those involved in your answer to Exercise 20 came into being.
    b. From your materials collected from Exercises 4, 5, or 6, write a summary of the action of a play. Be sure you have a sound Proposition and a correct climax. List the necessary and suggested characters and state their basic use in the action.
22. Take the basic situation involving A, B, and the wife. Ask yourself the questions suggested in the preceding paragraph on page 170. Next, write the summary of a story about these three. Next, discarding the Proposition we have offered, make a Proposition out of your material. Finally, decide upon a climax. Your summary, of course, may be revised to any extent in the process.
23. Let us see what could be done with ideas suggested by this old English ballad, *Lord Rendal:*

"Where have you been wandering, Rendal, my son?
Where have you been wandering, my pretty one?"
"I've been to my sweetheart's, mother.
Make my bed soon, for I'm sick to the heart,
And I fain would lie down."

"What did she give you, Rendal, my son?
   What did she give you, my pretty one?"
"O, eels and eel-broth, mother!
Make my bed soon, etc."

"What was their color, Rendal, my son?
What was their color, my pretty one?"
"O, spickit and sparkit,* mother!
Make my bed soon, etc."

"Where did she find them, Rendal, my son?
Where did she find them, my pretty one?"
"In hedges and ditches, mother!
Make my bed soon, etc."

* speckled and spotted.

"What will you leave your mother, Rendal, my son?
What will you leave your mother, my pretty one?"
"My lands and houses, mother!
Make my bed soon, etc."

"What will you leave your sweetheart, Rendal, my son?
What will you leave your sweetheart, my pretty one?"
"A rope for to hang her, mother!
Make my bed soon, etc."

This old ballad, with that marvelous mixture of the crude and the subtle which is characteristic of the English ballads, tells a story of betrayal. Rendal has been poisoned by his sweetheart; he has been fed not eels, which are found in the water and are not "spickit and sparkit," but snakes. Here the snake is used aptly as the traditional symbol of treachery. With the ballad as a starting point, work out a story of betrayal. Write a summary of the action. Make a Proposition. Decide upon a climax. (Do not feel in any way bound by the details of the ballad. Modernize the setting if you wish.)

CHAPTER EIGHT

24. As you read each one-act play, identify:
    a. The central character (He will not always be the focus of interest in the play.)
    b. The second character
    c. The climax
    d. The Proposition
25. Choose one of the subjects here indicated as suitable for a one-act play. Plan the play; make a summary of the action; reframe the material until you have a Proposition and a climax; and so forth. Then write the play.
26. Write a set of several descriptions of interesting pantomime with which a play might open. (You may get an idea for a play from such attempts, too.)
27. Make a list, for future reference, of masculine and feminine names such as you feel have strong associational character values. Jot down beside each name what you feel these values are.

CHAPTER NINE

28. a. Examine the materials you have used in answer to Exercise 25. Are your chief characters people whose nature is in opposition to the circumstances in which they are involved? If so, describe how. If not, try writing another play on the same subject, this time conceiving your characters' temperaments as in opposition to the circumstances.

   b. Choose another of the subjects mentioned in connection with Exercise 25. Make this a play in which the characters' traits are in opposition to their situation.

29. a. Write a series of such biographical sketches for each of the significant characters in:

   (1) *Othello* or *Hedda Gabler* or *The Cherry Orchard* or *The Chalk Garden*

   and

   (2) *The Importance of Being Earnest* or *The Circle* or *As You Desire Me* or *Biography* or *Born Yesterday*

   b. Write a series of such biographical sketches for each of the significant characters in the play planned in Exercise 28(b) or in another play you are planning.

30. Write a piece of dialogue which will characterize someone.

31. Write an incident in which someone shows his character traits by what he does.

32. Write a scene in which three people are present. Be sure you characterize at least two of them.

CHAPTER TEN

33. Revise one of the longer dramatic scripts written as an exercise before this, to improve the dialogue by dispensing with some of the shorter sentences in the dialogue.

34. Write a series of individual speeches whose rhythm will convey:
   a. Surliness
   b. Exaltation
   c. Numb grief
   d. Caution
   e. Impatience

f. Wrath

35. Write a script (or else rewrite one already composed for these exercises) in which you substitute the language of imagery for abstract expression.

36. Revise several of your earlier scripts by rearranging the dialogue so that the more forceful phrases are at the beginning and end of speeches.

37. Revise the dialogue of several of your scripts in the light of what you now know about the length of speeches.

CHAPTER ELEVEN

38. Consider the possibilities of one of the following as material for a tragedy:
    a. Ariadne (central character) and Theseus
    b. Patroclus (central character) and Achilles
    c. Hector (central character) and Andromache
    d. Saul (central character) and David
    e. Samson (central character) and Delilah
    f. Jephtha (central character) and his daughter
    Feel free to translate, if you prefer, these stories into a modern setting. Make a summary of the action. Construct a Proposition. Invent a climax. Arrange the action within the scope of a three-act play. Write a biographical passage on each important character. Identify the hero's tragic flaw. Then, if you feel ambitious, write the play.

39. Make the summary of the action for a comedy. Identify the central character. Construct a Proposition. Invent a climax. Write a biographical passage on each important character.

40. Do the same as in Exercise 39 for a play of grave experience.

41. Do the same as in Exercise 39 for a melodrama or a farce. If you like, take the story of some mystery novel for the purposes of the melodrama.

CHAPTER TWELVE

42. Find an interesting dramatic idea from history or legend, an idea that has considerable scope, and after making all the preliminary preparations (Proposition, climax, biographical

sketches, and so forth), write an outline of the action of each scene for a play of multiple scenes.

43. *The Three Sisters* makes superb use of symbolism. Trace the symbols employed by Chekhov for the characters of Solenyi and Natasha. Why are they as appropriate as they are for the meaning of the play?

44. Reconsider one of your favorite scripts. Identify for yourself the theme. Then decide on a prevailing image which will cooperate with that theme, and revise some of the dialogue, at significant places, to incorporate the image.

CHAPTER THIRTEEN

45. Make a Proposition and identify the climax of the following from *The Merchant of Venice:*
   a. The Antonio-Shylock-Portia story
   b. The story of the wooing of Portia
   c. The Jessica-Lorenzo story
   d. The Gratiano-Nerissa story
   e. The Launcelot Gobbo story

46. Make a Proposition and identify the climax of the subplot of *Six Characters in Search of an Author.*

47. State Proposition and climax from the point of view of:
   a. Gina
   b. Hedvig

48. Make a Proposition and identify the climax from the point of view of the following characters in *Hamlet:*
   a. Claudius
   b. Gertrude
   c. Polonius
   d. Ophelia
   e. Laertes

49. State Proposition and climax for the following relationships in Behrman's *Biography:*
   a. Kurt and Marion
   b. Kurt and Nolan
   c. Nolan and Marion

50. State Proposition and climax for the leading secondary figures in one of your more successful scripts.

INDEX

379